D0107101

BUY THE
RIGHT
WINE
EVERY TIME

THE NO-FUSS
NO-VINTAGE
WINE GUIDE

STERLING EPICURE
New York

An Imprint of Sterling Publishing
387 Park Avenue South
New York, NY 10016

STERLING EPICURE is a trademark of Sterling Publishing Co., Inc.
The distinctive Sterling logo is a registered trademark of Sterling Publishing Co., Inc.

© 2014 by Tom Stevenson

ISBN 978-1-4027-6341-0

Library of Congress Cataloging-in-Publication Data

Stevenson, Tom, 1951-
  Buy the right wine every time : the no-fuss, no-vintage
wine guide / Tom Stevenson.
    pages cm
  ISBN 978-1-4027-6341-0
  1. Wine and wine making. I. Title.
  TP548.S7238 2014
  663'.2--dc23

                                                2013013433

Distributed in Canada by Sterling Publishing
c/o Canadian Manda Group, 165 Dufferin Street
Toronto, Ontario, Canada M6K 3H6
Distributed in the United Kingdom by GMC Distribution Services
Castle Place, 166 High Street, Lewes, East Sussex, England BN7 1XU
Distributed in Australia by Capricorn Link (Australia) Pty. Ltd.
P.O. Box 704, Windsor, NSW 2756, Australia

For information about custom editions, special sales, and premium
and corporate purchases, please contact Sterling Special Sales
at 800-805-5489 or specialsales@sterlingpublishing.com.

Manufactured in China

2 4 6 8 10 9 7 5 3 1

www.sterlingpublishing.com

T his is a guide to the best, most widely available wines found in restaurants and wine shops globally. Inevitably the most widely available wines include many of the cheapest brands, an area of wine habitually avoided by critics. As such wines are almost exclusively purchased by most wine drinkers, those critics (myself included) have effectively disenfranchised most wine consumers. That is something I want to correct, but how do you interest people who are content with just one or two brands? How do you write a book for people who do not want to read about wine? That has always been the conundrum. I'm not sure that there was ever a eureka moment, but gradually the answer seemed obvious: create a guide that does not teach or, heaven forbid, preach wine. Most people enjoy many things in life that they do not want to study. I love driving my Range Rover up and down the steepest vineyards in Europe, but I have absolutely no interest in what's going on under the hood. To appeal to the wine-consumer equivalent of this particular Range Rover driver, I needed to write a guide to the world's cheapest and most widely distributed wines that would be useful, but not heavy on the sort of detail that wine geeks like to devour.

When I started this project, I did not imagine in my wildest dreams that I would end up recommending the likes of White Zinfandel or Blossom Hill, let alone White Zinfandel from Blossom Hill. Rightly or wrongly, Blossom Hill is one of the brands most denigrated by wine snobs (there are other equally maligned brands, the book is full of them...), but my tastings demonstrated that Blossom Hill has worked very hard on the fruit, freshness and, above all, consistency of its best-selling White Zinfandel over the past ten years or so. On the other hand, I discovered that the quality of other, often more highly rated, brands did not live up to their reputation. I found that some of the most famous brands were, at best, inconsistent from vintage to vintage. A branded wine should be consistent by definition. You might not like the taste, but you should be able to rely on it having that taste year in and year out. That is why one of the primary features of this guide is to recommend wines you can buy with confidence, whatever vintage they happen to be, and that is why some famous brand wines cannot be found in this book. As the old John West advert used to go, "It's the fish that John West rejects, that makes John West the best!"

This guide also includes some more expensive wines. Take Champagne, for example. There cannot be a restaurant or wine shop anywhere in the world that does not offer at least one brand of genuine French Champagne. Many offer it by the glass. If this is to be a guide to the most widely available wines in the world, then it must include some of the biggest-selling Champagne brands. Almost the same could be said for the most widely available Burgundy, Rhône, Chianti, etc. Some of these wines, even at entry level, could hardly be described as cheap, but they must be covered by this guide as the most widely available wines of their type.

In a rut?

It's easy to get stuck in a rut over the choice of what to drink. It might be an enjoyable rut, but it's a rut nonetheless—a bit like going to your favorite restaurant and ordering the same dish every time. We've all done it and at sometime during the meal, often just after we've ordered, there is often a tinge of regret that we did not order this or that. With this guide, you can easily find "this" and "that" wines that are very similar to those you habitually drink, and they will be at least as good.

If you cannot find your favorite wine in this book, this will be due to one of three different reasons. First, it could merely mean that it is not widely available, although it might be well distributed in your own area. Secondly, it could be that I had some concern about its consistency, and the producer was unwilling (or claimed to be unable) to provide samples of past, present and forthcoming releases of said wine. This was a rare experience, as most producers were confident enough in the quality of their brand to provide samples without quibble, particularly as the guide would not be featuring any wines I could not recommend, but it occasionally happened and when it did I could not risk its inclusion. Thirdly, it could simply be that the wine failed my tasting test. If I did not like a wine you like, you should not take offence. It's not a matter of my being right and your being wrong. You are entitled to enjoy whatever you like. Nobody has the right to say you should not enjoy any particular wine, just as no one has the right to say that you should not enjoy a specific food, music, work of art or whatever. We all have different tastes and some individuals have very different tastes indeed. However, once I know the type and style of wine you prefer, I should be able to recommend something similar that you will enjoy even more, and that is what this guide attempts to do.

Tom Stevenson

What's In This Book?

You will find the wines are quality-rated as Recommended, Highly Recommended and To Die For. Under **Wines By Style**, just before the main section of the guide, all the wines are compactly grouped by style, making it very simple to identify other widely available wines of a similar style. Even if your own favorite wine is not included, you should easily be able to identify the style group in which it fits. Each wine is also categorized by price category:

$	Up to $10 retail
$$	$10–$25 retail
$$$	Over $25 retail

These price categories are approximate. In some localities a $ wine can be $$, or the reverse, and wine in restaurants gets a much greater markup, of course, but all in all the price categories act as a rough guide to what wine is likely to be cheap, premium priced or expensive.

This is the first level at which *The Timeless Wine Guide* works. Even readers who have no desire to learn anything about wine can search out wines that will be similar to and at least as enjoyable as the wines they currently restrict themselves to, just using the quality ratings in the **Wines By Style** section.

The next level of usage is the **A–Z of Wines** that are "Recommended," "Highly Recommended," and "To Die For" and, hands up, it does involve a little learning, but it's all focused and usefully informative, rather than generalized text. Just a brief explanation of what the wine is and what it tastes like. Nothing about what's going on under the hood. It can be useful to know what you are drinking, even if it's little more than the grape variety, where it's grown, and whether there is any oak in the wine. It's all compartmentalized, so there is no obligation to read this before getting to the description of what the wine actually tastes like. There is a bit of winespeak in the description, but every specialist subject has its own vocabulary, and "body" or "length" is no more pretentious than a car magazine's "torque" or "revs." However, as previously stated, it's all optional. If you do not want to know what the wine is or what it tastes like, you can skip over both.

Want to dip your toe in the world of fine wine?

Even for just a one-off special occasion? Well, you can use this guide to transport you directly from your regular, reliable branded wine to the perfect step up in quality, something truly special of an essentially similar style. I have lost count of the number of people who have tried a so-called fine wine only to be bitterly disappointed. Why pay heaps more for a wine you like less than your favorite inexpensive tipple or, worse still, a wine you positively dislike? Sometimes this disappointment is due to circumstance. Most people who find Champagne too acidic, for example, have tasted it only at weddings with the wedding cake (never drink dry wine with anything sweet!). If that was my only experience, I would also find Champagne too acidic. More often, however, people who are disappointed by an Old World classic or New World superstar have inadvertently tried an inappropriate wine. Their favorite brand might, for example, be a dry white wine and so they feel that any classic dry white would be fine for a treat, but it depends on so many different factors: whether the wine is light or full-bodied, soft or acidic, intensely or subtly flavored, fruit-driven, oaky, bottle-matured, etc. Within each of these stylistic categories, there are further differences. A fruit-driven dry Riesling, for example, could not be more different from Chardonnay, even if it is unoaked and fruit-driven, and a young fruit-driven dry Riesling varies enormously from a fruit-driven dry Riesling with a few years bottle-aging. It is possible to find radically different styles from the same grape variety grown in the same geographical region, and a very similar style from totally different grape varieties grown in different countries.

So, how do you avoid that sort of disappointment and find a truly fine wine you can be confident you will enjoy? It's not easy. Think of a room with thousands of doors, each of which takes you to a different part of the world of fine wine. Of these, there will be only half a dozen doors that will lead you to fine wines of the type you are seeking. As I said, not easy, especially if you are the sort of person who wants to drink, not *think* about, wine and has never been interested in learning about the subject. Unless, that is, you have a copy of *The Timeless Wine Guide*. Just skip down to "If you like this, then try with confidence..." and you will see one or more wines under three self-explanatory headings:

- » For greater quality and greater intensity
- » For greater quality and less intensity
- » For something completely different to suit this taste profile

PART 1

WINES BY STYLE

KEY
Red Wine
White Wine
Fortified Wine
Sparkling Wine
Rosé Wine

All the wines in the main section of this book (**Part 2, A–Z of Wines**) are grouped here by style. When you find one of your favorite wines in the **A–Z of Wines** and want to locate other widely available wines of a similar style, simply take a note of the style category of the wine in question (located in the color bar), then look up that group on the pages here in **Wines By Style**. Any one of the wines you find here can be tried with confidence that it will appeal directly to you personally, but to increase that likelihood, check out your personal preferences with the introductory advice under the Style Category heading in question. Even if your own favorite wine is not recommended in the **A–Z of Wines**, you should be able to find a similarly named wine in one of the style categories in which it fits.

Price-quality ratio
Under each category, the wines are listed in order of recommendation. It is interesting to note the effect this has on the price categories, with most of the $$$ and $$ wines stacked at the top of these lists, and most of the $ wines toward the bottom. From this we can reasonably conclude that for most wines, you get what you pay for. However, there are more than a few anomalies where lower-priced wines have outperformed higher-priced wines. It might be obvious, but it is always worth saying: you have to pay for quality, but higher prices do not always guarantee higher quality.

Aromatic White

If you regularly drink the off-dry Rosemount, and you are looking for a similar touch of sweetness, the off-dry Hugel and the almost off-dry Trivento will be the closest in taste. However, both are considerably more alcoholic, so if low alcohol is more important, then you should either try a much sweeter Moscato (see the still version in the Moscato style category) or go for something completely different under "If you like this ..."

Highly Recommended

$$ **Hugel Gewurztraminer Hugel** 13.5%

Recommended

$ **Trivento Reserve Torrontés** 13%
$ **Rosemount Traminer Riesling** 9%
$ **Alamos Torrontés** 13.5%

Cabernet Sauvignon

The more expensive the category, the fuller-bodied the wine, and the greater intensity it has.

To Die For

$$$ **Col Solare** 14.5%
$$$ **Yalumba The Signature** 14.5%
$$$ **Beringer Private Reserve Cabernet Sauvignon** 14.5%
$$$ **Silver Oak Alexander Valley Cabernet Sauvignon** 14%

Highly Recommended

$$$ **Cakebread Cabernet Sauvignon** 14%
$$$ **Caymus Cabernet Sauvignon** 14.5%
$$$ **Clos du Val Cabernet Sauvignon Stags Leap District** 14.5%
$$$ **Clos du Val Cabernet Sauvignon** 13.5%

$$$	Duckhorn Vineyards Cabernet Sauvignon 14.5%
$$$	Jordan Cabernet Sauvignon 13.5%
$$$	Stag's Leap Wine Cellars Artemis Cabernet Sauvignon 14.5%
$$	Jacob's Creek Cabernet Sauvignon Reserve Coonawarra 14%
$$	Wolf Blass Gold Label Cabernet Sauvignon 14.5%
$$	Lapostolle Cuvée Alexandre Cabernet Sauvignon 14%
$$	MontGras Reserva Cabernet Sauvignon 14%
$$	Chateau Ste Michelle Cabernet Sauvignon 13.5%
$	Alamos Cabernet Sauvignon 14%
$	Beringer Cabernet Sauvignon 13.5%

Recommended

$$	Wolf Blass Yellow Label Cabernet Sauvignon 13.5%
$$	Hardy's Nottage Hill Cabernet-Shiraz 14%
$$	Maculan Brentino 13.5%
$$	Kendall Jackson Cabernet Sauvignon Vintner's Reserve 13.5%
$$	Louis M. Martini Sonoma Cabernet Sauvignon 13.5%
$$	Columbia Crest Grand Estates Cabernet Sauvignon 13.5%
$	Banrock Station Cabernet Sauvignon 13.5%
$	Hardy's Stamp of Australia Cabernet Sauvignon 13.5%
$	Rosemount Cabernet Sauvignon 13.5%
$	Trivento Reserve Cabernet Sauvignon 14%
$	Mouton Cadet Bordeaux Rouge 13.5%
$	Barefoot Cellars Cabernet Sauvignon 13%
$	Beaulieu Vineyards BV Coastal Estate Cabernet Sauvignon 13.5%
$	Blossom Hill Winemaker's Reserve Cabernet Sauvignon 13%
$	Gallo Family Vineyards Cabernet Sauvignon 13%
$	Redwood Creek Cabernet Sauvignon 13%
$	Robert Mondavi Private Selection Cabernet Sauvignon 13.5%
$	Turning Leaf Cabernet Sauvignon 13%
$	Woodbridge Cabernet Sauvignon 13.5%

$ Concha y Toro Casillero del Diablo Reserva Cabernet Sauvignon 13.5%

$ Santa Rita Cabernet Sauvignon 120 13.5%

Cabernet-Shiraz or Shiraz-Cabernet

Decent wines, but much of a muchness. If you want more excitement, go straight to "If you like this …"

Recommended

$$ Banrock Station Reserve Cabernet Sauvignon-Shiraz 14%

$ Hardy's Stamp of Australia Shiraz-Cabernet Sauvignon 13.5%

$ Penfolds Koonunga Shiraz-Cabernet 13.5%

Carmenère

Much of a muchness again. Chile's number one red wine grape, but if you want to see how great it can be, go straight to "If you like this …"

Recommended

$$ Lapostolle Cuvée Alexandre Carmenère 14.5%

$$ MontGras Reserva Carmenère 14.5%

$ Concha y Toro Casillero del Diablo Reserva Carmenère 13.5%

Chardonnay

The more expensive the category, the fuller-bodied and more intense the wine, particularly from California and Australia. The To Die For Burgundies are rich, but not as big as some of the Highly Recommended Chardonnay, but they do exude quality, class and finesse. If you prefer more acidity and purity, and a less big and buttery Chardonnay, try the Chablis, Bramìto and Jacob's Creek Adelaide Hills.

$$$ Château Fuissé Pouilly-Fuissé Les Brulés 13.5%

$$$ Olivier Leflaive Chassagne-Montrachet 13.5%

Highly Recommended

$$$ Louis Latour Chassagne-Montrachet 13.5%

$$$ Jordan Chardonnay 13.5%

$$$ Rombauer Chardonnay 14.5%

$$$ Drouhin Vaudon Chablis Premier Cru 12.5%

$$ Bramìto Chardonnay Castello della Salla 13%

$$ Jacob's Creek Chardonnay Adelaide Hills 12.5%

$$ Clos du Val Chardonnay 13.5%

$$ Christian Moreau Chablis 13%

$$ Simmonet-Fèbvre Chablis 12.5%

$$ Lapostolle Cuvée Alexandre Chardonnay 14.5%

$$ Louis Latour Grand Ardèche Chardonnay 13.5%

$$ Villa Maria Chardonnay Marlborough Reserve 13.5%

$ Banrock Station Colombard-Chardonnay 11%

$ Beringer Chardonnay 13.5%

$ Bogle Chardonnay 13.5%

$ Lapostolle Casa Chardonnay 14%

Recommended

$$$ Joseph Drouhin Puligny-Montrachet 13.5%

$$$ Louis Latour Meursault 13.5%

$$$ Louis Latour Puligny-Montrachet 13.5%

$$$ Villa Maria Chardonnay Marlborough Cellar Selection 13.5%

$$ Banrock Station Reserve Chardonnay-Verdelho 13%

$$ Hardy's Nottage Hill Chardonnay 13%

$$ Wolf Blass Yellow Label Chardonnay 13.5%

$$ Catena Chardonnay 14%

$$ Louis Latour Pouilly-Fuissé 13%

$$ Kendall Jackson Chardonnay Vintner's Reserve 13.5%

$$ **La Crema Chardonnay Monterey** 13.5%

$$ **Sonoma Cutrer Chardonnay** 14%

$$ **Drouhin Vaudon Chablis** 12.5%

$$ **Simonnet-Fèbvre Chablis 1er Cru Vaillons** 13.5%

$$ **Louis Latour Duet Chardonnay-Viognier** 13.5%

$$ **Villa Maria Chardonnay East Coast Private Bin** 13.5%

$$ **Chateau Ste Michelle Chardonnay** 13.5%

$$ **Columbia Crest Grand Estates Chardonnay** 13.5%

$ **Torres Gran Viña Sol** 12.5%

$ **Banrock Station Chardonnay** 14%

$ **Hardy's Stamp of Australia Chardonnay** 13.5%

$ **Hardy's Stamp of Australia Chardonnay-Semillon** 12.5%

$ **Jacob's Creek Chardonnay** 13%

$ **Lindeman's Bin 65 Chardonnay** 13.5%

$ **Penfolds Koonunga Hill Chardonnay** 12%

$ **Rosemount Chardonnay** 13%

$ **Wyndham Estate Bin 222 Chardonnay** 13%

$ **Yellow Tail Chardonnay** 12.5%

$ **Barefoot Chardonnay** 13%

$ **Beaulieu Vineyards BV Coastal Estate Chardonnay** 13.5%

$ **Fetzer Sundial Chardonnay** 13.5%

$ **Mirassou Chardonnay** 13.5%

$ **Redwood Creek Chardonnay** 13.5%

$ **Robert Mondavi Private Selection Chardonnay** 13.5%

$ **Turning Leaf Chardonnay** 13.5%

$ **Woodbridge Chardonnay** 13.5%

$ **Concha y Toro Casillero del Diablo Reserva Chardonnay** 13.5%

Chianti & Chianti Style

If you have been put off by rather rustic Chianti in the past, try the top-end Chiantis here, which are really smooth and sleek.

Highly Recommended

$$$	Castello Banfi Brunello di Montalcino	13.5%
$$	Pèppoli Chianti Classico Antinori	13%
$$	Rocca delle Macie Chianti Classico	12.5%
$$	Rocca delle Macie Rubizzo Sangiovese di Toscana	13.5%
$$	Ruffino Chianti Classico Riserva Ducale Oro	13.5%
$$	Santa Cristina Chianti Superiore Antinori	13%
$$	Villa Antinori Toscana	13.5%
$	Ruffino Chianti Classico Riserva Ducale	13.5%

Recommended

$$	Rocca delle Macie SASYR	13.5%
$	Piccini Chianti	12.5%
$	Ruffino Chianti	12.5%
$	Santa Cristina Toscana Antinori	13%

Fortified (Full, Dry, Sherry)

For the world's finest fino you really should treat yourself to a Spanish holiday and try it straight from the cask.

Recommended

$$	Gonzalez Byass Alfonso Oloroso Seco	18%
$$	Gonzalez Byass Leonor Palo Cortado	20%

Fortified (Full, Sweet)

The hierarchy here is not just a matter of quality, as the three Highly Recommended wines are significantly sweeter than the two that are Recommended.

Highly Recommended

$$$	Blandy's 10-Year Malmsey	19%
$$	Gonzalez Byass Solera 1847 Oloroso Dulce	18%
$$	Gonzalez Byass Nectar Pedro Ximénez	15.5%

Recommended

$$	Blandy's Alvada 5-Year Madeira	19%
$$	Gonzalez Byass Cristina Oloroso Abocado	17.5%

Fortified (Ruby Port Style)

Some excellent value here. None of these wines will disappoint.

To Die For

$$$	Smith Woodhouse Late Bottled Vintage	20%

Highly Recommended

$$	Dow's Late Bottled Vintage	19.5%
$$	Dow's Vale do Bomfim	14%
$$	Graham's Six Grapes Reserve Porto	19.5%

Recommended

$$	Cockburn's Special Reserve	19.5%
$$	Fonseca Bin 27 Porto	20%
$$	Sandeman Founders Reserve	20%
$$	Sandeman Late Bottled Vintage	20.5%

Fortified (Tawny)

Glorious wines, but you have to pay a glorious price! As these are all truly great quality wines, you should not start your journey to discover even greater wines until you have tried all of these.

To Die For

$$$	**Taylor Fladgate 10-Year Tawny Port**	20%
$$$	**Sandeman Twenty Years Old Tawny**	20%
$$$	**Taylor Fladgate 20-Year Tawny**	20%

Highly Recommended

$$$	**Churchill's 10-Year Tawny**	19.5%
$$$	**Dow's 10-Year Tawny**	20%
$$$	**Graham's 10-Year Tawny**	20%
$$$	**Sandeman Ten Years Old Tawny**	20%
$$$	**Graham's 20-Year Tawny**	20%

Gamay

Cheap, widely available Beaujolais is one of the most difficult wines to recommend, unless it is from a great vintage.

Highly Recommended

$$	**Henry Fessy Beaujolais-Villages**	12.5%
$$	**Henry Fessy Morgon**	13.5%

Recommended

$$	**Henry Fessy Brouilly**	13%
$$	**Henry Fessy Moulin à Vent**	13.5%

Malbec Pure & Blended

The more expensive the category, the fuller-bodied the wine and the greater intensity it has. Argentina's iconic red wine variety.

Highly Recommended

$$ **Alamos Selección Malbec** 14.5%
$$ **Bodega Norton Malbec Reserva** 14.5%
$$ **Gascon Malbec** 14%
$$ **Terrazas de los Andes Reserva Malbec** 14%
$$ **Bodega Norton Privada** 14.5%

Recommended

$$ **Altos las Hormigas Malbec** 14%
$$ **Catena Malbec** 14%
$$ **Graffigna Malbec Reserve** 14%
$$ **Luigi Bosca Malbec** 14%
$ **Trapiche Malbec** 13.5%
$ **Trivento Reserve Malbec** 14%

Merlot

The more expensive the category, the fuller-bodied the wine and the greater intensity it has.

To Die For

$$ **Villa Maria Merlot Reserve** 13.5%

Highly Recommended

$$$ **Clos du Val Merlot** 13.5%
$$ **Lapostolle Cuvée Alexandre Merlot** 15%
$$ **Chateau Ste Michelle Canoe Ridge Estate Merlot** 14.5%
$$ **Chateau Ste Michelle Merlot** 13.5%
$ **Blackstone Merlot** 13%

$ **Rex-Goliath Merlot**   13.5%

$ **Robert Mondavi Private Selection Merlot**   13.5%

Recommended

$$ **Columbia Crest Grand Estates Merlot**   13.5%

$ **B & G Merlot Pays d'Oc IGP**   12%

$ **Banrock Station Merlot**   13.5%

$ **Hardy's Stamp of Australia Merlot**   13.5%

$ **Kumala Merlot-Ruby Cabernet**   13.5%

$ **Barefoot Cellars Merlot**   13%

$ **Bogle Merlot**   13.5%

$ **Redwood Creek Merlot**   13.5%

$ **Turning Leaf Merlot**

Moscato (Still & Sparkling)

Invariably low in alcohol with a very sweet taste, Moscato is the most floral, grapiest grape in the world.

Highly Recommended

$$ **Fontanafredda Asti**   7%

$$ **Castello de Poggio Moscato d'Asti**   5.5%

$$ **Castello de Poggio Moscato Provincia di Pavia**   5%

$$ **Zonin Moscato Puglia**   7%

$ **Banrock Station Moscato**   5.5%

$ **Jacob's Creek Moscato**   8%

Recommended

$ **Barefoot Moscato**   9%

$ **Mirassou Moscato**   8%

Other Dry White

If you want the richest, fattest and most floral of these other dry white wines, try the pure Viognier Vidal-Fleury Condrieu or the Marsanne-dominated E. Guigal Crozes-Hermitage. The Viognier from Yalumba is also very rich, but has a higher acidity. For lighter, try Vidal-Fleury Côtes-du-Rhône; for softer, try Planeta La Segreta; with the Mouton for lighter and crisper and the Simonsig Chenin Blanc for something zesty.

Highly Recommended

$$$	**Vidal-Fleury Condrieu** 13.5%
$$	**E. Guigal Crozes-Hermitage Blanc** 13%
$$	**E. Guigal Côtes-du-Rhône Blanc** 14%
$$	**Vidal-Fleury Côtes-du-Rhône Blanc** 13.5%
$$	**Yalumba Eden Valley Viognier** 13.5%
$	**Simonsig Chenin Blanc** 14.5%
$	**Planeta La Segreta Blanca** 13.5%

Recommended

$	**Mouton Cadet Bordeaux Blanc** 13%

Other Red

If you want bigger, try the Barolo; for higher acidity, soft tannins and lighter weight, the Barbera; and for higher acidity but richer than the Barbera, the Chinon. Planeta is an excellent producer, but this particular wine is somewhat rustic.

Highly Recommended

$$$	**Fontanafredda Serralunga d'Alba Barolo** 14%
$$	**Fontanafredda Briccotondo Barbera** 13.5%
$$	**Remy Pannier Chinon** 13%

Recommended

$ **Planeta La Segreta Rosso**   13.5%

Pinot Grigio & Other Light White Wines

The Albariño and the Pinot Grigio from New Zealand are the crispest and most zesty of this bunch, while the Trimbach and Italian Pinot Grigio are the softest. The Robert Mondavi Private Selection Pinot Grigio is easily the best value.

Highly Recommended

$$ **Santiago Ruiz Albariño**   12%

$$ **Spy Valley Marlborough Pinot Gris**   14%

$ **Robert Mondavi Private Selection Pinot Grigio**   12.5%

Recommended

$$$ **Villa Maria Pinot Gris Cellar Selection**   13.3%

$$ **Hugel Gentil**   12.5%

$$ **Martín Codáx Albariño**   13%

$$ **Trimbach Pinot Blanc**   12.5%

$$ **Graffigna Pinot Grigio Reserve**   13%

$$ **Maso Canali Pinot Grigio**   13%

$$ **Villa Maria Pinot Gris East Coast Private Bin**   13%

$ **Barefoot Cellars Pinot Grigio**   12.5%

$ **Cavit Pinot Grigio**   12%

$ **Forest Glen Pinot Grigio Tehachapi Clone**   12.5%

$ **Rosemount Pinot Grigio**   12.5%

$ **Ruffino Pinot Grigio**   12%

$ **Turning Leaf Pinot Grigio**   12.5%

Pinot Noir

Because this is the lightest-bodied of all the world's greatest varietal wines, it has to rely on elegance and finesse, consequently Pinot Noir is the most difficult wine to get right at the cheaper and mid-price end of the scale. Any $$ Pinot Noir that is Highly Recommended is an amazing success, but for Robert Mondavi Private Selection Pinot Noir to warrant Highly Recommended is nothing short of a miracle.

Highly Recommended

$$$	**Clos du Val Pinot Noir** 13.5%
$$$	**Villa Maria Pinot Noir Cellar Selection** 14%
$$	**Jacob's Creek Reserve Pinot Noir Adelaide Hills** 13.5%
$$	**Louis Latour Marsannay** 13%
$$	**Nicolas Potel Bourgogne Pinot Noir** 12.5%
$$	**Brancott Estate Pinot Noir** 13%
$$	**Spy Valley Pinot Noir** 14%
$$	**Villa Maria Pinot Noir Reserve** 14%
$	**Robert Mondavi Private Selection Pinot Noir** 13.5%

Recommended

$$$	**Louis Latour Aloxe-Corton 1er Cru Les Chaillots** 13%
$$$	**Louis Latour Pommard** 13.5%
$$	**Louis Latour Pinot Noir Bourgogne** 13%
$$	**La Crema Pinot Noir Monterey** 13.5%
$$	**MacMurray Ranch Sonoma Coast Pinot Noir** 14%
$$	**Louis Latour Domaine de Valmoissine Pinot Noir** 13.5%
$$	**Coopers Creek Marlborough Pinot Noir** 14%
$$	**Kim Crawford Pinot Noir** 14%
$$	**Matua Valley Pinot Noir** 13.5%
$$	**Villa Maria Pinot Noir Private Bin** 13.5%
$	**Jacob's Creek Pinot Noir** 12.5%

$ **Rosemount Pinot Noir**   13.5%
$ **Forest Glen Pinot Noir**   12.5%
$ **Mirassou Pinot Noir**   13%
$ **Redwood Creek Pinot Noir**   13.5%
$ **Turning Leaf Pinot Noir**   13%

Pinotage

You would not want to taste the Pinotage that did not qualify for recommendation! There are, however, some amazing versions of this unique South African if you consult "If you like this …"

Recommended

$$ **Graham Beck Pinotage**   13.5%
$$ **Simonsig Pinotage Redhill Stellenbosch**   14.5%
$$ **Simonsig Pinotage**   14%

Rhône Style Red & Rosé

A very successful and often extremely good value style. The Côtes-du-Rhônes, including Paul Jaboulet Aîné Parallèle 45, make the ideal starting point.

Highly Recommended

$$$ **E. Guigal Châteauneuf-du-Pape**   14%
$$$ **Jacob's Creek St Hugo Barossa Grenache Shiraz Mataro**   14.1%
$$$ **Vidal-Fleury Châteauneuf-du-Pape**   14.5%
$$ **E. Guigal Côtes-du-Rhône Rosé**   13.5%
$$ **Yalumba Bush Vine Grenache**   14%
$$ **E. Guigal Côtes-du-Rhône**   14%
$$ **M. Chapoutier Bila-Haut Côtes du Roussillon Villages**   14%
$$ **Paul Jaboulet Aîné Parallèle 45**   13.5%
$$ **Vidal-Fleury Côtes-du-Rhône**   13.5%

Recommended

$$$ **M. Chapoutier La Ciboise Lubéron** 14%

$ **M. Chapoutier Belleruche Côtes-du-Rhône** 14%

Riesling (Dry)

Not all the Rieslings qualified, but of those that did, the low-est quality rating was Highly Recommended, illustrating the potential of this world-class grape. Riesling repays a few years bottle-age more than any other white wine variety, yet most is consumed before it reaches anywhere near its peak. Try buying an older vintage every now and then.

To Die For

$$$ **Pewsey Vale Riesling The Contours Museum Reserve** 13%

$$ **Jacob's Creek Steingarten Riesling** 11%

Highly Recommended

$$$ **Villa Maria Riesling Cellar Selection** 12.5%

$$ **Hugel Riesling Hugel** 12%

$$ **Trimbach Riesling** 13%

$$ **Jacob's Creek Riesling Reserve Barossa** 12%

$$ **Wolf Blass Gold Label Riesling** 13%

$$ **Coopers Creek Marlborough Riesling** 12%

$$ **Spy Valley Riesling** 13%

$$ **Villa Maria Dry Riesling Private Bin** 12.5%

$$ **Villa Maria Riesling Reserve** 12%

$ **Chateau Ste Michelle Dry Riesling** 13%

Rioja & Other Spanish Tempranillo

The more expensive the category, the fuller-bodied the wine and the greater intensity it has, yet even the relatively light-bodied Marqués de Cáceres has a lovely lunchtime claret quality, making it an excellent quaffer.

To Die For

$$$	Bodegas Lan Rioja Culmen Reserva	14%

Highly Recommended

$$$	O. Fournier Spiga	14.5%
$$	Bodegas Lan Rioja Reserva	13.5%
$$	Campo Viejo Rioja Reserva	13.5%
$$	Coto de Imaz Rioja Reserva	13.5%
$$	Marqués de Riscal Rioja Gran Reserva	14.5%
$$	Marqués de Riscal Rioja Reserva	14%
$$	Ysios Rioja Reserva	13.5%
$	Campo Viejo Rioja	13.5%

Recommended

$$$	Bodegas Lan Rioja Viña Lanciano Reserva	13.5%
$$	Faustino V Rioja Reserva	13%
$$	Marqués de Cáceres Rioja Crianza	13%
$$	Marqués de Cáceres Rioja Reserva	14%
$	Bodegas Lan Rioja Crianza	13.5%

Rosé, *see* Rhône Style Red & Rosé

Sauvignon Blanc

New Zealand Sauvignon Blanc is the best and most consistent in the world, particularly when it's from Marlborough.

Highly Recommended

$$$	**Cloudy Bay Sauvignon Blanc**	13.5%
$$	**Drylands Sauvignon Blanc**	13%
$$	**Kim Crawford Sauvignon Blanc**	13.5%
$$	**Matua Valley Paretai Sauvignon Blanc**	13.5%
$$	**Nederburg Winemaster's Reserve Sauvignon Blanc**	13.5%
$$	**Nobilo Sauvignon Blanc**	13%
$$	**Spy Valley Sauvignon Blanc**	13.5%
$$	**Starborough Sauvignon Blanc**	13.5%
$$	**Stoneleigh Sauvignon Blanc**	12.5%
$$	**Villa Maria Sauvignon Blanc Private Bin**	13.5%
$$	**Villa Maria Sauvignon Blanc Reserve Clifford Bay**	13%
$$	**Villa Maria Sauvignon Blanc Reserve Wairau Valley**	13%
$	**Robert Mondavi Sauvignon Blanc**	12.5%

Recommended

$$$	**Villa Maria Sauvignon Blanc Cellar Selection**	13.5%
$$	**Coopers Creek Marlborough Sauvignon Blanc**	13%
$$	**Matua Valley Sauvignon Blanc**	13%
$$	**MontGras Reserva Sauvignon Blanc**	14%
$$	**Nobilo Icon Sauvignon Blanc**	14%
$$	**O. Fournier B Crux Sauvignon Blanc**	12%
$$	**O. Fournier Centauri Sauvignon Blanc**	12.5%
$$	**Pascal Jolivet Sancerre**	12.5%
$	**Blossom Hill Winemaker's Reserve Sauvignon Blanc**	12.5%
$	**Brancott Estate Sauvignon Blanc**	12.5%
$	**Mirassou Sauvignon Blanc**	13.5%
$	**Rosemount Sauvignon Blanc**	12%

$ **Santa Rita Sauvignon Blanc 120**   13.5%

$ **Woodbridge Sauvignon Blanc**   13%

Sparkling Wine (Rosé)

For all the wines immediately below, and for most pink sparkling wine in general, the color is purely visual. Put the wine in a black glass so you cannot see the color and serve it to most people and they would be unable to distinguish what color it is. Not that it should matter. A visual attribute is perfectly valid.

Highly Recommended

$$ **Codorníu Cava Pinot Noir Brut Rosé**   11.5%

$$ **Freixenet Elyssia Pinot Noir Brut**   11.5%

$$ **Simmonet-Fèbvre Crémant de Bourgogne Brut Rosé**   12%,

Recommended

$$$ **Lanson NV Brut Rosé**   12.5%

$ **Freixenet Cordon Rosado Brut**   12%

Sparkling Wine (White)

Those who are used to drinking Champagne find it very difficult to take other sparkling wines seriously. It has to do with the often unique character of Champagne's aromas, its body, greater intensity, length and acidity, after which anything else comes up rather short, but if you cannot afford Champagne prices, there are some very good Proseccos and Cavas.

To Die For

$$$ **Charles Heidsieck NV Brut Reserve**   12%

$$$ **Dom Pérignon**   12.5%

$$$ **Louis Roederer NV Brut Premier**   12%

$$	Nino Franco Grave di Stecca Prosecco 11.5%
$$$	Lanson Black Label NV Brut 12.5%
$$$	Mumm NV Cordon Rouge Brut 12%
$$$	Pol Roger NV Reserve Brut 12.5%
$$$	Talttlnger NV Brut 12%
$$$	Mumm Napa Blanc de Blancs 12.5%
$$$	Mumm Napa DVX Brut 12.5%
$$	Bisol Jeio Prosecco 11.5%
$$	Segura Viudas Heredad Brut Reserva 12%
$$	Gloria Ferrer Blanc de Noirs 13%
$$	Simonnet-Fèbvre Crémant de Bourgogne Brut 12%

Recommended

$$$	Moët & Chandon NV Brut Impérial 12%
$$$	Perrier-Jouët NV Grand Brut 12%
$$$	Veuve Clicquot NV Brut Yellow Label 12%
$$	Nino Franco Rustico Prosecco 11.5%
$$	Codorníu Cava Anna de Codorníu Brut Reserva 11.5%
$$	Gonzalez Byass Tio Pepe 15%
$$	Domaine Chandon Brut Classic NV 12%
$$	Domaine Ste Michelle Blanc de Blancs 12%
$$	Domaine Ste Michelle Brut 11.5%
$$	Gloria Ferrer Sonoma Brut 12.5%
$$	Graham Beck NV Brut 12%
$$	Mumm Napa NV Brut Prestige 12.5%
$	Adami Prosecco Bosco del Gica 11%
$	Adami Prosecco Garbèl 11%
$	Codorníu Cava Brut Original 11.5%
$	Freixenet Cordon Negro Brut 12%
$	Segura Viudas Brut Reserva 11.5%

Sparkling Wine (Off-Dry)

Most Prosecco is off-dry.

Highly Recommended

$$ **Nino Franco Primo Prosecco** 11.5%

Recommended

$$ **LaMarca Prosecco** 11.5%
$ **Zardetto Prosecco Treviso** 11.5%
$ **Zonin Prosecco** 11%

Sweet & Medium-Sweet

In this section, you won't find anything sweeter than De Bortoli Noble One or anything finer than Eroica. Theoretically, the Chateau Ste Michelle Riesling is the best bargain, but for me the Dr. L Riesling is even greater value.

To Die For

$$$ **De Bortoli Noble One** 10%
$$ **Chateau Ste Michelle Riesling Eroica** 12.5%

Highly Recommended

$$ **Ken Forrester Old Vine Reserve Chenin Blanc** 14.5%
$$ **Dr. L Riesling** 8.5%
$ **Chateau Ste Michelle Riesling** 11%

Recommended

$$ **Remy Pannier Vouvray** 11.5%
$ **Blossom Hill White Zinfandel** 10%
$ **Mirassou Riesling** 12.5%
$ **Gallo Family Vineyards White Zinfandel** 9.5%
$ **Sutter Home White Zinfandel** 10%

Syrah, Shiraz & Petite Sirah

The more expensive the category, the fuller-bodied the wine and the greater intensity it has, particularly in Australia, but try the French for finesse.

To Die For

$$$	**Penfolds RWT Shiraz**	14.5%
$$$	**Vidal-Fleury Côte Rôtie La Chatillonne**	13%
$$	**E. Guigal Crozes-Hermitage**	13%

Highly Recommended

$$$	**Penfolds Bin 28 Kalimna Shiraz**	14.5%
$$$	**Wolf Blass Platinum Label Shiraz**	14.5%
$$	**Bogle Phantom**	14.5%
$$	**Jacob's Creek Shiraz Reserve Barossa**	14%
$$	**Paul Jaboulet Aîné Crozes Hermitage**	13%
$$	**Vidal-Fleury St. Joseph**	13%

Recommended

$$	**Nederburg Winemaster's Reserve Shiraz**	14.5%
$$	**Wolf Blass Yellow Label Shiraz**	13.5%
$$	**Wyndham Estate Bin 555 Shiraz**	13.5%
$$	**Vidal-Fleury Crozes-Hermitage**	13.5%
$	**Bogle Petite Sirah**	13.5%
$	**Banrock Station Shiraz**	13%
$	**Hardy's Stamp of Australia Shiraz**	13.5%
$	**Lindeman's Bin 50 Shiraz**	13.5%
$	**Yellow Tail Shiraz**	13.5%
$	**Trivento Reserve Syrah**	14%

Valpolicella

These are not your normal light-bodied, wishy-washy Valpolicellas with a bitter finish. They are, instead, deep-colored, powerfully flavored Amarone (made from grapes that have been dried and concentrated for six months) or Ripasso (refermented on Amarone grape skins) wines. Different animals indeed.

Highly Recommended

$$$	Allegrini Amarone della Valpolicella Classico	15.5%
$$	Allegrini Palazzo Della Torre	14%
$$	Santi Valpolicella Ripasso Classico Superiore Solane	13.5%
$$	Zonin Amarone della Valpolicella	14%
$$	Zonin Valpolicella Ripasso Superiore	13%

Zinfandel

All amazingly inexpensive!

Highly Recommended

$	Bogle Old Vines Zinfandel	14.5%
$	Ravenswood Zinfandel Vintners Blend	13.5%

Recommended

$$	Kendall Jackson Zinfandel Vintner's Reserve	13.5%
$	Barefoot Cellars Zinfandel	13%
$	Fetzer Valley Oaks Zinfandel	14%
$	Gallo Family Vineyards Zinfandel	13.5%
$	Rex-Goliath Zinfandel	13.5%
$	Robert Mondavi Private Selection Zinfandel	13.5%

PART 2

A–Z
OF
WINES

KEY
 Red Wine
White Wine
 Fortified Wine
 Sparkling Wine
Rosé Wine

Adami Prosecco Bosco del Gica

Recommended	$	11%

What is it?

A dry sparkling white wine made from predominantly
the Glera grape (plus 3–7% Chardonnay) grown in Prosecco,
in the Veneto region of northeastern Italy. Charmat method
with no lees aging to retain fresh fruit character.

What does it taste like?

Extremely fresh, richer than the Garbèl,
with fruitier aromas, but just as crisp

If you like this, then try with confidence . . .

Greater quality, greater intensity

Champagne Pol Roger Blanc de Blancs

Greater quality, less intensity

Champagne Duval-Leroy Blanc de Blancs

Try something completely different

Ridgeview Grosvenor

Adami Prosecco Garbèl

Recommended	$	11%

What is it?

A dry sparkling white wine made from
the Glera grape grown in Treviso, in
the Veneto region of northeastern Italy.
Charmat method with no lees aging to
retain fresh fruit character.

What does it taste like?

Elegant, fresh, floral aromas, crisp finish

If you like this, then try with confidence . . .

Greater quality, greater intensity

Champagne Pol Roger Blanc de Blancs

Greater quality, less intensity

Champagne Duval-Leroy Blanc de Blancs

Try something completely different

Ridgeview Grosvenor

Alamos Cabernet Sauvignon

Highly Recommended	$	14%

What is it?

A dry red wine made from the Cabernet Sauvignon grape grown in Mendoza, Argentina. Aged in French and American oak for 6–9 months.

What does it taste like?

Nice varietal character and intensity, with black cherry and smoke aromas and a persistent finish

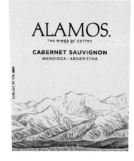

If you like this, then try with confidence . . .

Greater quality, greater intensity

Catena Alta Cabernet Sauvignon

Greater quality, less intensity

Etchart Cafayate Cabernet Sauvignon

Try something completely different

Malbec, Argentina's signature red wine, from the best producers, such as Archával Ferrer, Catena, O Fournier and Tikal

Alamos Selección Malbec

Highly Recommended	$$	14.5%

What is it?

A dry red wine made from the Malbec grape grown in Mendoza, Argentina. Aged in French and American oak for 9–12 months.

What does it taste like?

Classic Malbec, with sweet spice, ripe raspberry and mocha flavors. Rich, creamy and long on the palate.

If you like this, then try with confidence . . .

Greater quality, greater intensity

Luigi Bosca Vistalba Malbec and Nicolas Catena Zapata Malbec Argentino, then Flichman Parcelo 26 for the ultimate monster Malbec

Greater quality, less intensity

Colomé Malbec from Salta (very precise, pure and elegant expression of Malbec) or Bodegas Lagarde Agrelo and Terrazas Afincado single-vineyard Malbecs (for a softer, more savoury style), and Yacochuya Estate in Salta for the ultimate precision Malbec

Try something completely different

Cahors from Clos Triguedina or Tannat Castel La Puebla Dayman from Stagnari in Uruguay

Alamos Torrontés

Recommended	$	13.5%

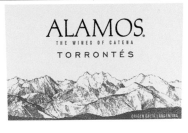

What is it?
  A dry white wine made from the Torrontés grape grown in Salta, Argentina

What does it taste like?
  Dry and pleasant with lingering apple flavors

If you like this, then try with confidence . . .
  Greater quality, greater intensity
  Fully fledged Muscat d'Alsace such as Trimbach, JosMeyer or Bruno Sorg Muscat d'Alsace
  Greater quality, less intensity
  Alsace Klevner de Heiligenstein starting with Zeyssolff Cuvée Z L'Opaline

Try something completely different
  Spicy-floral rather than fruity-floral, such as the lighter Gewürztraminer d'Alsace, such as JosMeyer Les Folastries

Allegrini Amarone della Valpolicella Classico

Highly Recommended	$$$	15.5%

What is it?
  A dry red wine made from a blend of grape varieties (80% Corvina, 15% Rondinella and 5% Oseleta) grown in Valpolicella, in the Veneto region of Italy. The grapes are dried prior to fermentation, and the wine is matured for 18 months, then in bottle for 14 months before release.

What does it taste like?
  Loads of chocolaty oak flavors with warm red fruits and raisin notes. A very well-balanced Amarone, not overdone in the least.

If you like this, then try with confidence . . .
  Greater quality, greater intensity
  Quintarelli Amarone della Valpolicella
  Greater quality, less intensity
  Corte Sant'Alda Amarone della Valpolicella

Try something completely different
  Avalon, a quirky Amarone-inspired blend of Pinotage and Shiraz from Asara in Stellenbosch, South Africa

Allegrini Palazzo Della Torre

Highly Recommended	$$	14%

What is it?

A dry red wine made from a blend of grapes (70% Corvina, 25% Rondinella, 5% Sangiovese) grown in Valpolicella, in the Veneto region of Italy. Fermented using the ripasso method. Aged in used French oak for 15 months.

What does it taste like?

Lovely rose petal aromas with dried black cherry, tobacco and grace notes of dried herb and black pepper with a ripe, velvety texture. Very consistent and delicious, over delivers.

If you like this, then try with confidence . . .

Greater quality, greater intensity
Allegrini Amarone della Valpolicella Classico
Greater quality, less intensity
Corte Sant'Alda Valpolicella Classico

Try something completely different

Margan Family Special Reserve Ripasso, a splendid Australian take on this classic wine

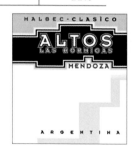

PALAZZO DELLA TORRE

Altos las Hormigas Malbec

Recommended	$$	14%

What is it? A dry red wine made from Malbec grapes grown in Mendoza, Argentina. Bottled after 3 months maturation in stainless steel in contact with inner staves of French and American oak.

What does it taste like? Deep, very focused bramble fruit, with a hint of chocolate. Rich and full-bodied.

If you like this, then try with confidence . . .

Greater quality, greater intensity
Luigi Bosca Vistalba Malbec and Nicolas Catena Zapata Malbec Argentino, then Flichman Parcelo 26 for the ultimate monster Malbec

Greater quality, less intensity
Colomé Malbec from Salta (very precise, pure and elegant) or Bodegas Lagarde Agrelo and Terrazas Afincado single-vineyard Malbecs (for a softer, more savory style), and Yacochuya Estate in Salta for the ultimate precision Malbec

Try something completely different

Cahors from Clos Triguedina or Tannat Castel La Puebla Dayman from Stagnari in Uruguay

Andes, *see* Terrazas de los Andes

Antinori, *see also* Bramìto, Pèppoli, Santa Cristina, and Villa Antinori

B & G Merlot Pays d'Oc IGP

Recommended	$	12%

What is it?
A dry red wine made from Merlot grapes grown in the Languedoc, France. A portion is aged in oak.

What does it taste like?
Simple, juicy blackberry fruit, light in body but very drinkable

If you like this, then try with confidence . . .
Greater quality, greater intensity
Petaluma Coonawarra Merlot
Greater quality, less intensity
Cullen Margaret River Red or Château d'Aiguilhe from the Côtes de Castillon

Try something completely different
Great Merlot-dominated blends from Pomerol, such as châteaux L'Evangile, La Fleur-Pétrus, Latour à Pomerol, Petit-Village, Trotanoy and, if you can afford them, Pétrus and Le Pin

Banfi, *see* Castello Banfi

Banrock Station Cabernet Sauvignon

| Recommended | $ | 13.5% |

What is it?

A dry red wine made from the Cabernet Sauvignon grape grown in Southeastern Australia with subtle oak influence

What does it taste like?

Good varietal character, with sage, black currant and eucalyptus flavors finishing with smooth tannins

If you like this, then try with confidence . . .

Greater quality, greater intensity

Wolf Blass Gold Label Cabernet Sauvignon

Greater quality, less intensity

Cape Mentelle Margaret River Cabernet Sauvignon

Try something completely different

Washington Merlot from the best producers, such as L'Ecole No. 41, Leonetti, Seven Hills and Woodward Canyon

Banrock Station Chardonnay

Recommended	$	14%

What is it?

A dry white wine made from the Chardonnay grape grown in Southeastern Australia with subtle oak influence

What does it taste like?

Just off-dry, with clean, simple apple and melon fruit. An easy-drinking style.

If you like this, then try with confidence . . .

Greater quality, greater intensity

Heemskerk Chardonnay, Tasmania

Greater quality, less intensity

Bay of Fires Chardonnay, Tasmania

Try something completely different

Fabulous Australian Marsanne, Roussanne and Marsanne-Roussanne blends from Yeringberg

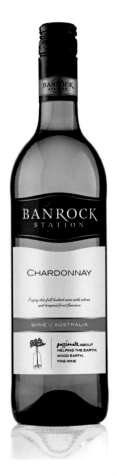

Banrock Station Colombard-Chardonnay

Highly Recommended	**$**	**11%**

What is it?

A dry white wine made from a blend of grapes (Colombard and Chardonnay) grown in Southeastern Australia with subtle oak influence

What does it taste like?

A refreshing wine with fruity peach and lime flavors that finishes clean and sprightly

If you like this, then try with confidence . . .

Greater quality, greater intensity
Heemskerk Chardonnay, Tasmania
Greater quality, less intensity
Bay of Fires Chardonnay, Tasmania

Try something completely different

Fabulous Australian Marsanne, Roussanne and Marsanne-Roussanne blends from Yeringberg

Banrock Station Merlot

Recommended	$	13.5%

What is it?

A dry red wine made from the Merlot grape grown in Southeastern Australia with subtle oak influence

What does it taste like?

Sweet entry of fruit, with red plum, black cherry and baking spice

If you like this, then try with confidence . . .

Greater quality, greater intensity

Petaluma Coonawarra Merlot

Greater quality, less intensity

Cullen Margaret River Red or Château d'Aiguilhe from the Côtes de Castillon

Try something completely different

Great Merlot-dominated blends from Pomerol, such as châteaux L'Evangile, La Fleur-Pétrus, Latour à Pomerol, Petit-Village, Trotanoy and, if you can afford them, Pétrus and Le Pin

Banrock Station Moscato

| **Highly Recommended** | **$** | **5.5%** |

What is it?

A medium-dry white wine made from the Moscato grape grown in Southeastern Australia

What does it taste like?

Lovely, sweet, fresh and typical, with fresh white grapes, rose petals and peaches

If you like this, then try with confidence . . .

Greater quality, greater intensity

A richer, sweeter Moscato d'Asti, such as Marchesi di Grésy or Villa Lunata

Greater quality, less intensity

Drier, but not bone-dry, Rolly Gassmann Muscat d'Alsace and drier still, Bruno Sorg Muscat d'Alsace

Try something completely different

The light-as-a-dime fortified Muscat de Beaumes-de-Venise from top producers such as Domaine des Bernardins or Durban

Banrock Station Reserve Cabernet Sauvignon-Shiraz

Recommended	$$	14%

What is it?

A dry red wine made from a blend of grapes (Cabernet Sauvignon and Shiraz) grown in Southeastern Australia with subtle oak influence

What does it taste like?

Mouth-filling red currant and red cherry flavors, with light oak holding out the finish

If you like this, then try with confidence . . .

Greater quality, greater intensity

Yalumba The Signature or Wolf Blass Black Label Cabernet Sauvignon Shiraz Malbec

Greater quality, less intensity

Brangayne of Orange Tristan Cabernet Sauvignon Shiraz Merlot

Try something completely different

Pure Cabernet Sauvignon from Washington (Andrew Will, Woodward Canyon), Australia (Houghton's Jack Mann, Balnaves The Tally) and Spain (Marqués de Griñon)

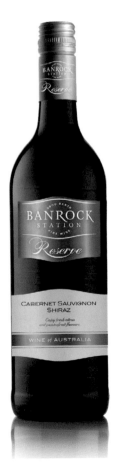

Banrock Station Reserve Chardonnay-Verdelho

Recommended	$$	13%

What is it?

A dry white wine made from a blend of grapes (Chardonnay and Verdelho) grown in Southeastern Australia with subtle oak influence

What does it taste like?

Medium-bodied with a round mid-palate and flavors of ripe tree fruits and nectarine

If you like this, then try with confidence . . .

Greater quality, greater intensity
Heemskerk Chardonnay, Tasmania
Greater quality, less intensity
Bay of Fires Chardonnay, Tasmania

Try something completely different

Fabulous Australian Marsanne, Roussanne and Marsanne-Roussanne blends from Yeringberg

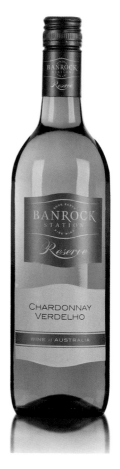

Banrock Station Shiraz

| Recommended | $ | 13% |

What is it?
A dry red wine made from the Shiraz grape grown in Southeastern Australia with subtle oak influence

What does it taste like?
Full-bodied and smooth, with smoky blackberry and meaty aromas

If you like this, then try with confidence . . .
Greater quality, greater intensity
Penfolds St Henri and various Bin numbers (28, 128, 150, 389), culminating in RWT and Grange or Henschke Hill of Grace
Greater quality, less intensity
Clonakilla Shiraz-Viognier

Try something completely different
Zinfandel (especially those by Ridge), Petite Syrah (Ridge Vineyards Dynamite Hill, Rosenblum Rockpile, Turley Cellars Hayne Vineyard or Lava Cap Grand Hill) or even an Australian Zinfandel (such as Cape Mentelle)

Barefoot Cellars Cabernet Sauvignon

Recommended	$	13%

What is it?
A dry red wine made from the Cabernet Sauvignon grape grown in California with subtle oak influence

What does it taste like?
Medium-bodied with grippy tannins, low acidity and spicy blackberry fruit

If you like this, then try with confidence . . .
Greater quality, greater intensity
Caymus Special Selection Cabernet Sauvignon or Dunn Vineyards Howell Mountain Cabernet Sauvignon
Greater quality, less intensity
Stag's Leap Cask 23 Estate Cabernet Sauvignon

Try something completely different
For a classic Bordeaux to match the intensity and voluptuousness of top California Cabernet Sauvignon, try a Merlot-dominated Pomerol such as châteaux L'Evangile, La Fleur-Pétrus, Latour à Pomerol, Petit-Village, Trotanoy and, if you can afford them, Pétrus and Le Pin

Barefoot Cellars Merlot

Recommended	$	13%

What is it?
A dry red wine made from the Merlot grape grown in California with subtle oak influence

What does it taste like?
Straightforward and friendly, with cherry, plum and chocolate flavors

If you like this, then try with confidence . . .
Greater quality, greater intensity
Great Merlot from California (Pahlmeyer, Paloma and Pride) or Washington (L'Ecole No. 41, Leonetti, Seven Hills and Woodward Canyon)
Greater quality, less intensity
Raphael Rosé of Merlot from Long Island

Try something completely different
Great Merlot-dominated blends from Pomerol, such as châteaux L'Evangile, La Fleur-Pétrus, Latour à Pomerol, Petit-Village, Trotanoy and, if you can afford them, Pétrus and Le Pin

Barefoot Cellars Pinot Grigio

| Recommended | $ | 12.5% |

PINOT GRIGIO

What is it?
A dry white wine made from the Pinot Grigio grape grown in California

What does it taste like?
Just off-dry, clean and fruity, with flavors of apples, melons and peaches

If you like this, then try with confidence . . .
Greater quality, greater intensity
JosMeyer Pinot Gris 1854 Fondation or Trimbach Pinot Gris Réserve with a few years additional bottle-age
Greater quality, less intensity
JosMeyer Pinot Blanc Les Lutins or Domaine Weinbach Pinot Blanc

Try something completely different
A good Soave such as Pieropan or Inama, perhaps even Chasselas from Blaise Duboux in Switzerland or, for the very adventurous, a super-soft Koshu from Japan, such as Misawa Private Reserve from Grace

Barefoot Cellars Zinfandel

| Recommended | $ | 13% |

ZINFANDEL
LODI. CALIFORNIA

What is it?
A dry red wine made from the Zinfandel grape grown in California with subtle oak influence

What does it taste like?
Easy-drinking with pleasant red fruit and bramble flavors and a smooth finish

If you like this, then try with confidence . . .
Greater quality, greater intensity
Ravenswood Lodi Old Vine Zinfandel, then single-vineyard Zinfandels from Ravenswood or Rosenblum
Greater quality, less intensity
Kendall Jackson Zinfandel Vintners Reserve, then single-vineyard Zinfandels by Ridge

Try something completely different
Zinfandel is a Croatian grape variety (Tribidrag, a.k.a. Crljenak Kastelanski) that is also grown in Puglia, Italy (as Primitivo), producing intensely ripe, full-bodied red wines at moderate prices.

Barefoot Chardonnay

Recommended   **$**   **13%**

What is it?
A dry white wine made from the Chardonnay grape grown in California with subtle oak influence

What does it taste like?
Sweet spice, peach and vanilla flavors with a dry, clean finish

If you like this, then try with confidence . . .
Greater quality, greater intensity
Jacobs Creek Chardonnay Adelaide Hills
Greater quality, less intensity
The very best from the basic Mâcon-Villages appellation, such as Mâcon Solutré Clos des Bertillones Denogent

Try something completely different
The best Pinot Blanc from Alsace, starting with Domaine Weinbach or Collio Pinot Blanco from Schiopetto from Veneto in Italy

Barefoot Moscato

Recommended   **$**   **9%**

What is it?
A medium-dry white wine made from the Moscato grape grown in Southeastern Australia

What does it taste like?
Still wine bursting with rose petal and jasmine aromas plus fresh grapes and peaches

If you like this, then try with confidence . . .
Greater quality, greater intensity
A richer, sweeter Moscato d'Asti, such as Marchesi di Grésy or Villa Lunata
Greater quality, less intensity
Drier, but not bone-dry, Rolly Gassmann Muscat d'Alsace and drier still, Bruno Sorg Muscat d'Alsace

Try something completely different
The light-as-a-dime fortified Muscat de Beaumes-de-Venise from top producers such as Domaine des Bernardins or Durban

Beaulieu Vineyards BV Coastal Estate Cabernet Sauvignon

Recommended	$	13.5%

What is it?
A dry red wine made predominantly from the
Cabernet Sauvignon grape grown in California
with subtle oak influence

What does it taste like?
Bright black currant and black cherry, with hints
of cigar and toast. Firm tannins but generous
dark fruits on the palate.

If you like this, then try with confidence . . .
Greater quality, greater intensity
Caymus Special Selection Cabernet Sauvignon
or Dunn Vineyards Howell Mountain Cabernet
Sauvignon
Greater quality, less intensity
Stag's Leap Cask 23 Estate Cabernet Sauvignon

Try something completely different
For a classic Bordeaux to match the intensity and voluptuousness of top
California Cabernet Sauvignon, try a Merlot-dominated Pomerol such as
châteaux L'Evangile, La Fleur-Pétrus, Latour à Pomerol, Petit-Village, Trotanoy
and, if you can afford them, Pétrus and Le Pin

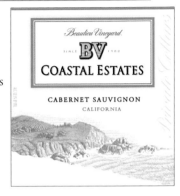

Beaulieu Vineyards BV Coastal Estates Chardonnay

| Recommended | $ | 13.5% |

What is it?

A dry white wine made from the Chardonnay grape grown in California with subtle oak influence. Half of the wine underwent malolactic fermentation to soften the acidity, and regular lees stirring to impart a creamy texture.

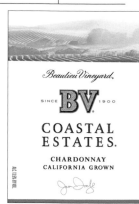

What does it taste like?

Ripe melon and red apple, with subtle vanilla and cream notes, full-bodied and creamy-textured

If you like this, then try with confidence . . .

Greater quality, greater intensity
Jacobs Creek Chardonnay Adelaide Hills
Greater quality, less intensity
The very best from the basic Mâcon-Villages appellation, such as Mâcon Solutré Clos des Bertillones Denogent

Try something completely different

The best Pinot Blanc from Alsace, starting with Domaine Weinbach or Collio Pinot Blanco from Schiopetto from Veneto in Italy

Beringer Cabernet Sauvignon

Highly Recommended	$	13.5%

What is it?

A dry red wine made from the Cabernet Sauvignon grape grown in California. Aged 8 months in American and French oak.

What does it taste like?

Juicy, with good intensity of sweet black cherry fruit, nice balance and drinkability

If you like this, then try with confidence . . .

Greater quality, greater intensity

Caymus Special Selection Cabernet Sauvignon or Dunn Vineyards Howell Mountain Cabernet Sauvignon

Greater quality, less intensity

Stag's Leap Cask 23 Estate Cabernet Sauvignon

Try something completely different

For a classic Bordeaux to match the intensity and voluptuousness of top California Cabernet Sauvignon, try a Merlot-dominated Pomerol such as châteaux L'Evangile, La Fleur-Pétrus, Latour à Pomerol, Petit-Village, Trotanoy and, if you can afford them, Pétrus and Le Pin

Beringer Chardonnay

Highly Recommended	**$**	**13.5%**

What is it?

A dry white wine made from the Chardonnay grape grown in California with subtle oak influence

What does it taste like?

Medium-bodied with spicy oak and sweet fruit. Notes of fig and melon with good length.

If you like this, then try with confidence . . .

Greater quality, greater intensity

Jacobs Creek Chardonnay Adelaide Hills

Greater quality, less intensity

The very best from the basic Mâcon-Villages appellation, such as Mâcon Solutré Clos des Bertillones Denogent

Try something completely different

The best Pinot Blanc from Alsace, starting with Domaine Weinbach or Collio Pinot Blanco from Schiopetto from Veneto in Italy

Beringer Private Reserve Cabernet Sauvignon

To Die For	$$$	14.5%

What is it?

A dry red wine made from the Cabernet Sauvignon grape grown in Napa, California. Aged in new French oak for 22 months.

What does it taste like?

Voluptuous and layered, with classic Cabernet fruit of black currant, cassis, black cherry jam and hints of toasty oak and eucalyptus. Full-bodied and powerful, with a very long finish.

If you like this, then try with confidence . . .

Greater quality, greater intensity

Caymus Special Selection Cabernet Sauvignon or Dunn Vineyards Howell Mountain Cabernet Sauvignon

Greater quality, less intensity

Stag's Leap Cask 23 Estate Cabernet Sauvignon

Try something completely different

For a classic Bordeaux to match the intensity and voluptuousness of top California Cabernet Sauvignon, try a Merlot-dominated Pomerol such as châteaux L'Evangile, La Fleur-Pétrus, Latour à Pomerol, Petit-Village, Trotanoy and, if you can afford them, Pétrus and Le Pin

Bisol Jeio Prosecco

Highly Recommended	$$	11.5%

What is it?

An off-dry sparkling wine made from predominantly the Glera grape (plus 5–7% Chardonnay) grown in Prosecco, in the Veneto region of northeastern Italy. Charmat method with no lees aging to retain fresh fruit character.

What does it taste like?

Longer, richer, fresher and better than most other Prosecco, and after a bar crawl through Venice I'm convinced Jeio makes the best Bellini in the world!

If you like this, then try with confidence . . .

Greater quality, greater intensity

Cru and Vintage Prosecco from Bisol (especially Cru Garnei and the Cartizze)

Greater quality, less intensity

Champagne De Venoge Vin du Paradis

Try something completely different

Veuve Clicquot Vintage Rich

Blackstone Merlot

Highly Recommended	$	13%

What is it?

A dry red wine made from a blend of grapes (82% Merlot, 10% Syrah and 18% other varieties) grown in California. Aged in French and American oak barrels (80% new) for 11 months.

What does it taste like?

A big, chunky wine full of blackberry and plum fruits, very soft and rich on the palate

If you like this, then try with confidence . . .

Greater quality, greater intensity

Great Merlot from California (Pahlmeyer, Paloma and Pride) or Washington (L'Ecole No. 41, Leonetti, Seven Hills and Woodward Canyon)

Greater quality, less intensity

Raphael Rosé of Merlot from Long Island

Try something completely different

Great Merlot-dominated blends from Pomerol, such as châteaux L'Evangile, La Fleur-Pétrus, Latour à Pomerol, Petit-Village, Trotanoy and, if you can afford them, Pétrus and Le Pin

Blandy's 10-Year Malmsey

Highly Recommended	$$$	19%

What is it?

A sweet fortified wine made from the Malmsey grape grown in Madeira, Portugal. Aged an average of 10 years in oak.

What does it taste like?

Intense nose of orange peel, roasted walnuts, with a thick texture and mouthwatering acidity

If you like this, then try with confidence . . .

Greater quality, greater intensity

Vintage Malmsey from Blandy's, Justino's and Quinta & Vineyard

Greater quality, less intensity

Vintage Verdelho from Blandy's and 15-Year-Old Verdelho from Henriques & Henriques

Try something completely different

Richer, alternative fortified wines, such as Australian Topaque (formerly called Liqueur Tokay) or, for a fresher, lighter, fruitier style, fortified Muscats of southern France

Blandy's Alvada 5-Year Madeira

Recommended	$$	19%

What is it?

A sweet fortified wine made from a blend of grapes (Malmsey and Bual) grown in Madeira, Portugal. Aged an average of 5 years in oak.

What does it taste like?

Very appealing, with lightly roasted walnut, juicy acidity and good length. Quite sweet.

If you like this, then try with confidence . . .

Greater quality, greater intensity

Blandy's 10-Year Malmsey, then start exploring vintage Boal and Malmsey Madeiras

Greater quality, less intensity

Henriques & Henriques 15-Year-Old Boal or 15-Year-Old Verdelho

Try something completely different

Richer, alternative fortified wines, such as Australian Topaque (formerly called Liqueur Tokay) or, for a fresher, lighter, fruitier style, fortified Muscats of southern France

Blossom Hill White Zinfandel

Recommended	$	10%

What is it?
A medium-sweet rosé wine made from the Zinfandel grape grown in California

What does it taste like?
Lots of clean fresh summer fruits

If you like this, then try with confidence . . .
Greater quality, greater intensity
A Kir, but made from a fine Moscato d'Asti rather than a dry white Burgundy, and the tiniest possible dash of Cassis for color
Greater quality, less intensity
Chateau de la Varière Cabernet d'Anjou Demi-Sec or dry rosés such as E. Guigal Côtes du-Rhône Rosé, or the fruitier Garnacha-based rosado of Navarra in Spain

Try something completely different
Riesling Kabinett or Spätlese from Germany

Blossom Hill Winemaker's Reserve Cabernet Sauvignon

Recommended	$	13%

What is it?

A dry red wine made from the Cabernet Sauvignon grape grown in California

What does it taste like?

Juicy, vibrant black cherry fruit, very pure and refreshing. Not too heavy.

If you like this, then try with confidence . . .

Greater quality, greater intensity

Caymus Special Selection Cabernet Sauvignon or Dunn Vineyards Howell Mountain Cabernet Sauvignon

Greater quality, less intensity

Stag's Leap Cask 23 Estate Cabernet Sauvignon

Try something completely different

For a classic Bordeaux to match the intensity and voluptuousness of top California Cabernet Sauvignon, try a Merlot-dominated Pomerol such as châteaux L'Evangile, La Fleur-Pétrus, Latour à Pomerol, Petit-Village, Trotanoy and, if you can afford them, Pétrus and Le Pin

Blossom Hill Winemaker's Reserve Sauvignon Blanc

Recommended	$	12.5%

What is it?

A dry white wine made from the Sauvignon Blanc grape grown in California

What does it taste like?

Very fresh, with herbs, grass, nettles and grapefruit flavors. Crisp and mouthwatering.

If you like this, then try with confidence . . .

Greater quality, greater intensity

Iconic Marlborough Sauvignon Blanc, such as Cloudy Bay, Craggy Range Avery Vineyard, Hunter's, Isabel Estate, Koura Whaleback, Nobilo Icon and Palliser Estate

Greater quality, less intensity

The finest, most elegant Pouilly-Fumé, such as Didier Dagueneau Silex and Pur Sang

Try something completely different

Lean, linear Riesling from Alsace (Trimbach Clos Ste Hune or JosMeyer Grand Cru Hengst) and Mosel (Maximin Grünhaus Abtsberg Alte Reben Trocken)

Bodega Norton Malbec Reserva

Highly Recommended	$$	14.5%

What is it?

A dry red wine made from the Malbec grape grown in Mendoza, Argentina. Aged in first- and second-use French oak barrels for 12 months plus 10 months in bottle prior to release.

What does it taste like?

Opaque purple. Boysenberry jam on the nose and a touch of graphite. Delicious, some oak on the finish, very creamy and rich texture with mild tannins.

If you like this, then try with confidence . . .

Greater quality, greater intensity

Luigi Bosca Vistalba Malbec and Nicolas Catena Zapata Malbec Argentino, then Flichman Parcelo 26 for the ultimate monster Malbec

Greater quality, less intensity

Colomé Malbec or Yacochuya Estate from Salta, Bodegas Lagarde Agrelo and Terrazas Afincado single-vineyard Malbecs

Try something completely different

Cahors from Clos Triguedina or Tannat Castel La Puebla Dayman from Stagnari in Uruguay

Bodega Norton Privada

Highly Recommended	**$$**	**14.5%**

What is it?

A dry red wine made from a blend of grapes (Malbec, Merlot and Cabernet Sauvignon) grown in Mendoza, Argentina. Aged in new French oak barrels for 16 months followed by 1 year in bottle prior to release.

What does it taste like?

Opaque ruby-purple. Dense fruit and texture, with black cherry jam and cassis flavors with well-integrated, ripe tannins.

If you like this, then try with confidence . . .

Greater quality, greater intensity

Nicolas Catena Zapata Malbec Argentino, then Flichman Parcelo 26

Greater quality, less intensity

Colomé Malbec or Yacochuya Estate from Salta, Bodegas Lagarde Agrelo and Terrazas Afincado single-vineyard Malbecs

Try something completely different

Cahors from Clos Triguedina or Tannat Castel La Puebla Dayman from Stagnari in Uruguay

Bodegas Lan Rioja Crianza

Recommended	**$**	**13.5%**

What is it?

A dry red wine made from the Tempranillo grape grown in Rioja, Spain. Aged in American and French oak barrels for 12 months, followed by several months in bottle prior to release.

What does it taste like?

Limestone minerality shines through with light cherry flavors, tea leaf tannins and bright acidity. Clean and consistent.

If you like this, then try with confidence . . .

Greater quality, greater intensity

Rioja from Finca Allende, Artadi, Lealtanza, Manzanos, Marqués de Griñon, Nekeas, Palacios Remondo, La Rioja Alta, San Vicente and Bodegas Ysios, then the very best wines of Barón de Ley, Luis Canas, Contino, Marqués de Murrieta, Marqués de Riscal and Bodegas Muga for ultimate quality

Greater quality, less intensity

Reserva and Gran Reserva from La Rioja Alta Viña Ardanza, Marqués de Cáceres and Viña Tondonia Rioja or any rosado from a top Rioja producer

Try something completely different

Numanthia Termes then Numanthia Termanthia from Toro

Bodegas Lan Rioja Culmen Reserva

To Die For	$$$	14%

What is it?

A dry red wine made from the Tempranillo grape grown in Rioja, Spain.
Aged in new French oak barrels for 18 months followed by 18 months
in the bottle prior to release.

What does it taste like?

Gorgeous and precise, with texture, depth and a multifaceted range of flavors
that sail through to a long finish

If you like this, then try with confidence . . .

Greater quality, greater intensity

Rioja from Finca Allende, Artadi, Lealtanza,
Manzanos, Marqués de Griñon, Nekeas, Palacios
Remondo, La Rioja Alta, San Vicente and Bodegas
Ysios, then the very best wines of Barón de Ley, Luis
Canas, Contino, Marqués de Murrieta, Marqués de
Riscal and Bodegas Muga for ultimate quality

Greater quality, less intensity

Reserva and Gran Reserva from La Rioja Alta Viña
Ardanza, Marqués de Cáceres and Viña Tondonia
Rioja or any rosado from a top Rioja producer

Try something completely different

Numanthia Termes then Numanthia Termanthia
from Toro

Bodegas Lan Rioja Reserva

Highly Recommended $$ | 13.5%

What is it?

A dry red wine made from the Tempranillo grape grown in Rioja, Spain. Aged in American and French oak barrels for at least 12 months, followed by 24 months in bottle prior to release.

What does it taste like?

Traditional yet polished style. The density of fruit stands up to the oak aging, lending structure and character.

If you like this, then try with confidence . . .

Greater quality, greater intensity

Rioja from Finca Allende, Artadi, Lealtanza, Manzanos, Marqués de Griñon, Nekeas, Palacios Remondo, La Rioja Alta,
San Vicente and Bodegas Ysios, then the very best wines of Barón de Ley, Luis Canas, Contino, Marqués de Murrieta, Marqués de Riscal and Bodegas Muga for ultimate quality

Greater quality, less intensity

Reserva and Gran Reserva from La Rioja Alta Viña Ardanza, Marqués de Cáceres and Viña Tondonia Rioja or any rosado from a top Rioja producer

Try something completely different

Numanthia Termes then Numanthia Termanthia from Toro

Bodegas Lan Rioja Viña Lanciano Reserva

Recommended	$$$	13.5%

What is it?

A dry red wine made from the Tempranillo grape grown in Rioja, Spain. Aged in Russian oak barrels for 6 months and in French oak barrels for 12 months followed by 18 months in bottle prior to release.

What does it taste like?

Modern-style Rioja, with dense, extracted, raisined fruit, full body and mild acidity

If you like this, then try with confidence . . .

Greater quality, greater intensity

Rioja from Finca Allende, Artadi, Lealtanza, Manzanos, Marqués de Griñon, Nekeas, Palacios Remondo, La Rioja Alta, San Vicente and Bodegas Ysios, then the very best wines of Barón de Ley, Luis Canas, Contino, Marqués de Murrieta, Marqués de Riscal and Bodegas Muga for ultimate quality

Greater quality, less intensity

Reserva and Gran Reserva from La Rioja Alta Viña Ardanza, Marqués de Cáceres and Viña Tondonia Rioja or any rosado from a top Rioja producer

Try something completely different

Numanthia Termes then Numanthia Termanthia from Toro

Bogle Chardonnay

Highly Recommended	**$**	**13.5%**

What is it?

A dry white wine made from the Chardonnay grape grown in California. Fermented in 50% new American oak followed by aging 9 months in new American oak.

What does it taste like?

A well-balanced wine that has weight on the palate yet remains fresh, with tropical fruit flavors and a hint of vanilla oak

If you like this, then try with confidence . . .

Greater quality, greater intensity

Jacobs Creek Chardonnay Adelaide Hills

Greater quality, less intensity

The very best from the basic Mâcon-Villages appellation, such as Mâcon Solutré Clos des Bertillones Denogent

Try something completely different

The best Pinot Blanc from Alsace, starting with Domaine Weinbach or Collio Pinot Blanco from Schiopetto in Veneto, Italy

Bogle Merlot

Recommended	**$**	**13.5%**

What is it?

A dry red wine made from the Merlot grape grown in California. Aged in American oak for 12 months.

What does it taste like?

Medium-bodied with sweet spice and jammy raspberry and black cherry flavors and velvety tannins

If you like this, then try with confidence . . .

Greater quality, greater intensity

Great Merlot from California (Pahlmeyer, Paloma and Pride) or Washington (L'Ecole No. 41, Leonetti, Seven Hills and Woodward Canyon)

Greater quality, less intensity

Raphael Rosé of Merlot from Long Island

Try something completely different

Great Merlot-dominated blends from Pomerol, such as châteaux L'Evangile, La Fleur-Pétrus, Latour à Pomerol, Petit-Village, Trotanoy and, if you can afford them, Pétrus and Le Pin

Bogle Old Vines Zinfandel

Highly Recommended	$	14.5%

What is it?
A dry red wine made from the Zinfandel grape grown in Lodi and Amador Counties, California. Aged in American oak for 10 months.

What does it taste like?
Solid example, not overdone, with raspberry jam and vanilla flavors. Very drinkable.

If you like this, then try with confidence . . .
Greater quality, greater intensity
Ravenswood Lodi Old Vine Zinfandel, then single vineyard Zinfandels from Ravenswood or Rosenblum
Greater quality, less intensity
Kendall Jackson Zinfandel Vintners Reserve, then single-vineyard Zinfandels by Ridge

Try something completely different
Zinfandel is a Croatian grape variety (Tribidrag, aka Crljenak Kastelanski) that is also grown in Puglia, Italy (as Primitivo), producing intensely ripe, full-bodied red wines at moderate prices.

Bogle Petite Sirah

Recommended	$	13.5%

What is it?
A dry red wine made from the Petite Sirah grape grown in California. Aged in American oak for 12 months.

What does it taste like?
Quite toasty and dark with intense licorice, blackberry and fig aromas. Thick texture and soft tannins.

If you like this, then try with confidence . . .
Greater quality, greater intensity
Ridge Vineyards Dynamite Hill, Rosenblum Rockpile, Turley Cellars Hayne Vineyard or Lava Cap Grand Hill
Greater quality, less intensity
Field Stone Rosé of Petite Sirah from the Alexander Valley

Try something completely different
Classic Syrah from California, Australia (Shiraz) and France (Crozes-Hermitage, St-Joseph and Cornas, then Hermitage and Côte Rôtie)

Bogle Phantom

Highly Recommended   **$$** | **14.5%**

What is it?

A dry red wine made from a blend of grapes (53% Petite Sirah, 44% Zinfandel, 3% Mourvèdre) grown in Clarksburg, Lodi and Amador Counties, California. Aged 24 months in American oak.

What does it taste like?

Very flavorful, smooth, thick and powerful, with a good mix of toasty oak and ripe berry fruit

If you like this, then try with confidence . . .

Greater quality, greater intensity

Ridge Vineyards Dynamite Hill, Rosenblum Rockpile, Turley Cellars Hayne Vineyard or Lava Cap Grand Hill

Greater quality, less intensity

Field Stone Rosé of Petite Sirah from the Alexander Valley

Try something completely different

Classic Syrah from California, Australia (Shiraz) and France (Crozes-Hermitage, St-Joseph and Cornas, then Hermitage and Côte Rôtie)

Bortoli, *see* De Bortoli

Bosca, *see* Luigi Bosca

Bramìto Chardonnay Castello della Salla

Highly Recommended	$$	13%

What is it?
A dry white wine made from the
Chardonnay grape grown in Umbria, Italy

What does it taste like?
Beautifully sleek and fresh Chardonnay,
with delicious orchard fruits and a lingering
vanilla finish

If you like this, then try with confidence . . .
Greater quality, greater intensity
Domaine Leflaive Puligny-Montrachet
Greater quality, less intensity
The very best from Mâcon, such as Mâcon
Solutré Clos des Bertillones Denogent

Try something completely different
White wines from cru classé châteaux in Pessac-Léognan

CASTELLO DELLA SALA

BRAMÌTO
del Corvo

CHARDONNAY
Umbria
Indicazione Geografica Tipica

Brancott Estate Pinot Noir

Highly Recommended	$$	13%

What is it?
A dry red wine made from the Pinot Noir grape
grown in Marlborough, New Zealand with subtle
oak influence

What does it taste like?
A fairly structured Pinot, with medium body, grippy
tannins and a solid core of red fruit

If you like this, then try with confidence . . .
Greater quality, greater intensity
Pinot Noir from Akarua, Ata Rangi, Craggy Range Te
Muna, Felton Road and Twin Paddocks
Greater quality, less intensity
Kim Crawford Marlborough New Zealand Pansy Rosé

Try something completely different
Fruit-driven Nebbiolo, such as Cascina Adelaide di
Amabile Drocco Barolo Fossati, Aldo Conterno Barolo Cicala, Parusso Barolo
Le Coste-Mosconi or G. D. Vajra Barolo Albe

BRANCOTT
ESTATE
NEW ZEALAND

MARLBOROUGH
PINOT NOIR
THE *Original* MARLBOROUGH PINOT NOIR

Brancott Estate Sauvignon Blanc

Recommended	$	12.5%

What is it?

A dry white wine made from the Sauvignon Blanc grape grown in Marlborough, New Zealand

What does it taste like?

Light nose, with peachy fruit and some herbal complexity

If you like this, then try with confidence . . .

Greater quality, greater intensity

Iconic Marlborough Sauvignon Blanc, such as Cloudy Bay, Craggy Range Avery Vineyard, Hunter's, Isabel Estate, Koura Whaleback, Nobilo Icon and Palliser Estate

Greater quality, less intensity

The finest, most elegant Pouilly-Fumé, such as Didier Dagueneau Silex and Pur Sang

Try something completely different

Lean, linear Riesling from Alsace (Trimbach Clos Ste Hune or JosMeyer Grand Cru Hengst) and Mosel (Maximin Grünhaus Abtsberg Alte Reben Trocken)

Cáceres, *see* **Marqués de Cáceres**

Cakebread Cabernet Sauvignon

Highly Recommended	$$$	14%

What is it?

A dry red wine made from a blend of grapes (76% Cabernet Sauvignon, 13% Merlot and 11% other varieties) grown in Napa, California. The wine is matured in French oak barrels (one-third new) for 18 months.

What does it taste like?

Deep ruby purple in color with aromas of cedar, freshly turned earth, dark chocolate and fresh black currant. Full-bodied but supple, with very fine tannins.

If you like this, then try with confidence . . .

Greater quality, greater intensity

Caymus Special Selection Cabernet Sauvignon or Dunn Vineyards Howell Mountain Cabernet Sauvignon

Greater quality, less intensity

Stag's Leap Cask 23 Estate Cabernet Sauvignon

Try something completely different

For a classic Bordeaux to match the intensity and voluptuousness of top California Cabernet Sauvignon, try a Merlot-dominated Pomerol such as châteaux L'Evangile, La Fleur-Pétrus, Latour à Pomerol, Petit-Village, Trotanoy and, if you can afford them, Pétrus and Le Pin

Cakebread Cellars

Napa Valley

Cabernet Sauvignon

ALCOHOL 14.1% BY VOLUME

Campo Viejo Rioja Reserva

Highly Recommended	$$	13.5%

What is it?
A dry red wine made from the Tempranillo grape grown in Rioja, Spain. Aged in American and French oak casks (half new) for 18 months followed by 18 months in bottle.

What does it taste like?
Good-intensity cranberry and dried strawberry flavors lead to grip, freshness and interest on the palate

If you like this, then try with confidence . . .
Greater quality, greater intensity
Rioja from Finca Allende, Artadi, Lealtanza, Manzanos, Marqués de Griñon, Nekeas, Palacios Remondo, La Rioja Alta, San Vicente and Bodegas Ysios, then the very best wines of Barón de Ley, Luis Canas, Contino, Marqués de Murrieta, Marqués de Riscal and Bodegas Muga for ultimate quality
Greater quality, less intensity
Reserva and Gran Reserva from La Rioja Alta Viña Ardanza, Marqués de Cáceres and Viña Tondonia Rioja or any rosado from a top Rioja producer

Try something completely different
Numanthia Termes then Numanthia Termanthia from Toro

Campo Viejo Rioja

Highly Recommended	$	13.5%

What is it?
A dry red wine made from the Tempranillo grape grown in Rioja, Spain. Aged in American oak barrels for 4 months.

What does it taste like?
Lovely purity, with fresh and flavorful strawberry and tobacco notes. Medium-bodied with a savory finish.

If you like this, then try with confidence . . .
Greater quality, greater intensity
Rioja from Finca Allende, Artadi, Lealtanza, Manzanos, Marqués de Griñon, Nekeas, Palacios Remondo, La Rioja Alta, San Vicente and Bodegas Ysios, then the very best wines of Barón de Ley, Luis Canas, Contino, Marqués de Murrieta, Marqués de Riscal and Bodegas Muga for ultimate quality
Greater quality, less intensity
Reserva and Gran Reserva from La Rioja Alta Viña Ardanza, Marqués de Cáceres and Viña Tondonia Rioja or any rosado from a top Rioja producer

Try something completely different
Numanthia Termes then Numanthia Termanthia from Toro

Casillero del Diablo, *see* **Concha y Toro Casillero del Diablo**

Castello Banfi Brunello di Montalcino

Highly Recommended	$$$	13.5%

What is it?

A dry red wine made from Sangiovese grapes. The wine is matured in small French and Slavonian oak barrels for 2 years, then in bottle for a further year before release.

What does it taste like?

Dried red cherry, touches of herb and dust, with fine but grippy tannins

If you like this, then try with confidence . . .

Greater quality, greater intensity

The richest Chianti Classico (Castello di Ama, Poggio al Sole Casasilia, Querciabella) and Brunello di Montalcino (Casanova di Neri, Case Basse, Mastrojanne, Siro Pacenti)

Greater quality, less intensity

Lighter and fruitier with Yalumba Y Series Sangiovese Rosé or Mitolo Jester McLaren Vale Sangiovese Rosé

Try something completely different

Check out Montepulciano d'Abruzzo (Valentini is best).

Castello de Poggio Moscato d'Asti

Highly Recommended	$$	5.5%

What is it?
A sweet white semi-sparkling wine made by Zonin from Moscato grapes grown in Asti, Piemonte, Italy

What does it taste like?
Rich and sweet, with exquisitely fresh, floral aromas and peachy fruit

If you like this, then try with confidence . . .
Greater quality, greater intensity
Richer, fully sparkling Asti from the very finest producers, such as Romano Dogliotti Asti La Selvatica or Cerutti Asti Cesare
Greater quality, less intensity
Marchesi di Grésy Moscato d'Asti

Try something completely different
The light-as-a-dime fortified Muscat de Beaumes-de-Venise from top producers such as Domaine des Bernardins or Durban

Castello de Poggio Moscato Provincia di Pavia

Highly Recommended	$$	5%

What is it?
A sweet white semi-sparkling wine made by Zonin from Moscato grapes grown in Asti, Piemonte, Italy

What does it taste like?
Intensely sweet, floral-musky fruit. Long and lingering.

If you like this, then try with confidence . . .
Greater quality, greater intensity
Richer, fully sparkling Asti from the very finest producers, such as Romano Dogliotti Asti La Selvatica or Cerutti Asti Cesare
Greater quality, less intensity
Castello de Poggio Moscato d'Asti

Try something completely different
The light-as-a-dime fortified Muscat de Beaumes-de-Venise from top producers such as Domaine des Bernardins or Durban

Catena Chardonnay

Recommended $$ 14%

What is it?

A dry white wine made from the Chardonnay grape grown in Mendoza, Argentina. The wine is fermented and aged for 9 months in small French oak barrels.

What does it taste like?

Banana, lemon and vanilla aromas, and a rich, creamy texture balanced by lively acidity

If you like this, then try with confidence . . .

Greater quality, greater intensity
Catena Angelica Zapata Chardonnay
Greater quality, less intensity
Catena Alta Chardonnay

Try something completely different

White wines from cru classé châteaux in Pessac-Léognan

Catena Malbec

Recommended $$ 14%

What is it?

A dry red wine made from the Malbec grape grown in Mendoza, Argentina. After a long maceration (both before and after the fermentation), the wine is matured in a mix of French and American small oak barrels for 14 months.

What does it taste like?

Deep purple, with intense dark bramble fruits with hints of violet, chocolate and vanilla. Full-bodied.

If you like this, then try with confidence . . .

Greater quality, greater intensity
Luigi Bosca Vistalba Malbec and Nicolas Catena Zapata Malbec Argentino, then Flichman Parcelo 26 for the ultimate monster Malbec
Greater quality, less intensity
Colomé Malbec or Yacochuya Estate from Salta, Bodegas Lagarde Agrelo and Terrazas Afincado single-vineyard Malbecs

Try something completely different

Cahors from Clos Triguedina or Tannat Castel La Puebla Dayman from Stagnari in Uruguay

Cavit Pinot Grigio

Recommended   **$**   **12%**

What is it?
A dry white wine made from the Pinot Grigio grape grown in Friuli-Venezia Giulia, Italy

What does it taste like?
Clean and fruity, with citrus and apple flavors.
An easy, friendly wine.

If you like this, then try with confidence . . .
Greater quality, greater intensity
JosMeyer Pinot Gris 1854 Fondation or Trimbach
Pinot Gris Réserve with a few years additional bottle-age
Greater quality, less intensity
JosMeyer Pinot Blanc Les Lutins or Domaine Weinbach Pinot Blanc

Try something completely different
A good Soave such as Pieropan or Inama, perhaps even Chasselas from Blaise Duboux in Switzerland or, for the very adventurous, a super-soft Koshu from Japan, such as Misawa Private Reserve from Grace

Caymus Cabernet Sauvignon

Highly Recommended   **$$$**   **14.5%**

What is it?
A dry red wine made from the Cabernet Sauvignon grape grown in Napa, California. Aged in French oak barrels for 16 months.

What does it taste like?
Very ripe, opulent style wrapped in new oak with vanilla and coffee aromas. Tannins are fine-grained, giving structure and a velvety texture. Long finish.

If you like this, then try with confidence . . .
Greater quality, greater intensity
Caymus Special Selection Cabernet Sauvignon or Dunn Vineyards Howell Mountain Cabernet Sauvignon
Greater quality, less intensity
Stag's Leap Cask 23 Estate Cabernet Sauvignon

Try something completely different
For a classic Bordeaux to match the intensity and voluptuousness of top California Cabernet Sauvignon, try a Merlot-dominated Pomerol such as châteaux L'Evangile, La Fleur Pétrus, Latour à Pomerol, Petit-Village, Trotanoy and, if you can afford them, Pétrus and Le Pin

Charles Heidsieck NV Brut Reserve

To Die For	$$$	12%

What is it?

A dry sparkling wine made from a blend of grapes (Pinot Noir, Chardonnay and Meunier) grown in Champagne, France. Traditional Method with lees aging for a minimum of 3 years and including a large proportion of reserve wines in the blend.

What does it taste like?

Very deep and rich yet vibrant, focused and fresh, with slowly evolving toasty notes. Layers and layers of flavors. Despite a steadily increasing price since 2012, this Champagne is superior to many vintage Champagnes and therefore remains an outstanding value.

If you like this, then try with confidence . . .

Greater quality, greater intensity

Charles Heidsieck Vintage or Charles Heidsieck Blanc des Millénaires

Greater quality, less intensity

Roederer NB Brut Premier

Try something completely different

The top sparkling wines from England (Camel Valley, Henners, Herbert Hall, Nyetimber, Ridgeview) and Tasmania (Bay of Fires, Clover Hill, Jansz, Stefano Lubiana, Pirie, Relbia)

Château-Fuissé Pouilly-Fuissé Les Brulés

To Die For	$$$	13.5%

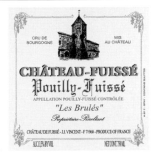

What is it?

A dry white wine made from the Chardonnay grape grown in Pouilly-Fuissé in Burgundy, France. Fermented and aged in new French oak for 12 months.

What does it taste like?

Good intensity on the nose with cream, smoke and ripe red apple aromas leading to a rich palate with peach fruit and fresh acidity

If you like this, then try with confidence . . .

Greater quality, greater intensity

Pouilly-Fuissé from Guffens-Heyen or Château-Fuissé Vieilles Vignes

Greater quality, less intensity

The very best from the basic Mâcon-Villages appellation, such as Mâcon Solutré Clos des Bertillones Denogent

Try something completely different

White wines from cru classé châteaux in Pessac-Léognan

Chateau Ste Michelle Cabernet Sauvignon

Highly Recommended	$$	13.5%

What is it?

A dry red wine made from the Cabernet Sauvignon grape grown in Columbia Valley, Washington. Aged in French and American oak (30% new) for 16 months.

What does it taste like?

Aromas of black currant, blackberry and charred oak with concentration and finesse on the palate. Medium-bodied with fine-grained tannins and a long finish.

If you like this, then try with confidence . . .

Greater quality, greater intensity

Leonetti or Quilceda Creek Cabernet Sauvignon

Greater quality, less intensity

Seven Hills and Woodward Canyon Cabernet Sauvignon

Try something completely different

For a classic Bordeaux to match the intensity of top Washington Cabernet Sauvignon, such as great Margaux, like châteaux Lascombes, Palmer and, if you can afford it, Château Margaux itself

Chateau Ste Michelle Canoe Ridge Estate Merlot

Highly Recommended	$$	14.5%

What is it?

A dry red wine made from the Merlot grape grown in Columbia Valley, Washington. Two thirds was aged in new oak (mostly French with a little American) for 18 months.

What does it taste like?

Intense spiced cake aromas, dark fruit and plush tannins

If you like this, then try with confidence . . .

Greater quality, greater intensity

Great Merlot from California (Pahlmeyer, Paloma and Pride) or Washington (L'Ecole No. 41, Leonetti, Seven Hills and Woodward Canyon)

Greater quality, less intensity

Raphael Rosé of Merlot from Long Island

Try something completely different

Great Merlot-dominated blends from Pomerol, such as châteaux L'Evangile, La Fleur-Pétrus, Latour à Pomerol, Petit-Village, Trotanoy and, if you can afford them, Pétrus and Le Pin

Chateau Ste Michelle Chardonnay

Recommended	$$	13.5%

What is it?

A dry white wine made from the Chardonnay grape grown in Columbia Valley, Washington. 100% of the wine went through malolactic fermentation and was aged on the lees for 6 months in French and American oak (10% new).

What does it taste like?

Ripe apple and melon flavors with a buttery, round texture

If you like this, then try with confidence . . .

Greater quality, greater intensity

Any white Burgundy from Domaine (not Olivier) Leflaive

Greater quality, less intensity

The very best from the basic Mâcon-Villages appellation, such as Mâcon Solutré Clos des Bertillones Denogent

Try something completely different

The best Pinot Blanc from Alsace, starting with Domaine Weinbach or Collio Pinot Blanco from Schiopetto from Veneto in Italy

Chateau Ste Michelle Dry Riesling

Highly Recommended	$	13%

What is it?

A dry white wine made from the Riesling grape grown in Columbia Valley, Washington

What does it taste like?

Fresh, light-bodied and slightly tangy, with white peach and white nectarine flavors

If you like this, then try with confidence . . .

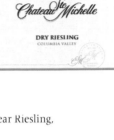

Greater quality, greater intensity

The best dry Australian Riesling, such as Pewsey Vale The Contours Museum Reserve, Grosset Polish Hill and Pressing Matters (R0 or R9)

Greater quality, less intensity

Observatory Hill Vintner's Reserve or, for a leaner, more linear Riesling, Puddleduck from Tasmania

Try something completely different

Dry Australian Semillon, particularly from the Hunter Valley, with several years bottle-age

Chateau Ste Michelle Merlot

Highly Recommended	$$	13.5%

What is it?

A dry red wine made from the Merlot grape grown in Columbia Valley, Washington. Aged in French and American oak (one-third new) for 16 months.

What does it taste like?

Nice depth of aroma, with smoky, sultry black plum and black cherry jam. Medium-full-bodied and plush with just enough tannic grip.

If you like this, then try with confidence . . .

Greater quality, greater intensity

Great Merlot from California (Pahlmeyer, Paloma and Pride) or Washington (L'Ecole No. 41, Leonetti, Seven Hills and Woodward Canyon)

Greater quality, less intensity

Raphael Rosé of Merlot from Long Island

Try something completely different

Great Merlot-dominated blends from Pomerol, such as châteaux L'Evangile, La Fleur-Pétrus, Latour à Pomerol, Petit-Village, Trotanoy and, if you can afford them, Pétrus and Le Pin

Chateau Ste Michelle Riesling Eroica

To Die For	$$	12.5%

What is it?

An off-dry white wine made from the Riesling grape grown in Columbia Valley, Washington. Residual Sugar 16 g/l.

What does it taste like?

Off-dry with laser beam acidity, and mouthwatering flavors of nectarine and lemon curd with surprising minerality; begs for food

If you like this, then try with confidence . . .

Greater quality, greater intensity

Dr. Loosen's own single-vineyard wines, especially Spätlese wines from Erdener Treppchen (and Prälat) and Wehlener Sonnenuhr

Greater quality, less intensity

Fine, off-dry whites in a more restrained style, such as single-vineyard Rieslings from Max Ferd Richter and J.J. Prüm

Try something completely different

High-quality Vouvray Demi-Sec from producers such as Domaine du Clos Naudin by Philippe Foreau

Chateau Ste Michelle Riesling

Highly Recommended	$	11%

What is it?
An off-dry white wine made from the Riesling grape grown in Columbia Valley, Washington. Residual Sugar 22 g/l.

What does it taste like?
Just delicious, with loads of fresh apples and peaches, and a precise balance of sweetness and vibrant acidity

If you like this, then try with confidence . . .
Greater quality, greater intensity
Chateau Ste Michelle Riesling Eroica
Greater quality, less intensity
Observatory Hill Vintner's Reserve or, for a leaner, more linear Riesling, Puddleduck from Tasmania

Try something completely different
Dry Australian Semillon, particularly from the Hunter Valley, with several years bottle-age

Christian Moreau Chablis

Highly Recommended	$$	13%

What is it?
A dry white wine made from the Chardonnay grape grown in Chablis, Burgundy, France

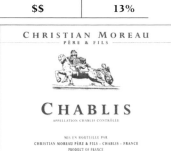

What does it taste like?
Fruity style, with a soft texture and juicy acidity. Crowd-pleasing, with ripe golden apple and lemon curd flavors and a hint of smoke.

If you like this, then try with confidence . . .
Greater quality, greater intensity
Premier, then Grand Cru Chablis from Michel Laroche
Greater quality, less intensity
The very best from the basic Mâcon-Villages appellation, such as Mâcon Solutré Clos des Bertillones Denogent

Try something completely different
The best Pinot Blanc from Alsace, starting with Domaine Weinbach or Collio Pinot Blanco from Schiopetto from Veneto in Italy

Churchill's 10-Year Tawny

| **Highly Recommended** | **$$$** | 19.5% |

What is it?

A sweet fortified wine made from a blend of grapes (Tinta Barroca, Tinta Roriz, Touriga Franca, Touriga Nacional and other traditional Port varieties) grown in Douro, Portugal. Aged an average of 10 years in oak.

What does it taste like?

Pronounced aromas of roasted walnut, candied orange rind and crème caramel. Full-bodied and creamy, with a long, balanced aftertaste.

If you like this, then try with confidence . . .

Greater quality, greater intensity
Taylor Fladgate 10-Year Tawny
Greater quality, less intensity
The best of the lower end of the scale Tawny Ports, such as Warre's King's Tawny or Delaforce Finest Tawny

Try something completely different

The tawny-like Fondillón, a 15-year-old Monastrell, with a non-fortified 16% of alcohol from Casta Diva in Alicante, Spain, or Penfolds Club Reserve Classic Tawny, then the truly iconic Penfolds Grandfather and Great Grandfather Rare Tawnies

Clicquot, *see* Veuve Clicquot

Clos du Val Cabernet Sauvignon Stags Leap District

Highly Recommended	**$$$**	**14.5%**

What is it?

A dry red wine made predominantly from the Cabernet Sauvignon grape grown in Stags Leap District, Napa, California. Aged 24 months in small French oak barrels (50% new).

What does it taste like?

Potent powerhouse wine packed with blackberry and cassis flavors and loads of toasty oak

If you like this, then try with confidence . . .

Greater quality, greater intensity

Caymus Special Selection Cabernet Sauvignon or Dunn Vineyards Howell Mountain Cabernet Sauvignon

Greater quality, less intensity

Stag's Leap Cask 23 Estate Cabernet Sauvignon

Try something completely different

For a classic Bordeaux to match the intensity and voluptuousness of top California Cabernet Sauvignon, try a Merlot-dominated Pomerol such as châteaux L'Evangile, La Fleur-Pétrus, Latour à Pomerol, Petit-Village, Trotanoy and, if you can afford them, Pétrus and Le Pin

Clos du Val Cabernet Sauvignon

Highly Recommended	$$$	13.5%

What is it?
A dry red wine made predominantly from the Cabernet Sauvignon grape grown in Napa, California. Aged 18 months in small French oak barrels (25% new).

What does it taste like?
Restrained style of Cabernet that is perfectly suited for food. Black cherry, black currant flavors, a hint of eucalyptus and toasty oak.

If you like this, then try with confidence . . .
Greater quality, greater intensity
Caymus Special Selection Cabernet Sauvignon or Dunn Vineyards Howell Mountain Cabernet Sauvignon
Greater quality, less intensity
Stag's Leap Cask 23 Estate Cabernet Sauvignon

Try something completely different
For a classic Bordeaux to match the intensity and voluptuousness of top California Cabernet Sauvignon, try a Merlot-dominated Pomerol such as châteaux L'Evangile, La Fleur-Pétrus, Latour à Pomerol, Petit-Village, Trotanoy and, if you can afford them, Pétrus and Le Pin

Clos du Val Chardonnay

Highly Recommended	**$$**	**13.5%**

What is it?

A dry white wine made from the Chardonnay grape grown in Carneros, California. The wine was fermented and aged for 10 months in small French oak barrels (20% new).

What does it taste like?

Restrained, elegant style with aromas of white figs and toast. Juicy acidity balances the viscosity. On the palate there's plenty of ripe pear and cinnamon, yet the oak is well integrated.

If you like this, then try with confidence . . .

Greater quality, greater intensity

Any white Burgundy from Domaine (not Olivier) Leflaive

Greater quality, less intensity

The very best from the basic Mâcon-Villages appellation, such as Mâcon Solutré Clos des Bertillones Denogent

Try something completely different

The best Pinot Blanc from Alsace, starting with Domaine Weinbach or Collio Pinot Blanco from Schiopetto from Veneto in Italy

Clos du Val Merlot

Highly Recommended	$$$	13.5%

What is it?

A dry red wine made predominantly from the Merlot grape grown in Napa, California. Aged 17 months in small French oak barrels (25% new).

What does it taste like?

Excellent varietal character with black cherry, black plum and complex hints of eucalyptus and tobacco with great structure and depth

If you like this, then try with confidence . . .

Greater quality, greater intensity

Great Merlot from California (Pahlmeyer, Paloma and Pride) or Washington (L'Ecole No. 41, Leonetti, Seven Hills and Woodward Canyon)

Greater quality, less intensity

Raphael Rosé of Merlot from Long Island

Try something completely different

Great Merlot-dominated blends from Pomerol, such as châteaux L'Evangile, La Fleur-Pétrus, Latour à Pomerol, Petit-Village, Trotanoy and, if you can afford them, Pétrus and Le Pin

Clos du Val Pinot Noir

Highly Recommended   **$$$** | **13.5%**

What is it?

A dry red wine made from the Pinot Noir grape grown in Carneros, California. Aged 14 months in small French oak barrels (20% new).

What does it taste like?

Rich cherry-cola, a hint of tree bark, with a satiny texture, excellent length and depth. Very balanced and classy.

If you like this, then try with confidence . . .

Greater quality, greater intensity

La Bauge au Dessus and other Pinot Noir from Au Bon Climat in Santa Barbara, California, or Le Grand Clos Pinot Noir from Le Clos Jordanne in Niagara, Canada

Greater quality, less intensity

The more elegant Oregon Pinot Noir, starting with Adelsheim, Bethel Heights and Rex Hill

Try something completely different

Fruit-driven Nebbiolo, such as Cascina Adelaide di Amabile Drocco Barolo Fossati, Aldo Conterno Barolo Cicala, Parusso Barolo Le Coste-Mosconi or G. D. Vajra Barolo Albe

Cloudy Bay Sauvignon Blanc

Highly Recommended	$$$	13.5%

What is it?

A dry white wine made from the Sauvignon Blanc grape grown in Marlborough, New Zealand

What does it taste like?

Often softer than other Marlborough Sauvignon Blanc, yet it still has plenty of pungent, herbaceous fruit, sometimes mingling with a little passion fruit, too; lively and refreshing, with a lingering, mouthwatering finish

If you like this, then try with confidence . . .

Greater quality, greater intensity

Iconic Marlborough Sauvignon Blanc, such as Cloudy Bay, Craggy Range Avery Vineyard, Hunter's, Isabel Estate, Koura Whaleback, Nobilo Icon and Palliser Estate

Greater quality, less intensity

The finest, most elegant Pouilly-Fumé, such as Didier Dagueneau Silex and Pur Sang

Try something completely different

Lean, linear Riesling from Alsace (Trimbach Clos Ste Hune or JosMeyer Grand Cru Hengst) and Mosel (Maximin Grünhaus Abtsberg Alte Reben Trocken)

Cockburn's Special Reserve

Recommended	$$	19.5%

What is it?

A sweet fortified red wine made from a blend of grapes (Tinta Barroca, Tinta Roriz, Touriga Franca, Touriga Nacional and other traditional Port varieties) grown in Douro, Portugal

What does it taste like?

Sweet with intense spicy fruit and warming alcohol

If you like this, then try with confidence . . .

Greater quality, greater intensity

The finest quality, most intense ruby-style wines such as Vintage Ports from Taylor's, Graham's and Fonseca

Greater quality, less intensity

The finest quality, least intense ruby style is Ferreira's Vintage Port, but try also single-quinta Ports and, the lightest of all, "pink" Port from Croft, Porto Cruz and Quinta & Vineyard

Try something completely different

Other sweet, ruby-style fortified wines, such as Banyuls from France or Australian Ruby and Australian Vintage (both formerly known as Australian Liqueur Port)

Codorníu Cava Anna de Codorníu Brut Reserva

Recommended	$$	11.5%

What is it?

A dry sparkling wine made from a blend of grapes (70% Chardonnay, 10% Macabeo, 10% Parellada, and 10% reserve wines), grown in Penedès, Spain. Made in the Traditional Method with aging on the lees for at least 9 months.

What does it taste like?

Vibrant lemon, white flowers and green apple, very fresh and light in body yet intense in flavor

If you like this, then try with confidence . . .

Greater quality, greater intensity

Charles Heidsieck NV Brut Réserve

Greater quality, less intensity

Pommery Cuvée Louise or, if you can afford it, Louis Roederer Cristal

Try something completely different

Ca'del Bosco Cuvée Annamaria Clementi after two or three years additional aging

Codorníu Cava Brut Original

Recommended	$	11.5%

What is it?

A dry sparkling wine made from a blend of grapes (40% Macabeo, 30% Parellada, 20% Xarel-lo and 10% blended base wines) grown in Penedès, Spain. Made in the Traditional Method and aged for 9 months on the lees.

What does it taste like?

Simple, clean and fresh citrus fruit with subtle smokiness. Light in body.

If you like this, then try with confidence . . .

Greater quality, greater intensity

Charles Heidsieck NV Brut Réserve

Greater quality, less intensity

Pommery Cuvée Louise or, if you can afford it, Louis Roederer Cristal

Try something completely different

Ca'del Bosco Cuvée Annamaria Clementi after two or three years additional aging

Codorníu Cava Pinot Noir Brut Rosé

Highly Recommended	$$	11.5%

What is it?

A dry sparkling rosé wine made from the Pinot Noir grape grown in Penedès, Spain. Made in the Traditional Method with aging on the lees for at least 9 months.

What does it taste like?

Freshly picked raspberries and strawberries, very lively and refreshing

If you like this, then try with confidence . . .

Greater quality, greater intensity

Charles Heidsieck Brut Rosé

Greater quality, less intensity

Billecart Salmon NV Brut Rosé

Try something completely different

Camel Valley Pinot Noir Brut

Col Solare

To Die For	$$$	14.5%

What is it?

A dry red wine made from a blend of grapes (75% Cabernet Sauvignon, 20% Merlot, 5% Cabernet Franc) grown in Columbia Valley, Washington. Malolactic fermentation occurred in new oak (mostly French with a little American) followed by a period of aging for 21 months in barrel.

What does it taste like?

Pronounced nose of black cherry, black currant, notes of herb, cedar and vanilla. Great palate structure, with judicious, ripe tannins.
A well-balanced, long and flavorful wine.

If you like this, then try with confidence . . .

Greater quality, greater intensity
Massive, tannic, intense Napa Cabernets, such as Abreu

Greater quality, less intensity
Penfolds Bin 407, or Cabernet-dominated Bordeaux left-bank wines such as Château Pichon-Baron and Château Mouton-Rothschild

Try something completely different

Pure Cabernet Sauvignon from Washington (Andrew Will, Woodward Canyon), Australia (Houghton's Jack Mann, Balnaves The Tally) and Spain (Marqués de Griñon)

Columbia Crest Grand Estates Cabernet Sauvignon

Recommended	$$	13.5%

What is it?
A dry red wine made from the Cabernet Sauvignon grape grown in Columbia Valley, Washington. Aged in French oak barrels (one-third new) for 16 months.

What does it taste like?
Rich, plush texture, quite ripe, jammy black cherry and blackberry fruit with smoky oak on the finish

If you like this, then try with confidence . . .
Greater quality, greater intensity
Leonetti or Quilceda Creek Cabernet Sauvignon
Greater quality, less intensity
Seven Hills and Woodward Canyon Cabernet Sauvignon

Try something completely different
For a classic Bordeaux to match the intensity of top Washington Cabernet Sauvignon, try a great Margaux, like châteaux Lascombes, Palmer and, if you can afford it, Château Margaux itself

Columbia Crest Grand Estates Chardonnay

Recommended	$$	13.5%

What is it?
A dry white wine made from the Chardonnay grape grown in Columbia Valley, Washington. A quarter of the wine was fermented in stainless steel while the rest was fermented in used American and French oak barrels before being aged a further 8 months in barrel.

What does it taste like?
Aromas of toast, vanilla and red apple, with good weight and length

If you like this, then try with confidence . . .
Greater quality, greater intensity
Any white Burgundy from Domaine (not Olivier) Leflaive
Greater quality, less intensity
The very best from the basic Mâcon-Villages appellation, such as Mâcon Solutré Clos des Bertillones Denogent

Try something completely different
The best Pinot Blanc from Alsace, starting with Domaine Weinbach or Collio Pinot Blanco from Schiopetto from Veneto in Italy

Columbia Crest Grand Estates Merlot

Recommended	$$	13.5%

What is it?
A dry red wine made from the Merlot grape grown in
Columbia Valley, Washington. Aged in French oak barrels
(one-third new) for 14 months.

What does it taste like?
Pronounced toasty oak aromas with dark cherry and plum
flavors and a rich, smooth texture

If you like this, then try with confidence . . .
Greater quality, greater intensity
Merlot from L'Ecole No. 41, Leonetti, Seven Hills and
Woodward Canyon
Greater quality, less intensity
Raphael Rosé of Merlot from Long Island

Try something completely different
Great Merlot-dominated blends from Pomerol, such as châteaux L'Evangile,
La Fleur-Pétrus, Latour à Pomerol, Petit-Village, Trotanoy and, if you can afford
them, Pétrus and Le Pin

Concha y Toro Casillero del Diablo Reserva Cabernet Sauvignon

Recommended	$	13.5%

What is it?
A dry red wine made from the Cabernet Sauvignon
grape grown in the Central Valley, Chile. Two thirds
is aged in American oak barrels for 8 months.

What does it taste like?
Ripe black currant and refreshing eucalyptus, with
hints of coffee. Juicy and medium-bodied.

If you like this, then try with confidence . . .
Greater quality, greater intensity
Louis Filipe Edwards Family Selection Gran Reserve
Cabernet Sauvignon
Greater quality, less intensity
Louis Filipe Edwards Pupilla Cabernet Sauvignon

Try something completely different
Washington Merlot from the best producers, such as L'Ecole No. 41, Leonetti,
Seven Hills and Woodward Canyon

Concha y Toro Casillero del Diablo Reserva Carmenère

Recommended		$	13.5%

What is it?

A dry red wine made from the Carmenère grape grown in Rapel Valley, Chile. Two thirds is aged in American oak barrels for 9 months.

What does it taste like?

Intense blackberry, red pepper, chocolate and spices. Rich and warming on the palate.

If you like this, then try with confidence . . .

Greater quality, greater intensity

Concha y Toro Terrunyo Carmenère

Greater quality, less intensity

Anakena Carmenère Single Vineyard

Try something completely different

Chilean Merlot or Cabernet Franc from Franciacorta in Italy

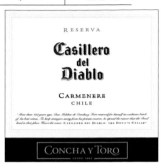

Concha y Toro Casillero del Diablo Reserva Chardonnay

Recommended		$	13.5%

What is it?

A dry white wine made from the Chardonnay grape grown in Casablanca and Limarí, Chile. One third is fermented and aged in small French barrels.

What does it taste like?

Pineapple and banana, with hints of yogurt and toast. Creamy texture.

If you like this, then try with confidence . . .

Greater quality, greater intensity

Any white Burgundy from Domaine (not Olivier) Leflaive

Greater quality, less intensity

The very best from the basic Mâcon-Villages appellation, such as Mâcon Solutré Clos des Bertillones Denogent

Try something completely different

White wines from cru classé châteaux in Pessac-Léognan

Coopers Creek Marlborough Pinot Noir

Recommended	$$	14%

What is it?

A dry red wine made from Pinot Noir grapes grown in Marlborough, New Zealand, with some oak aging

What does it taste like?

Richly flavored, supported by supple tannins, with black cherries and juicy ripe Victoria plums on the palate

If you like this, then try with confidence . . .

Greater quality, greater intensity

Pinot Noir from Akarua, Ata Rangi, Craggy Range Te Muna, Felton Road and Twin Paddocks

Greater quality, less intensity

Kim Crawford Marlborough New Zealand Pansy Rosé

Try something completely different

Fruit-driven Nebbiolo, such as Cascina Adelaide di Amabile Drocco Barolo Fossati, Aldo Conterno Barolo Cicala, Parusso Barolo Le Coste-Mosconi or G. D. Vajra Barolo Albe

Coopers Creek Marlborough Riesling

Highly Recommended	$$	12%

What is it?

A dry white wine made from the Riesling grape grown in Marlborough, New Zealand

What does it taste like?

Crisp, mouthwatering and off-dry with intense citrus fruit and extreme purity on the finish

If you like this, then try with confidence . . .

Greater quality, greater intensity

Pressing Matters R0 from Tasmania

Greater quality, less intensity

Observatory Hill Vintner's Reserve or, for a leaner, more linear Riesling, Puddleduck from Tasmania

Try something completely different

Dry Australian Semillon, particularly from the Hunter Valley, with several years bottle-age

Coopers Creek Marlborough Sauvignon Blanc

Recommended	$$	13%

What is it?

A dry white wine made from the Sauvignon Blanc grape grown in Marlborough, New Zealand. Vintages older than 2 years are easily found and should be avoided.

What does it taste like?

Classic Marlborough gooseberry, leaning toward citrus and passion fruit. Drink before two years old.

If you like this, then try with confidence . . .

Greater quality, greater intensity

Iconic Marlborough Sauvignon Blanc, such as Cloudy Bay, Craggy Range Avery Vineyard, Hunter's, Isabel Estate, Koura Whaleback, Nobilo Icon and Palliser Estate

Greater quality, less intensity

The finest, most elegant Pouilly-Fumé, such as Didier Dagueneau Silex and Pur Sang

Try something completely different

Lean, linear Riesling from Alsace (Trimbach Clos Ste Hune or JosMeyer Grand Cru Hengst) and Mosel (Maximin Grünhaus Abtsberg Alte Reben Trocken)

Coto de Imaz Rioja Reserva

Highly Recommended	$$	13.5%

What is it?

A dry red wine made from the Tempranillo grape grown in Rioja, Spain. Aged in small American oak barrels for 18 months followed by 24 months in the bottle prior to release.

What does it taste like?

Delicious strawberry fruit supported by structured, integrated oak. Additional flavors of herbs, leather and spice on the palate with a long, savory finish.

If you like this, then try with confidence . . .

Greater quality, greater intensity

Rioja from Finca Allende, Artadi, Lealtanza, Manzanos, Marqués de Griñon, Nekeas, Palacios Remondo, La Rioja Alta, San Vicente and Bodegas Ysios, then the very best wines of Barón de Ley, Luis Canas, Contino, Marqués de Murrieta, Marqués de Riscal and Bodegas Muga for ultimate quality

Greater quality, less intensity

Reserva and Gran Reserva from La Rioja Alta Viña Ardanza, Marqués de Cáceres and Viña Tondonia Rioja or any rosado from a top Rioja producer

Try something completely different

Numanthia Termes then Numanthia Termanthia from Toro

Crawford, *see* **Kim Crawford**

Crema, *see* **La Crema**

De Bortoli Noble One

To Die For	$$$	10%

What is it?

A sweet white wine made from botrytized Semillon grapes grown in New South Wales, Australia. A portion of the wine was aged in French oak (40% new, 30% used, 30% no oak).

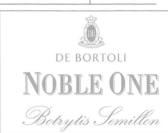

What does it taste like?

Intense aromas of honey, tinned apricot, beeswax, chamomile. Excellent balance between sugar and acidity that makes it a delight to consume.

If you like this, then try with confidence . . .

Greater quality, greater intensity

There are not many wines that can claim to be of greater intensity than this iconic botrytis wine. Maybe a PX Sherry, but that is so sweet it's better poured over ice cream!

Greater quality, less intensity

Good Sauternes, the original botrytized Sémillon, such as classed-growth châteaux like Coutet, Climens, Rieussec, Suduiraud and, if you can afford it, Yquem

Try something completely different

Great, unique, fortified sweet wines from the likes of Chambers, Morris and Stanton & Killeen in Rutherglen, Australia

Dom Pérignon

To Die For	**$$$**	**12.5%**

What is it?

A dry sparkling wine made from a blend of grapes (Pinot Noir and Chardonnay) grown in Champagne, France. Traditional Method with lees aging for 6–8 years.

What does it taste like?

Not exactly inexpensive, but it is the most widely distributed prestige cuvée in the world and, if given at least a further 2 years aging (to impart silkiness to the mousse and, through this, finesse to the wine), Dom Pérignon is, without doubt, one of the greatest Champagnes produced. A seamless blend of Pinot Noir and Chardonnay, this Champagne evolves slowly and gracefully, with tiny wisps of toastiness lifting the dried fruits, candied peel, allspice and creaminess on the palate.

If you like this, then try with confidence . . .

Greater quality, greater intensity

Dom Pérignon Oenotheque

Greater quality, less intensity

Taittinger Comtes de Champagne and Laurent Perrier Grand Siècle La Cuvée are also exceptionally elegant.

Try something completely different

The top sparkling wines from England (Camel Valley, Henners, Herbert Hall, Nyetimber, Ridgeview) and Tasmania (Bay of Fires, Clover Hill, Jansz, Stefano Lubiana, Pirie, Relbia)

Domaine Chandon Brut Classic NV

Recommended	$$	12%

What is it?
A dry white sparkling wine made from a blend of grapes (Chardonnay, Pinot Noir and Meunier) grown in California. The wine is made using the Traditional Method and is matured on its lees for a minimum of 12 months before disgorgement.

What does it taste like?
Fresh, attractively fruity and floral, with just a hint of yeast-induced complexity on the finish

If you like this, then try with confidence . . .
Greater quality, greater intensity
Moët & Chandon Grand Vintage
Greater quality, less intensity
Dom Pérignon

Try something completely different
The best American sparkling wines beyond California, such as Argyle in Oregon, Mountain Dome in Washington, L. Mawby in Michigan and Lamoreaux Landing in New York

Domaine Leflaive, see Olivier Leflaive

Domaine Ste Michelle Blanc de Blancs

Recommended	$$	12%

What is it?
A dry sparkling wine made from the Chardonnay grape grown in Columbia Valley, Washington. Traditional Method with lees aging for 18 months.

What does it taste like?
Clean, with light, pleasant biscuit and pear flavors

If you like this, then try with confidence . . .
Greater quality, greater intensity
Charles Heidsieck NV Brut Réserve
Greater quality, less intensity
Pommery Cuvée Louise or, if you can afford it, Louis Roederer Cristal

Try something completely different
Ca'del Bosco Cuvée Annamaria Clementi after two or three years additional aging

Domaine Ste Michelle Brut

Recommended	$$	11.5%

What is it?

A dry sparkling wine made from a blend of grapes (88% Chardonnay, 12% Pinot Noir) grown in Columbia Valley, Washington. Traditional Method with lees aging for 18 months.

What does it taste like?

Ripe fruit, with pear and apple flavors, just a hint of sweetness and a light, fresh finish

If you like this, then try with confidence . . .

Greater quality, greater intensity

Charles Heidsieck NV Brut Réserve

Greater quality, less intensity

Pommery Cuvée Louise or, if you can afford it, Louis Roederer Cristal

Try something completely different

Ca'del Bosco Cuvée Annamaria Clementi after two or three years additional aging

Dow's 10-Year Tawny

Highly Recommended	$$$	20%

What is it?

A sweet fortified wine made from a blend of grapes (Tinta Barroca, Tinta Roriz, Touriga Franca, Touriga Nacional and other traditional Port varieties) grown in Douro, Portugal. Aged an average of 10 years in oak.

What does it taste like?

Complex combination of dried fruit and nuts, very rich and luxurious

If you like this, then try with confidence . . .

Greater quality, greater intensity

Dow's 20-Year-Old Tawny or Taylor Fladgate 10-Year Tawny

Greater quality, less intensity

Taylor Fladgate 20-Year Tawny Port and Sandeman Twenty Years Old Tawny Port. Both are intensely flavored, but more elegant, complex and harmonious.

Try something completely different

The tawny-like Fondillón, a 15-year-old Monastrell, with a non-fortified 16% of alcohol from Casta Diva in Alicante, Spain, or Penfolds Club Reserve Classic Tawny, then the truly iconic Penfolds Grandfather and Great Grandfather Rare Tawnies

Dow's Late Bottled Vintage

| **Highly Recommended** | **$$** | **19.5%** |

What is it?

A sweet fortified red wine made from a blend of grapes (Tinta Barroca, Tinta Roriz, Touriga Franca, Touriga Nacional and other traditional Port varieties) grown in Douro, Portugal

What does it taste like?

Thick texture, but very balanced, with expressive dark red fruit and violet notes and well-integrated tannins

If you like this, then try with confidence . . .

Greater quality, greater intensity

The finest quality, most intense ruby-style wines such as Vintage Ports from Taylor's, Graham's and Fonseca

Greater quality, less intensity

The finest quality, least intense ruby style is Ferreira's Vintage Port, but try also single-quinta Ports and, the lightest of all, "pink" Port from Croft, Porto Cruz and Quinta & Vineyard

Try something completely different

Other sweet, ruby-style fortified wines, such as Banyuls from France or Australian Ruby and Australian Vintage (both formerly known as Australian Liqueur Port)

Dow's Vale do Bomfim Douro

Highly Recommended	**$$**	**14%**

VALE DO BOMFIM
DOURO D.O.C.

What is it?

A dry red wine made from a blend of grapes (Tinta Barroca, Tinta Roriz, Touriga Franca, Touriga Nacional and other traditional Port varieties) grown in Douro, Portugal with no oak influence

What does it taste like?

Full-bodied, yet gently structured and very appealing, with flavors of wild berries and violets and a complete finish

If you like this, then try with confidence . . .

Greater quality, greater intensity

The finest quality, most intense ruby-style wines such as Vintage Ports from Taylor's, Graham's and Fonseca

Greater quality, less intensity

The finest quality, least intense ruby style is Ferreira's Vintage Port, but try also single-quinta Ports and, the lightest of all, "pink" Port from Croft, Porto Cruz and Quinta & Vineyard

Try something completely different

Other sweet, ruby-style fortified wines, such as Banyuls from France or Australian Ruby and Australian Vintage (both formerly known as Australian Liqueur Port)

Dr. L Riesling

Highly Recommended	**$$**	**8.5%**

What is it?

A medium-sweet white wine made from the Riesling grape grown in the Mosel Valley, Germany. Low alcohol, made at the famous Dr. Loosen winery from locally sourced grapes.

What does it taste like?

Wonderfully fresh, crisp and delicious, with typical Mosel ripe green apple fruit, and a hint of grapefruit intensity.
This wine makes your mouth water just thinking about it. Ages beautifully.

If you like this, then try with confidence . . .

Greater quality, greater intensity

Dr. Loosen's own single-vineyard wines, especially Spätlese wines from Erdener Treppchen (and Prälat) and Wehlener Sonnenuhr

Greater quality, less intensity

Fine, off-dry whites in a more restrained style, such as single-vineyard Rieslings from Max Ferd Richter and J.J. Prüm

Try something completely different

Frogmore Creek FGR Riesling or Pressing Matters R69 from Tasmania

Drouhin Vaudon Chablis Premier Cru

Highly Recommended	$$$	12.5%

What is it?

A dry white wine made from the Chardonnay grape grown in Chablis, France. Fermented and aged in new French oak.

What does it taste like?

Medium-bodied, dry and vibrant, with a solid core of green apple and citrus fruit

If you like this, then try with confidence . . .

Greater quality, greater intensity

Premier, then Grand Cru Chablis from Michel Laroche

Greater quality, less intensity

The very best from the basic Mâcon-Villages appellation, such as Mâcon Solutré Clos des Bertillones Denogent

Try something completely different

The best Pinot Blanc from Alsace, starting with Domaine Weinbach or Collio Pinot Blanco from Schiopetto from Veneto in Italy

Drouhin Vaudon Chablis

Recommended   **$$** | **12.5%**

What is it?
A dry white wine made from the
Chardonnay grape grown in Chablis,
France

What does it taste like?
Crisp and light, with lemon and green
apple flavors and steely minerality

If you like this, then try with confidence . . .
Greater quality, greater intensity
Premier, then Grand Cru Chablis from
Michel Laroche
Greater quality, less intensity
The very best from the basic Mâcon-Villages appellation, such as Mâcon Solutré
Clos des Bertillones Denogent

Try something completely different
The best Pinot Blanc from Alsace, starting with Domaine Weinbach or Collio
Pinot Blanco from Schiopetto from Veneto in Italy

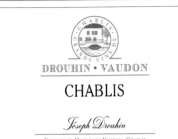

Drouhin, *see* **page 96 and above, and Joseph Drouhin**

Drylands Sauvignon Blanc

Highly Recommended	$$	13%

What is it?

A dry white wine made from the Sauvignon Blanc grape grown in Marlborough, New Zealand

What does it taste like?

Tangy and herbaceous style with ample lime zest flavors

If you like this, then try with confidence . . .

Greater quality, greater intensity

Iconic Marlborough Sauvignon Blanc, such as Cloudy Bay, Craggy Range Avery Vineyard, Hunter's, Isabel Estate, Koura Whaleback, Nobilo Icon and Palliser Estate

Greater quality, less intensity

The finest, most elegant Pouilly-Fumé, such as Didier Dagueneau Silex and Pur Sang

Try something completely different

Lean, linear Riesling from Alsace (Trimbach Clos Ste Hune or JosMeyer Grand Cru Hengst) and Mosel (Maximin Grünhaus Abtsberg Alte Reben Trocken)

Duckhorn Vineyards Cabernet Sauvignon

Highly Recommended	$$$	14.5%

What is it?

A dry red wine made from the Cabernet Sauvignon grape grown in the Napa Valley, California. The wine is aged in oak for 16 months.

What does it taste like?

Intense, focused black cherry, black olive, tobacco and clove; the palate is luxuriously silky yet full-bodied

If you like this, then try with confidence . . .

Greater quality, greater intensity

Caymus Special Selection Cabernet Sauvignon or Dunn Vineyards Howell Mountain Cabernet Sauvignon

Greater quality, less intensity

Stag's Leap Cask 23 Estate Cabernet Sauvignon

Try something completely different

For a classic Bordeaux to match the intensity and voluptuousness of top California Cabernet Sauvignon, try a Merlot-dominated Pomerol such as châteaux L'Evangile, La Fleur-Pétrus, Latour à Pomerol, Petit-Village, Trotanoy and, if you can afford them, Pétrus and Le Pin

E. Guigal Châteauneuf-du-Pape

Highly Recommended	$$$	14%

What is it?

A dry red wine made from a blend of grapes (70% Grenache, 20% Syrah, 5% Mourvèdre, 5% Other) grown in Châteauneuf-du-Pape, Southern Rhône, France. Aged 2 years in large used French oak barrels.

What does it taste like?

Full-bodied and well-structured, featuring stewed plum, wild strawberry and raisin flavors that open up to reveal notes of rosemary and smoke

If you like this, then try with confidence . . .

Greater quality, greater intensity

Domaine Pierre Usseglio Châteauneuf-du-Pape, then Château Rayas

Greater quality, less intensity

Domaine du Vieux Télégraphe Châteauneuf-du-Pape, then Château de Beaucastel Châteauneuf-du-Pape Hommage à Jacques Perrin

Try something completely different

Pure Garnacha from Navarra and Rioja in Spain

E. Guigal Côtes-du-Rhône Blanc

Highly Recommended	$$	13.5%

What is it?

A dry white wine made from a blend of grapes (55% Viognier, 20% Roussanne, 10% Marsanne, 5% Clairette, 5% Bourboulenc) grown in Côtes du Rhône, France with no oak influence

What does it taste like?

Juicy and perfumed, with exotic, ripe fruit and a round texture. Well-balanced wine with persistence on the finish.

If you like this, then try with confidence . . .

Greater quality, greater intensity

Coudoulet de Beaucastel Blanc, then Château de Beaucastel Blanc Vieilles Vignes

Greater quality, less intensity

Vieux Manoir du Frigoulas Côtes-du-Rhône Villages Blanc

Try something completely different

Matassa Blanc, from Roussillon, a blend of 70% Grenache Gris and 30% Macabéo

E. Guigal Côtes-du-Rhône Rosé

Highly Recommended	$$	14%

What is it?

A dry rosé wine made from a blend of grapes (50% Grenache, 40% Cinsault, 5% Mourvèdre, 5% Syrah) grown in Côtes-du-Rhône, France with no oak influence

What does it taste like?

Fruity yet dry and full-bodied, with strawberry and raspberry jam, underbrush and hint of pepper

If you like this, then try with confidence . . .

Greater quality, greater intensity

Charles Melton Barossa Valley Rosé of Virginia, Geoff Merrill Bush Vine McLaren Vale Grenache Rosé or Wirra Wirra Mrs Wigley McLaren Vale Grenache Rosé

Greater quality, less intensity

Château d'Esclans Garrus, consumed within two years of vintage

Try something completely different

The finest rosé with bubbles, such as Camel Valley Pinot Noir Brut from England or Pol Roger Brut Rosé from Champagne

E. Guigal Côtes-du-Rhône

Highly Recommended	$$	14%

What is it?
A dry red wine made from a blend of grapes
(45% Syrah, 52% Grenache, 3% Mourvèdre)
grown in Côtes-du-Rhône, France. Aged 18
months in large used French oak barrels.

What does it taste like?
Packed with ripe wild berry and dark mineral
flavors with excellent length

If you like this, then try with confidence . . .
Greater quality, greater intensity
Domaine Pierre Usseglio Châteauneuf-du-Pape, then Château Rayas
Greater quality, less intensity
E. Guigal Châteauneuf-du-Pape, then Domaine du Vieux Télégraphe
Châteauneuf-du-Pape

Try something completely different
Pure Grenache from Australia (Yalumba Bush Vine Grenache, Kilikanoon
The Duke Clare Valley Grenache) or France (Mas Foulaquier Le Petit Duc)

E. Guigal Crozes-Hermitage Blanc

Highly Recommended	$$	13%

What is it?
A dry white wine made from a blend of grapes
(95% Marsanne, 5% Roussanne) grown in Crozes-
Hermitage, Northern Rhône, France. Aged in used
French oak for 12 months.

What does it taste like?
Intense aromas of vanilla and hazelnut that lead to
marzipan on the palate. A very full, distinctive wine.

If you like this, then try with confidence . . .
Greater quality, greater intensity
Coudoulet de Beaucastel Blanc, then Château de Beaucastel Blanc Vieilles Vignes
Greater quality, less intensity
Vieux Manoir du Frigoulas Côtes-du-Rhône Villages Blanc

Try something completely different
Matassa Blanc, from Roussillon, a blend of 70% Grenache Gris and 30%
Macabéo

E. Guigal Crozes-Hermitage

To Die For	$$	13%

What is it?

A dry red wine made from the Syrah grape grown in Crozes-Hermitage, Northern Rhône, France. Aged 18 months in large French oak barrels.

What does it taste like?

Classic nose of violet, smoked meat, fresh blueberries and vanilla, with a rich, creamy palate and very fresh acidity

If you like this, then try with confidence . . .

Greater quality, greater intensity

Hermitage from Chapoutier (especially l'Ermite) and Marc Sorrel (Gréal), or fuller-style Côte Rôtie such as those by Guigal (Château d'Ampuis and the single-vineyard bottlings)

Greater quality, less intensity

René Rostaing and Yves Montez produce Côte Rôtie of exceptional quality, in a more elegant style and emphasizing freshness and florality.

Try something completely different

California Petite Sirah, the very best of which include Rosenblum Rockpile, Turley Cellars Hayne Vineyard or Lava Cap Grand Hill

Faustino V Rioja Reserva

Recommended	$$	13%

What is it?

A dry red wine made from the Tempranillo grape grown in Rioja, Spain. Aged 16 months in American oak barrels.

What does it taste like?

Traditional-style Rioja that features juiciness, structure, depth and balance

If you like this, then try with confidence . . .

Greater quality, greater intensity

Rioja from Finca Allende, Artadi, Lealtanza, Manzanos, Marqués de Griñon, Nekeas, Palacios Remondo, La Rioja Alta, San Vicente and Bodegas Ysios, then the very best wines of Barón de Ley, Luis Canas, Contino, Marqués de Murrieta, Marqués de Riscal and Bodegas Muga for ultimate quality

Greater quality, less intensity

Reserva and Gran Reserva from La Rioja Alta Viña Ardanza, Marqués de Cáceres and Viña Tondonia Rioja or any rosado from a top Rioja producer

Try something completely different

Numanthia Termes then Numanthia Termanthia from Toro

Ferrer, *see* **Gloria Ferrer**

Fessy, *see* **Henry Fessy**

Fetzer Sundial Chardonnay

Recommended	$	13.5%

What is it?

A dry white wine made from a blend of grape varieties (89% Chardonnay, 5% Viognier and 6% other varieties) grown in California. The wine was fermented in stainless steel with a small portion fermented and matured in oak.

What does it taste like?

Fresh, precise tropical banana and mango, crisp and light on the palate

If you like this, then try with confidence . . .

Greater quality, greater intensity

Jacob's Creek Chardonnay Adelaide Hills

Greater quality, less intensity

The very best from the basic Mâcon-Villages appellation, such as Mâcon Soluté Clos des Bertillones Denogent

Try something completely different

The best Pinot Blanc from Alsace, starting with Domaine Weinbach or Collio Pinot Blanco from Schiopetto from Veneto in Italy

Fetzer Valley Oaks Zinfandel

Recommended	$	14%

What is it?

A dry red wine made from a blend of grapes (87% Zinfandel, 10% Petite Sirah, 3% Syrah) grown in California, with subtle oak treatment

What does it taste like?

Ripe plum, black cherry and black olive, with sweet peppery spiciness. Full-bodied with soft tannins.

If you like this, then try with confidence . . .

Greater quality, greater intensity

Ravenswood Lodi Old Vine Zinfandel, then single-vineyard Zinfandels from Ravenswood or Rosenblum

Greater quality, less intensity

Kendall Jackson Zinfandel Vintners Reserve, then single-vineyard Zinfandels by Ridge

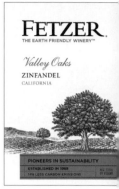

Try something completely different

Zinfandel is a Croatian grape variety (Tribidrag, a.k.a. Crljenak Kastelanski) that is also grown in Puglia, Italy (as Primitivo), producing intensely ripe, full-bodied red wines at moderate prices

Fonseca Bin 27 Porto

Recommended	$$	20%

What is it?
A sweet fortified red wine made from a blend
of grapes (Tinta Barroca, Tinta Roriz, Touriga
Franca, Touriga Nacional and other traditional
Port varieties) and matured for a short period
in large oak barrels

What does it taste like?
Intense spicy dark fruits, sweet and warming

If you like this, then try with confidence . . .
Greater quality, greater intensity
The finest quality, most intense ruby-style wines such as Vintage Ports
from Taylor's, Graham's and Fonseca
Greater quality, less intensity
The finest quality, least intense ruby style is Ferreira's Vintage Port, but
try also single-quinta Ports and, the lightest of all, "pink" Port from Croft,
Porto Cruz and Quinta & Vineyard

Try something completely different
Other sweet, ruby-style fortified wines, such as Banyuls from Franc
or Australian Ruby and Australian Vintage (both formerly known
a Australian Liqueur Port)

Fontanafredda Asti

Highly Recommended	$$	7%

What is it?
A sweet white sparkling wine made
from Moscato grapes grown in Asti,
Piemonte, Italy

What does it taste like?
Fresh, floral and easy to drink

If you like this, then try with confidence . . .
Greater quality, greater intensity
Romano Dogliotti Asti La Selvatica
Greater quality, less intensity
Cerutti Asti Cesare

Try something completely different
Moscato d'Asti, such as Marchesi di Grésy or Villa Lunata (Moscato d'Asti is
sweeter and more intense, but has much less fizz than Asti plain and simple)

Fontanafredda Briccotondo Barbera

Highly Recommended	$$	13.5%

What is it?
A dry red wine made from the Barbera grape grown in Piemonte, Italy

What does it taste like?
Brilliant. Perfectly typical, with juicy, bold sour cherry and plum fruit, complex and long.

If you like this, then try with confidence . . .
Greater quality, greater intensity
Braida Barbera d'Asti Bricco dell'Uccellone
Greater quality, less intensity
Mascarello Barbera Scudetto

Try something completely different
Fruity vibrant reds, such as good-quality
Cru Beaujolais like Henry Fessy Brouilly

Fontanafredda Serralunga d'Alba Barolo

Highly Recommended   **$$$**   **14%**

What is it?

A dry red wine made from the Nebbiolo grape grown in
Barolo, Piemonte, Italy. Aged for 24 months in a mix of
French and Slavonian oak, then at least 12 months in bottle.

What does it taste like?

An attractive, medium-depth crimson color, an alluring
aroma of roses, violets and an abundance of fresh red and
black cherry fruit, chocolate, liquorice and spice, supported
by plenty of supple tannin structure and naturally high,
refreshing acidity

If you like this, then try with confidence . . .

Greater quality, greater intensity
Paolo Scavino Barolo, then Gaja Sorì Tildìn
Greater quality, less intensity
Mascarello Barolo Monprivato

Try something completely different

Greek Xinomavro such as Naoussa from Boutari (Grande Reserve), Chrisohoou
and Thimiopoulos, or Alpha Estate in Amynteo

Forest Glen Pinot Grigio Tehachapi Clone

Recommended   **$**   **12.5%**

What is it?

An off-dry white wine made primarily from a white-
skinned mutation of the Pinot Grigio grape, with a
1%–2% splash of Muscat Canelli, grown in California

What does it taste like?

Highly floral aroma, with a soft, fruity palate, no hint
of spice, and a kiss of sweetness on the finish

If you like this, then try with confidence . . .

Greater quality, greater intensity
JosMeyer Pinot Gris 1854 Fondation or Trimbach Pinot Gris Réserve with a few
years additional bottle-age
Greater quality, less intensity
JosMeyer Pinot Blanc Les Lutins or Domaine Weinbach Pinot Blanc

Try something completely different

A good Soave such as Pieropan or Inama, perhaps even Chasselas from Blaise
Duboux in Switzerland or, for the very adventurous, a super-soft Koshu from
Japan, such as Misawa Private Reserve from Grace

Forest Glen Pinot Noir

Recommended	$	12.5%

What is it?

A medium-bodied, dry red wine made from the Pinot Noir grape grown in California

What does it taste like?

Not the juiciest or fruitiest of New World Pinot Noirs, more like a cheap Bourgogne Rouge from Burgundy in France, but whether that is judged as good or bad will depend on the buyer

If you like this, then try with confidence . . .

Greater quality, greater intensity

La Bauge au Dessus and other Pinot Noir from Au Bon Climat in Santa Barbara, California, or Le Grand Clos Pinot Noir from Le Clos Jordanne in Niagara, Canada

Greater quality, less intensity

The more elegant Oregon Pinot Noir, starting with Adelsheim, Bethel Heights and Rex Hill

Try something completely different

Fruit-driven Nebbiolo, such as Cascina Adelaide di Amabile Drocco Barolo Fossati, Aldo Conterno Barolo Cicala, Parusso Barolo Le Coste-Mosconi or G. D. Vajra Barolo Albe

Forrester, *see* **Ken Forrester**

Fournier, *see* **O. Fournier**

Franco, *see* **Nino Franco**

Freixenet Cordon Negro Brut

Recommended	$	12%

What is it?

A dry sparkling white wine made from a blend of grapes (35% Macabeo, 25% Xarel-lo, 40% Parellada) grown in Penedès, Spain. Traditional Method with lees aging for 18–24 months.

What does it taste like?

Refreshing and fruity, with light bread and golden apple flavors

If you like this, then try with confidence . . .

Greater quality, greater intensity

Charles Heidsieck NV Brut Réserve

Greater quality, less intensity

Pommery Cuvée Louise or, if you can afford it, Louis Roederer Cristal

Try something completely different

Ca'del Bosco Cuvée Annamaria Clementi after two or three years additional aging

Freixenet Cordon Rosado Brut

Recommended	$	12%

What is it?

A dry sparkling rosé wine made from a blend of grapes (Trepat and Garnacha) grown in Penedès, Spain. Traditional Method with lees aging for 12–18 months.

What does it taste like?

Fruity and bright, with notes of strawberry

If you like this, then try with confidence . . .

Greater quality, greater intensity

Charles Heidsieck Brut Rosé

Greater quality, less intensity

Billecart Salmon NV Brut Rosé

Try something completely different

Camel Valley Pinot Noir Brut

Freixenet Elyssia Pinot Noir Brut

Highly Recommended	$$	11.5%

What is it?

A dry sparkling rosé wine made from the Pinot Noir grape grown in Penedès, Spain. Traditional Method with lees aging for at least 9 months.

What does it taste like?

Lots of flavor and interest, with yeast-complexed watermelon fruit, gorgeous texture and length

If you like this, then try with confidence . . .

Greater quality, greater intensity
Charles Heidsieck Brut Rosé
Greater quality, less intensity
Billecart Salmon NV Brut Rosé

Try something completely different
Camel Valley Pinot Noir Brut

Gallo Family Vineyards Cabernet Sauvignon

Recommended	$	13%

What is it?

A dry red wine made from the Cabernet Sauvignon grape grown in California with subtle oak influence

What does it taste like?

Baking spices, soft black cherry and blackberry flavors with a smooth, easy-drinking texture

If you like this, then try with confidence . . .

Greater quality, greater intensity
Caymus Special Selection Cabernet Sauvignon or Dunn Vineyards Howell Mountain Cabernet Sauvignon
Greater quality, less intensity
Stag's Leap Cask 23 Estate Cabernet Sauvignon

Try something completely different
For a classic Bordeaux to match the intensity and voluptuousness of top California Cabernet Sauvignon, try a Merlot-dominated Pomerol such as châteaux L'Evangile, La Fleur-Pétrus, Latour à Pomerol, Petit-Village, Trotanoy and, if you can afford them, Pétrus and Le Pin

Gallo Family Vineyards White Zinfandel

Recommended	$	9.5%

What is it?
A medium-sweet rosé wine made from the Zinfandel grape grown in California

What does it taste like?
Medium-sweet, with watermelon rind and dried strawberry fruit with nice sugar-acid balance

If you like this, then try with confidence . . .
Greater quality, greater intensity
A Kir, but made from a fine Moscato d'Asti rather than a dry white Burgundy, and the tiniest possible dash of Cassis for color
Greater quality, less intensity
Chateau de la Varière Cabernet d'Anjou Demi-Sec or dry rosés such as E. Guigal Côtes-du-Rhône Rosé, or the fruitier Garnacha-based rosado of Navarra in Spain

Try something completely different
Riesling Kabinett or Spätlese from Germany

Gallo Family Vineyards Zinfandel

Recommended	$	13.5%

What is it?
A dry red wine made from the Zinfandel grape grown in California with subtle oak influence

What does it taste like?
Easy-drinking, medium-bodied with pure red fruit jelly flavors and a hint of sweet spice

If you like this, then try with confidence . . .
Greater quality, greater intensity
Ravenswood Lodi Old Vine Zinfandel, then single-vineyard Zinfandels from Ravenswood or Rosenblum
Greater quality, less intensity
Kendall Jackson Zinfandel Vintners Reserve, then single-vineyard Zinfandels by Ridge

Try something completely different
Zinfandel is a Croatian grape variety (Tribidrag, aka Crljenak Kastelanski) that is also grown in Puglia, Italy (as Primitivo), producing intensely ripe, full-bodied red wines at moderate prices

Gascon Malbec

Highly Recommended	$$	14%

What is it?
A dry red wine made from the Malbec grape grown in
Mendoza, Argentina

What does it taste like?
Excellent example, very well balanced, with blackberry
and boysenberry flavors and a rich, supple texture

If you like this, then try with confidence . . .
Greater quality, greater intensity
Luigi Bosca Vistalba Malbec and Nicolas Catena Zapata
Malbec Argentino, then Flichman Parcelo 26 for the
ultimate monster Malbec
Greater quality, less intensity
Colomé Malbec or Yacochuya Estate from Salta, Bodegas
Lagarde Agrelo and Terrazas Afincado single-vineyard
Malbecs

Try something completely different
Cahors from Clos Triguedina or Tannat Castel La Puebla Dayman from Stagnari
in Uruguay

Gloria Ferrer Blanc de Noirs

Highly Recommended	$$	13%

What is it?
A dry sparkling white wine made from a blend of
grapes (90% Pinot Noir, 10% Chardonnay) grown in
Carneros, California. Traditional Method with lees
aging for 18 months.

What does it taste like?
Pronounced watermelon, cherry skin and toast
aromas with subtle bubbles that deliver freshness to the palate

If you like this, then try with confidence . . .
Greater quality, greater intensity
Champagne Bollinger Vieilles Vignes Françaises or Krug Clos d'Ambonnay, if
you can afford either of them!
Greater quality, less intensity
Champagne Serge Mathieu Tradition Blanc de Noirs or Champagne De Venoge
Blanc de Noirs

Try something completely different
Coal Valley Vineyards Sparkling Pinot Noir from Tasmania

Gloria Ferrer Sonoma Brut

Recommended	$$	12.5%

What is it?

A dry sparkling white wine made from a blend of grapes (91% Pinot Noir, 9% Chardonnay) grown in Carneros, California. Traditional Method with aging lees for 18 months.

What does it taste like?

Full-bodied with light yeast-complexed fruit, rounded apple notes, medium acidity and good length

If you like this, then try with confidence . . .

Greater quality, greater intensity

Charles Heidsieck NV Brut Réserve

Greater quality, less intensity

Pommery Cuvée Louise or, if you can afford it, Louis Roederer Cristal

Try something completely different

The best American sparkling wines beyond California, such as Argyle in Oregon, Mountain Dome in Washington, L. Mawby in Michigan and Lamoreaux Landing in New York

Gonzalez Byass Alfonso Oloroso Seco

Recommended	$$	18%

What is it?

A dry fortified white wine made from the Palomino grape grown in Jerez, Spain. Aged an average of 8 years in American oak in the Solera. Residual Sugar less than 4 g/l.

What does it taste like?

Quite enjoyable, with good depth of cinnamon and walnut flavors and a savory, dry finish

If you like this, then try with confidence . . .

Greater quality, greater intensity

Aged genuinely dry Oloroso, such as Hidalgo Oloroso Viejo or Bodegas Tradición 30-Year-Old Oloroso VORS

Greater quality, less intensity

Valdespino Amontillado Tío Diego or Domecq Palo Cortado Capuchino

Try something completely different

Cossart Colheita Sercial

ALFONSO
JEREZ XÉRÈS SHERRY

OLOROSO
Seco

PALOMINO

GONZALEZ BYASS
DESDE 1835

Gonzalez Byass Cristina Oloroso Abocado

Recommended	$$	17.5%

What is it?

A sweet fortified white wine made from a blend of grapes (87% Palomino, 13% Pedro Ximénez) grown in Jerez, Spain. Aged an average of 7 years in American oak in the Solera. Residual Sugar 50 g/l.

What does it taste like?

Pleasant and balanced, with burnt-orange peel and roasted walnut flavors

If you like this, then try with confidence . . .

Greater quality, greater intensity
Osborne Palo Cortado Abocado Solera
Greater quality, less intensity
Lustau Almacenista Oloroso Pata de Gallina (García Jarana) or Williams & Humbert 20 Years Old Palo Cortado Dos Cortardos

Try something completely different

Henriques and Henriques 15-Year-Old Verdelho or Blandy's Colheita Verdelho

CRISTINA
JEREZ XERES SHERRY
OLOROSO
Abocado
PALOMINO
PEDRO XIMENEZ

Gonzalez Byass Leonor Palo Cortado

Recommended	$$	20%

What is it?

A dry fortified white wine made from the Palomino grape grown in Jerez, Spain. Aged an average of 12 years in American oak in the Solera. Residual Sugar 6 g/l.

What does it taste like?

Briny, nutty and dry with caramel and cream flavors on the finish. Good length and breadth.

If you like this, then try with confidence . . .

Greater quality, greater intensity

Aged genuinely dry Oloroso, such as Hidalgo Oloroso Viejo or Bodegas Tradición 30-Year-Old Oloroso VORS

Greater quality, less intensity

Valdespino Amontillado Tío Diego or Domecq Palo Cortado Capuchino

Try something completely different

Cossart Colheita Sercial

Gonzalez Byass Nectar Pedro Ximénez

Highly Recommended | **$$** | **15.5%**

What is it?

A sweet fortified white wine made from the Pedro Ximénez grape grown in Jerez, Spain. Aged an average of 7 years in American oak in the Solera. Residual Sugar over 400 g/l.

What does it taste like?

Perfect example with raisin, orange rind, caramel and an unctuous, sticky finish

If you like this, then try with confidence . . .

Greater quality, greater intensity

It is unlikely you will find a more intensely flavored wine than this, but other equally rich wines worth trying include Gonzales Byass Noe Pedro Ximénez VORS and other VOS and VORS Pedro Ximénez wines generally.

Greater quality, less intensity

The very finest VOS (20-year-old) and VORS (30-year-old) Oloroso Dulce, such as Gonzalez Byass Matúsalem

Try something completely different

Ancient Rutherglen fortified such as Calliope Rare Liqueur Topaque or Calliope Rare Liqueur Muscat

Gonzalez Byass Solera 1847 Oloroso Dulce

Highly Recommended $$ 18%

What is it?
A sweet fortified white wine made from a blend of grapes (75% Palomino, 25% Pedro Ximénez) grown in Jerez, Spain. Aged an average of 8 years in American oak in the Solera.

What does it taste like?
Aromas of coriander, celery seed, chamomile and orange marmalade with toasted walnut and Marconi almond on the palate and sweet tobacco nuances. Not cloying, great texture, delicious.

If you like this, then try with confidence . . .
Greater quality, greater intensity
Gonzalez Byass Oloroso Matúsalem, Valdespino Oloroso Solera 1842, Lustau Oloroso Emperatriz Eugenia or Sandeman Royal Ambrosante 20-Year-Old Pedro Ximénez
Greater quality, less intensity
Equipo Navazos La Bota No 28 Oloroso Fernando de Castilla

Try something completely different
Great Malmsey Madeira (Blandy's, Justino's and Quinta & Vineyard) or St Julien Solera Cream Sherry from Michigan!

Gonzalez Byass Tio Pepe

Recommended	$$	15%

What is it?
A dry fortified white wine made from the Palomino
grape grown in Jerez, Spain. Aged an average of 5 years
in American oak under flor in the Solera.

What does it taste like?
Typical, fresh and dry, with aromas of olive brine, green
apple skin and blanched almonds

If you like this, then try with confidence . . .
Greater quality, greater intensity
Tio Pepe En Rama
Greater quality, less intensity
Go to Jerez de la Frontera in southwest Spain and
taste it fresh from the barrel!

Try something completely different
Vin Jaune, such as Jacques Puffeney and André Mireille Tisot, or Château-Chalon,
like Baud Père & Fils and Jean Macle, both from the Jura in eastern France

Graffigna Malbec Reserve

Recommended	$$	14%

What is it?
A dry red wine made from the Malbec grape grown in
San Juan, Argentina. Matured in oak (mostly French
with a small portion of American) for 12 months.

What does it taste like?
Meaty and fruity, with a smooth finish

If you like this, then try with confidence . . .
Greater quality, greater intensity
Luigi Bosca Vistalba Malbec and Nicolas Catena Zapata
Malbec Argentino, then Flichman Parcelo 26 for the
ultimate monster Malbec
Greater quality, less intensity
Colomé Malbec or Yacochuya Estate from Salta, Bodegas
Lagarde Agrelo and Terrazas Afincado single-vineyard Malbecs

Try something completely different
Cahors from Clos Triguedina or Tannat Castel La Puebla Dayman from Stagnari
in Uruguay

Graffigna Pinot Grigio Reserve

Recommended   **$$**   **13%**

What is it?

A dry white wine made from the Pinot Grigio grape grown in San Juan, Argentina

What does it taste like?

Ripe melon fruit with cleansing acidity

If you like this, then try with confidence . . .

Greater quality, greater intensity

JosMeyer Pinot Gris 1854 Fondation or Trimbach Pinot Gris Réserve with a few years additional bottle-age

Greater quality, less intensity

JosMeyer Pinot Blanc Les Lutins or Domaine Weinbach Pinot Blanc

Try something completely different

A good Soave such as Pieropan or Inama, perhaps even Chasselas from Blaise Duboux in Switzerland or, for the very adventurous, a super-soft Koshu from Japan, such as Misawa Private Reserve from Grace

Graham Beck NV Brut

Recommended   **$$**   **12%**

What is it?

A dry white sparkling wine made from a blend of grape varieties (53% Chardonnay and 47% Pinot Noir) grown in the Western Cape, South Africa. Made using the Traditional Method and aged on its lees for 15–18 months before disgorgement.

What does it taste like?

Lime, lemon and toasted bread aromas, light in body and very crisp

If you like this, then try with confidence . . .

Greater quality, greater intensity

Charles Heidsieck NV Brut Réserve

Greater quality, less intensity

Pommery Cuvée Louise or, if you can afford it, Louis Roederer Cristal

Try something completely different

Ca'del Bosco Cuvée Annamaria Clementi after two or three years additional aging

Graham Beck Pinotage

Recommended	$$	13.5%

What is it?

A dry red wine made from the Pinotage grape grown in the Western Cape, South Africa. Matured in seasoned oak for 10 months.

What does it taste like?

Full-bodied, with super-ripe blackberry and prune fruit, some leather and earth and intense spiciness. Very full-bodied.

If you like this, then try with confidence . . .

Greater quality, greater intensity
Kaapzicht Pinotage, then their Steytler Pinotage
Greater quality, less intensity
Southern Right Pinotage

Try something completely different

Southern Italian reds made from Primitivo (a.k.a. Zinfandel) or Nero d'Avola

Graham's 10-Year Tawny

Highly Recommended	$$$	20%

What is it?

A sweet fortified red wine made from a blend of grapes (Tinta Barroca, Tinta Roriz, Touriga Franca, Touriga Nacional and other traditional Port varieties) grown in Douro, Portugal. Aged an average of 10 years in oak.

What does it taste like?

Aromas of roasted coffee and burnt sugar with walnut on the persistent finish. Very solid, with good texture and balance.

If you like this, then try with confidence . . .

Greater quality, greater intensity
Graham's 20-Year-Old Tawny or Taylor Fladgate 10-Year Tawny
Greater quality, less intensity
Graham's 20-Year-Old Tawny Port, or Taylor Fladgate 20-Year Tawny Port

Try something completely different

The tawny-like Fondillón, a 15-year-old Monastrell, with a non-fortified 16% of alcohol from Casta Diva in Alicante, Spain, or Penfolds Club Reserve Classic Tawny, then the truly iconic Penfolds Grandfather and Great Grandfather Rare Tawnies

Graham's 20-Year Tawny

Highly Recommended	$$$	20%

What is it?

A sweet fortified red wine made from a blend of grapes (Tinta Barroca, Tinta Roriz, Touriga Franca, Touriga Nacional and other traditional Port varieties) grown in Douro, Portugal. Aged an average of 20 years in oak.

What does it taste like?

Loads of flavor, with toffee and sandalwood notes and a rich texture

If you like this, then try with confidence . . .

Greater quality, greater intensity

The 20-Year-Old Tawny from Taylor Fladgate or Ramos Pinto (Quinta do Bom Retiro)

Greater quality, less intensity

Older Tawny Ports are not necessarily better, and some can be rather tired, but the best (such as those from Quinta do Noval) are complex, retain sufficient freshness and show incredible harmony and elegance.

Try something completely different

The tawny-like Fondillón, a 15-year-old Monastrell, with a non-fortified 16% of alcohol from Casta Diva in Alicante, Spain, or Penfolds Club Reserve Classic Tawny, then the truly iconic Penfolds Grandfather and Great Grandfather Rare Tawnies

Graham's Six Grapes Reserve Porto

Highly Recommended	$$	19.5%

What is it?

A sweet fortified red wine made from a blend of grapes (Tinta Barroca, Tinta Roriz, Touriga Franca, Touriga Nacional and other traditional Port varieties) grown in Douro, Portugal. Aged 3 years in barrel.

What does it taste like?

Opaque purple color. Aromas of dark figs, licorice and roasted espresso bean. Fresh on the palate, with a dense fruit core and somewhat firm tannins on the finish.

If you like this, then try with confidence . . .

Greater quality, greater intensity

The finest quality, most intense ruby-style wines such as Vintage Ports from Taylor's, Graham's and Fonseca

Greater quality, less intensity

The finest quality, least intense ruby style is Ferreira's Vintage Port, but try also single-quinta Ports and, the lightest of all, "pink" Port from Croft, Porto Cruz and Quinta & Vineyard

Try something completely different

Other sweet, ruby-style fortified wines, such as Banyuls from France or Australian Ruby and Australian Vintage (both formerly known as Australian Liqueur Port)

Hardy's Nottage Hill Cabernet-Shiraz

Recommended	$$	14%

What is it?

A dry red wine made from a blend of grapes (Cabernet Sauvignon and Shiraz) grown in Southeastern Australia with subtle oak influence

What does it taste like?

Fresh berries, mouthwatering and fruit-forward with supple tannins and moderate length

If you like this, then try with confidence . . .

Greater quality, greater intensity

Yalumba The Signature or Wolf Blass Black Label Cabernet Sauvignon Shiraz Malbec

Greater quality, less intensity

Brangayne of Orange Tristan Cabernet Sauvignon Shiraz Merlot

Try something completely different

Pure Cabernet Sauvignon from Washington (Andrew Will, Woodward Canyon), Australia (Houghton's Jack Mann, Balnaves The Tally) and Spain (Marqués de Griñon)

Hardy's Nottage Hill Chardonnay

Recommended	$$	13%

What is it?

A dry white wine made from the Chardonnay grape grown in Southeastern Australia with subtle oak influence

What does it taste like?

Quite fruity and tropical, with moderate acidity and light oak notes

If you like this, then try with confidence . . .

Greater quality, greater intensity
Hardy's Eileen Hardy Chardonnay
Greater quality, less intensity
Hardy's HRB Chardonnay

Try something completely different

Fabulous Australian Marsanne, Roussanne and Marsanne-Roussanne blends from Yeringberg

Hardy's Stamp of Australia Cabernet Sauvignon

Recommended	$	13.5%

What is it?

A dry red wine made from the Cabernet Sauvignon grape grown in Southeastern Australia

What does it taste like?

Soft plum, pepper and blackberry fruit with cedar backbone. Structured tannins on the long, smoky finish.

If you like this, then try with confidence . . .

Greater quality, greater intensity
Reynella Basket Pressed McLaren Vale Cabernet Sauvignon or Hardy's Thomas Hardy Cabernet Sauvignon

Greater quality, less intensity
Wolf Blass Grey Label Langhorne Creek Cabernet Sauvignon

Try something completely different

Washington Merlot from the best producers, such as L'Ecole No. 41, Leonetti, Seven Hills and Woodward Canyon

Hardy's Stamp of Australia Chardonnay

Recommended	$	13.5%

What is it?

A dry white wine made from the Chardonnay grape with subtle oak influence

What does it taste like?

Quite drinkable, fruity, soft style with tropical fruit flavors

If you like this, then try with confidence . . .

Greater quality, greater intensity
Hardy's Eileen Hardy Chardonnay
Greater quality, less intensity
Hardy's HRB Chardonnay

Try something completely different

Fabulous Australian Marsanne, Roussanne and
Marsanne-Roussanne blends from Yeringberg

Hardy's Stamp of Australia Chardonnay-Semillon

Recommended	$	12.5%

What is it?

A dry white wine made from a blend of grapes (Semillon and Chardonnay) grown in Southeastern Australia with subtle oak influence

What does it taste like?

Very drinkable, with medium body, zesty acidity and pleasant citrus and apple flavors

If you like this, then try with confidence . . .

Greater quality, greater intensity
Hardy's Eileen Hardy Chardonnay
Greater quality, less intensity
Hardy's HRB Chardonnay

Try something completely different

Fabulous Australian Marsanne, Roussanne and Marsanne-Roussanne blends from Yeringberg

Hardy's Stamp of Australia Merlot

Recommended	$	13.5%

What is it?

A dry red wine made from the Merlot grape grown in Southeastern Australia

What does it taste like?

Light, juicy cherry and plum flavors with supporting acidity and smooth tannins. Moderate oak support allows fruit to shine through.

If you like this, then try with confidence . . .

Greater quality, greater intensity

Petaluma Coonawarra Merlot

Greater quality, less intensity

Cullen Margaret River Red or Château d'Aiguilhe from the Côtes de Castillon

Try something completely different

Great Merlot-dominated blends from Pomerol, such as châteaux L'Evangile, La Fleur-Pétrus, Latour à Pomerol, Petit-Village, Trotanoy and, if you can afford them, Pétrus and Le Pin

Hardy's Stamp of Australia Shiraz

Recommended	$	13.5%

What is it?

A dry red wine made from the Shiraz grape grown in Southeastern Australia with subtle oak influence

What does it taste like?

Jammy, raisiny fruit with smoky complexity. A straightforward and solid wine.

If you like this, then try with confidence...

Greater quality, greater intensity

Penfolds St Henri and various Bin numbers (28, 128, 150, 389), culminating in RWT and Grange or Henschke Hill of Grace

Greater quality, less intensity

Clonakilla Shiraz-Viognier

Try something completely different

Zinfandel (especially those by Ridge), Petite Syrah (Ridge Vineyards Dynamite Hill, Rosenblum Rockpile, Turley Cellars Hayne Vineyard or Lava Cap Grand Hill) or even an Australian Zinfandel (such as Cape Mentelle)

Hardy's Stamp of Australia Shiraz-Cabernet Sauvignon

Recommended	$	13.5%

What is it?

A dry red wine made from a blend of grapes (85% Shiraz, 15% Cabernet Sauvignon) grown in Southeastern Australia with subtle oak influence

What does it taste like?

Perfumed and easy-drinking, with complex flavors of sweet blueberry, blackberry, black cherry and a hint of smoked meat

If you like this, then try with confidence . . .

Greater quality, greater intensity

Lindeman's Limestone Ridge Vineyard Shiraz Cabernet or Penfolds Koonunga Hill Seventy Six Shiraz Cabernet

Greater quality, less intensity

Hardy's Chronicle No. 1 Twice Lost Shiraz Cabernet Rosé

Try something completely different

Search out Sangiovese-dominated blends, such as The Mongrel from Hugh Hamilton in McLaren Vale

Henry Fessy Beaujolais-Villages

| Highly Recommended | $$ | 12.5% |

What is it?
A dry red wine made from the Gamay grape grown in Beaujolais, France. Fermented by partial carbonic maceration with no oak influence.

What does it taste like?
Exuberant and juicy, a perfect example of its style

If you like this, then try with confidence . . .
Greater quality, greater intensity
Domaine Pardon Cuvée de L'Ermitage Beaujolais-Villages
Greater quality, less intensity
Philippe Deschamps Coreau du Cornillon Beaujolais-Villages

Try something completely different
Castello del Poggio Barbera D'Asti or Vietti La Crena Barbera d'Asti

Henry Fessy Brouilly

| Recommended | $$ | 13% |

What is it?
A dry red wine made from the Gamay grape grown in Brouilly, Beaujolais, France, with no oak influence

What does it taste like?
Good, solid example, with soft dark cherry jelly and granite flavors, and a bright finish

If you like this, then try with confidence . . .
Greater quality, greater intensity
Jean Claude Lapalu Brouilly La Croix des Rameaux
Greater quality, less intensity
Jean-Claude Lapalu Vieilles Vignes Brouilly

Try something completely different
Castello del Poggio Barbera D'Asti or Vietti La Crena Barbera d'Asti

Henry Fessy Morgon

Highly Recommended $$ | 13.5%

What is it?

A dry red wine made from the Gamay grape grown in Morgon, France, with no oak influence

What does it taste like?

Quite floral and expressive, with delineated fruit, beautiful acid structure and flavor

If you like this, then try with confidence . . .

Greater quality, greater intensity

Georges Duboeuf Jean Descombes Morgon

Greater quality, less intensity

Louis Latour Morgon Les Charmes

Try something completely different

Castello del Poggio Barbera D'Asti or Vietti La Crena Barbera d'Asti

Morgon

HENRY FESSY
CRUS DU BEAUJOLAIS

Henry Fessy Moulin à Vent

Recommended $$ | 13.5%

What is it?

A dry red wine made from the Gamay grape grown in Moulin à Vent, France, with no oak influence

What does it taste like?

Typical and delicious, with festive black cherry jelly flavors and nice structure

If you like this, then try with confidence . . .

Greater quality, greater intensity

Louis Jadot Château des Jacques Moulin-à-Vent Clos des Thorins

Greater quality, less intensity

Château des Jacques Moulin-à-Vent Clos du Grand Carquelin

Try something completely different

Castello del Poggio Barbera D'Asti or Vietti La Crena Barbera d'Asti

Moulin-à-Vent

HENRY FESSY
CRUS DU BEAUJOLAIS

Hugel Gentil

Recommended	$$	12.5%

What is it?

An off-dry white wine made from a blend of grapes
(45% Gewürztraminer, 10% Muscat, 20% Riesling,
15% Pinot Gris, 10% Sylvaner) grown in Alsace,
France

What does it taste like?

Off-dry style with a soft texture and ripe orchard fruits

If you like this, then try with confidence . . .

Greater quality, greater intensity

Hugel Gewürztraminer Jubilée, then Trimbach Seigneurs de Ribeaupierre
Gewürztraminer for strength or Joseph Cattin Gewürztraminer Grand Cru
Hatschbourg for a more voluptuous rendition

Greater quality, less intensity

Alsace Klevner de Heiligenstein starting with Zeyssolff L'Opaline

Try something completely different

The Alsace-inspired Knappstein Three Clare Valley Gewürztraminer Riesling
Pinot Gris

Hugel Gewurztraminer Hugel

Highly Recommended	$$	13.5%

What is it?

An off-dry white wine made from the
Gewürztraminer grape grown in Alsace, France

What does it taste like?

Off-dry style, very aromatic and fresh, with good
typicity and balance

If you like this, then try with confidence . . .

Greater quality, greater intensity

Hugel Gewürztraminer Jubilée, then Trimbach
Seigneurs de Ribeaupierre Gewürztraminer for strength or Joseph Cattin
Gewurztraminer Grand Cru Hatschbourg for a more voluptuous rendition

Greater quality, less intensity

Alsace Klevner de Heiligenstein starting with Zeyssolff L'Opaline or a fine Alsace
Pinot Gris (JosMeyer, Paul Blanck, Domaine Weinbach, etc.) with two or three
years additional bottle-age to encourage a light spiciness

Try something completely different

The aromatic, complex blends of Marcel Deiss (Alsace, France), starting with
Engelgarten

Hugel Riesling Hugel

Highly Recommended | **$$** | **12%**

What is it?
A dry white wine made from the Riesling grape grown in Alsace, France

What does it taste like?
Dry, with excellent expression and clarity of fruit and bracing acidity

If you like this, then try with confidence . . .
Greater quality, greater intensity
Hugel Riesling Jubilée
Greater quality, less intensity
JosMeyer Riesling Les Pierrets

Try something completely different
Dry Australian Semillon, particularly from the Hunter Valley, with several years bottle-age

Imaz, *see* Coto de Imaz

Jaboulet Aîné, see Paul Jaboulet Aîné

Jacob's Creek Cabernet Sauvignon Reserve Coonawarra

Highly Recommended	$$	14%

What is it?
A dry red wine made from predominantly the Cabernet Sauvignon grape grown in Coonawarra, South Australia. Aged in large French oak barrels for 18 months.

What does it taste like?
Beautiful aromas of cassis, cedar and mint with a full-bodied palate that features supportive, integrated tannins and acidity

If you like this, then try with confidence . . .
Greater quality, greater intensity
Balnaves of Coonawarra The Tally Reserve Cabernet Sauvignon
Greater quality, less intensity
Wynns Coonawarra Estate Cabernet Sauvignon

Try something completely different
Washington Merlot from the best producers, such as L'Ecole No. 41, Leonetti, Seven Hills and Woodward Canyon

Jacob's Creek Reserve Chardonnay Adelaide Hills

Highly Recommended	$$	12.5%

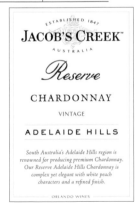

What is it?
A dry white wine made from the Chardonnay grape grown in Adelaide Hills, Australia. Fermented with native yeasts in partial new French oak barrels following malolactic fermentation, then aged on the lees with bâtonnage to impart creaminess and texture.

What does it taste like?
This wine manages to be lively, with a mouthwatering acidity and creamy texture all at once. Well-defined golden apple and mango fruit with a long finish.

If you like this, then try with confidence . . .
Greater quality, greater intensity
Domaine Leflaive Puligny-Montrachet
Greater quality, less intensity
The very best from Mâcon, such as Mâcon Solutré Clos des Bertillones Denogent

Try something completely different
Fabulous Australian Marsanne, Roussanne and Marsanne-Roussanne blends from Yeringberg

Jacob's Creek Chardonnay

Recommended	$	13%

What is it?
A dry white wine made from the Chardonnay grape grown in Southeastern Australia with subtle oak influence

What does it taste like?
Medium-bodied and straightforward, with tropical and peach flavors and a round texture

If you like this, then try with confidence . . .
Greater quality, greater intensity
Jacob's Creek Reeves Point Chardonnay
Greater quality, less intensity
The very best from Mâcon, such as Mâcon Solutré Clos des Bertillones Denogent

Try something completely different
Fabulous Australian Marsanne, Roussanne and Marsanne-Roussanne blends from Yeringberg

Jacob's Creek Moscato

Highly Recommended	$	8%

What is it?
A medium-dry slightly sparkling white wine made from the Moscato grape grown in Southeastern Australia

What does it taste like?
Fizzy and juicy with floral and peachy flavors. Really drinkable.

If you like this, then try with confidence . . .
Greater quality, greater intensity
Richer, fully sparkling Asti from the very finest producers, such as Romano Dogliotti Asti La Selvatica or Cerutti Asti Cesare
Greater quality, less intensity
Silvan Ridge Semi-Sparkling Early Muscat

Try something completely different
The light-as-a-dime fortified Muscat de Beaumes-de-Venise from top producers such as Domaine des Bernardins or Durban

Jacob's Creek Pinot Noir

Recommended	$	12.5%

What is it?
A medium-bodied, dry wine made from the Pinot Noir grape grown in Southeastern Australia

What does it taste like?
Easy-drinking Pinot Noir, which is more than can be said for most entry-level red Burgundy!

If you like this, then try with confidence . . .
Greater quality, greater intensity
Top Australian Pinot Noir from By Far, Farr Rising, Freycinet and Kooyong
Greater quality, less intensity
Yering Station ED Yarra Valley Pinot Noir Rosé or Shelmerdine Vineyards Yarra Valley Pinot Noir Rosé

Try something completely different
Fruit-driven Nebbiolo, such as Cascina Adelaide di Amabile Drocco Barolo Fossati, Aldo Conterno Barolo Cicala, Parusso Barolo Le Coste-Mosconi or G. D. Vajra Barolo Albe

Jacob's Creek Reserve Pinot Noir Adelaide Hills

Highly Recommended	$$	13.5%

What is it?
A medium-bodied, dry wine made from the Pinot Noir grape grown in Adelaide Hills, South Australia. Light use of oak.

What does it taste like?
Rhubarb and strawberry fruit, with notes of red and black cherry, a subtle use of oak and supple tannins

If you like this, then try with confidence . . .
Greater quality, greater intensity
Top Australian Pinot Noir from By Far, Farr Rising, Freycinet and Kooyong
Greater quality, less intensity
Yering Station ED Yarra Valley Pinot Noir Rosé or Shelmerdine Vineyards Yarra Valley Pinot Noir Rosé

Try something completely different
Fruit-driven Nebbiolo, such as Cascina Adelaide di Amabile Drocco Barolo Fossati, Aldo Conterno Barolo Cicala, Parusso Barolo Le Coste-Mosconi or G. D. Vajra Barolo Albe

Jacob's Creek Riesling Reserve Barossa

Highly Recommended   **$$** | **12%**

What is it?
A dry white wine made from the Riesling grape grown in Barossa, South Australia

What does it taste like?
Excellent zesty, floral aromas, with lime-influenced citrus fruits on the palate; tight, dry and crisp, with refreshing acidity

If you like this, then try with confidence . . .
Greater quality, greater intensity
Pewsey Vale Riesling The Contours Museum Reserve, Grosset Polish Hill and Pressing Matters (R0 or R9)
Greater quality, less intensity
Observatory Hill Vintner's Reserve or, for a leaner, more linear Riesling, Puddleduck from Tasmania

Try something completely different
Dry Australian Semillon, particularly from the Hunter Valley, with several years bottle-age

Jacob's Creek Shiraz Reserve Barossa

Highly Recommended   **$$** | **14%**

What is it?
A dry red wine made from the Shiraz grape grown in Barossa, South Australia. Aged in new and used American and French oak barrels for 20 months.

What does it taste like?
Textbook Barossa Shiraz, with all of the blue- and blackberry fruit, sweet spice and rich texture one would expect without the heaviness or jamminess. Well done.

If you like this, then try with confidence . . .
Greater quality, greater intensity
Penfolds St Henri and various Bin numbers (28, 128, 150, 389), culminating in RWT and Grange or Henschke Hill of Grace
Greater quality, less intensity
Clonakilla Shiraz-Viognier

Try something completely different
Zinfandel (especially those by Ridge), Petite Syrah (Ridge Vineyards Dynamite Hill, Rosenblum Rockpile, Turley Cellars Hayne Vineyard or Lava Cap Grand Hill) or even an Australian Zinfandel (such as Cape Mentelle)

Jacob's Creek St Hugo Barossa Grenache Shiraz Mataro

| Highly Recommended | $$$ | 14.1% |

What is it?

A dry red wine made from a blend of grapes (Grenache, Shiraz and Mataro) grown in Barossa, South Australia. The Grenache comes from very old vines (40 and 83 years for the first vintage in 2010). Mataro is better known in France as the Mourvèdre grape. Aged in new and used American and French oak barrels for 14 months. Already a well-established gold medal winner.

What does it taste like?

Very rich and long without being too heavy, this recently introduced super-premium wine has spicy red and black fruits on the palate, with soft and silky tannins on the finish.

If you like this, then try with confidence . . .

Greater quality, greater intensity

Cape Barren McLaren Vale Native Goose GSM

Greater quality, less intensity

Despite increasingly disappointing performance from Rosemount generally, this once solid brand still has a few consistent gems, such as Rosemount GSM McLaren Vale.

Try something completely different

Pure Grenache from Australia (Yalumba Bush Vine Grenache, Kilikanoon The Duke Clare Valley Grenache) or France (Mas Foulaquier Le Petit Duc)

Jacob's Creek Steingarten Riesling

To Die For	$$	11%

What is it?

A dry white wine made from the Riesling grape grown in Barossa Ranges, South Australia

What does it taste like?

Extraordinary minerality of citrus fruit, with a laserlike focus and an intense, crisply dry finish that can be quite honeyed some years

If you like this, then try with confidence . . .

Greater quality, greater intensity

Pewsey Vale Riesling The Contours Museum Reserve, Grosset Polish Hill and Pressing Matters (R0 or R9)

Greater quality, less intensity

Observatory Hill Vintner's Reserve or, for a leaner, more linear Riesling, Puddleduck from Tasmania

Try something completely different

Dry Australian Semillon, particularly from the Hunter Valley, with several years bottle-age

Jolivet, *see* Pascal Jolivet

Jordan Cabernet Sauvignon

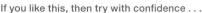

Highly Recommended $$$ | 13.5%

What is it?

A dry red wine made primarily from Cabernet Sauvignon grown in Alexander Valley, California. Aged 12 months in oak barrels (two-thirds French, one-third American).

What does it taste like?

Completely classic and reliable, this is the epitome of elegance. Black currant and black cherry flavors mingle nicely with well-integrated oak and a fine tannin structure.

If you like this, then try with confidence . . .

Greater quality, greater intensity

Caymus Special Selection Cabernet Sauvignon or Dunn Vineyards Howell Mountain Cabernet Sauvignon

Greater quality, less intensity

Stag's Leap Cask 23 Estate Cabernet Sauvignon

Try something completely different

Merlot-dominated Pomerol such as châteaux L'Evangile, La Fleur-Pétrus, Latour à Pomerol, Petit-Village, Trotanoy and, if you can afford them, Pétrus and Le Pin

Jordan Chardonnay

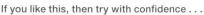

Highly Recommended $$$ | 13.5%

What is it?

A dry white wine made from the Chardonnay grape grown in the Russian River Valley in California. Aged in new French oak for 5 months.

What does it taste like?

Exceptionally well balanced and appealing, the judicious use of oak complements the round texture and fresh, ripe tree fruit qualities

If you like this, then try with confidence . . .

Greater quality, greater intensity

Any white Burgundy from Domaine (not Olivier) Leflaive

Greater quality, less intensity

The very best from the basic Mâcon-Villages appellation, such as Mâcon Solutré Clos des Bertillones Denogent

Try something completely different

The best Pinot Blanc from Alsace, starting with Domaine Weinbach or Collio Pinot Blanco from Schiopetto from Veneto in Italy

Joseph Drouhin Puligny-Montrachet

Recommended	$$$	13.5%

What is it?

A dry white wine made from the Chardonnay grape grown in Puligny-Montrachet, Burgundy, France. Fermented and aged in new French oak.

What does it taste like?

Rich, smoky, creamy and nutty, with red apple fruit, moderate weight and acidity

If you like this, then try with confidence . . .

Greater quality, greater intensity

Louis Jadot Puligny-Montrachet Premier Cru La Garenne, then Domaine Leflaive Montrachet Grand Cru

Greater quality, less intensity

The very best from the basic Mâcon-Villages appellation, such as Mâcon Solutré Clos des Bertillones Denogent

Try something completely different

Top-end Australian Semillon or oaked white Bordeaux Pessac-Léognan, such as Château de Chevalier or its reliable second wine Esprit de Chevalier

Jouët, *see* Perrier-Jouët

Ken Forrester Old Vine Reserve Chenin Blanc

Highly Recommended	**$$**	**14.5%**

What is it?

A dry white wine made from the Chenin Blanc grape grown in Stellenbosch, South Africa. A portion is barrel fermented and the wine is matured on its lees for 6–9 months in small French oak.

What does it taste like?

Gorgeously expressive ripe melon and apple, with a leesy creaminess and beautifully integrated spicy oak

If you like this, then try with confidence . . .

Greater quality, greater intensity
Ken Forrester The FMC Chenin Blanc
Greater quality, less intensity
Oak-fermented Chenin Blanc from Clos Rougrard in Saumur

Try something completely different

Modern-style white Rioja, for vibrant and interesting fruit aromas and prominent oak

Kendall-Jackson Cabernet Sauvignon Vintner's Reserve

Recommended	$$	13.5%

What is it?

A dry red wine made predominantly from the Cabernet Sauvignon grape grown in California. Aged 15 months in 61% French, 39% American oak.

What does it taste like?

Medium-bodied wine featuring red currant, black olive and cedar notes with dusty tannins on the finish

If you like this, then try with confidence . . .

Greater quality, greater intensity

Caymus Special Selection Cabernet Sauvignon or Dunn Vineyards Howell Mountain Cabernet Sauvignon

Greater quality, less intensity

Stag's Leap Cask 23 Estate Cabernet Sauvignon

Try something completely different

For a classic Bordeaux to match the intensity and voluptuousness of top California Cabernet Sauvignon, try a Merlot-dominated Pomerol such as châteaux L'Evangile, La Fleur-Pétrus, Latour à Pomerol, Petit-Village, Trotanoy and, if you can afford them, Pétrus and Le Pin

Kendall-Jackson Chardonnay Vintner's Reserve

Recommended	$$	13.5%

What is it?

A dry white wine made from the Chardonnay grape grown in California. Fermented and aged in French and American oak barrels on the lees with lees-stirring to impart creaminess and texture.

What does it taste like?

Butterscotch and spiced apple flavors with good weight and a creamy texture

If you like this, then try with confidence . . .

Greater quality, greater intensity

Any white Burgundy from Domaine (not Olivier) Leflaive

Greater quality, less intensity

The very best from the basic Mâcon-Villages appellation, such as Mâcon Solutré Clos des Bertillones Denogent

Try something completely different

The best Pinot Blanc from Alsace, starting with Domaine Weinbach or Collio Pinot Blanco from Schiopetto from Veneto in Italy

Kendall-Jackson Zinfandel Vintner's Reserve

Recommended	$$	13.5%

What is it?

A dry red wine made from the Zinfandel grape grown in California. Aged in small French and American oak barrels (including a small portion of new barrels) for at least 6 months.

What does it taste like?

Medium-bodied with raisin and raspberry flavors, low acidity and firm tannin structure

If you like this, then try with confidence . . .

Greater quality, greater intensity

Ravenswood Lodi Old Vine Zinfandel, then single-vineyard Zinfandels from Ravenswood or Rosenblum

Greater quality, less intensity

Kendall Jackson Zinfandel Vintners Reserve, then single-vineyard Zinfandels by Ridge

Try something completely different

Zinfandel is a Croatian grape variety (Tribidrag, aka Crljenak Kastelanski) that is also grown in Puglia, Italy (as Primitivo), producing intensely ripe, full-bodied red wines at moderate prices

Kim Crawford Pinot Noir

Recommended	$$	14%

What is it?

A dry red wine made from the Pinot Noir grape grown in Marlborough, New Zealand. Aged in French oak for 5 months.

What does it taste like?

A medium-bodied Pinot with dark and spicy red fruit flavors and cleansing acidity

If you like this, then try with confidence . . .

Greater quality, greater intensity

Pinot Noir from Akarua, Ata Rangi, Craggy Range Te Muna, Felton Road and Twin Paddocks

Greater quality, less intensity

Kim Crawford Marlborough New Zealand Pansy Rosé

Try something completely different

Fruit-driven Nebbiolo, such as Cascina Adelaide di Amabile Drocco Barolo Fossati, Aldo Conterno Barolo Cicala, Parusso Barolo Le Coste-Mosconi or G. D. Vajra Barolo Albe

Kim Crawford Sauvignon Blanc

Highly Recommended	$$	13.5%

What is it?

A dry white wine made from the Sauvignon Blanc grape grown in Marlborough, New Zealand

What does it taste like?

Really nice balance of lean and ripe with citrus and tropical flavors and notes of herb. Good weight, texture and intensity.

If you like this, then try with confidence . . .

Greater quality, greater intensity

Iconic Marlborough Sauvignon Blanc, such as Cloudy Bay, Craggy Range Avery Vineyard, Hunter's, Isabel Estate, Koura Whaleback, Nobilo Icon and Palliser Estate

Greater quality, less intensity

The finest, most elegant Pouilly-Fumé, such as Didier Dagueneau Silex and Pur Sang

Try something completely different

Lean, linear Riesling from Alsace (Trimbach Clos Ste Hune or JosMeyer Grand Cru Hengst) and Mosel (Maximin Grünhaus Abtsberg Alte Reben Trocken)

Kumala Merlot-Ruby Cabernet

Recommended   **$**   **13.5%**

What is it?

A dry red wine made from a blend of grape varieties (Merlot and Ruby Cabernet) grown in the Western Cape, South Africa

What does it taste like?

Deep, jammy, ripe plum and blackberry, warming and generous

If you like this, then try with confidence . . .

Greater quality, greater intensity

Bein Merlot Reserve

Greater quality, less intensity

Bein Little Merlot

Try something completely different

Great Merlot-dominated blends from Pomerol, such as châteaux L'Evangile, La Fleur-Pétrus, Latour à Pomerol, Petit-Village, Trotanoy and, if you can afford them, Pétrus and Le Pin

La Crema Chardonnay Monterey

Recommended	$$	13.5%

What is it?

A dry white wine made from the Chardonnay grape grown in Monterey, California. Aged for 6 months in oak barrels 75% French, 25% American, including a portion of new barrels).

What does it taste like?

A buttery, smooth, creamy wine with baked apple and pineapple flavors. The finish is just bright enough to keep it balanced and refreshing.

If you like this, then try with confidence . . .

Greater quality, greater intensity

Any white Burgundy from Domaine (not Olivier) Leflaive

Greater quality, less intensity

The very best from the basic Mâcon-Villages appellation, such as Mâcon Solutré Clos des Bertillones Denogent

Try something completely different

The best Pinot Blanc from Alsace, starting with Domaine Weinbach or Collio Pinot Blanco from Schiopetto from Veneto in Italy

La Crema Pinot Noir Monterey

Recommended	$$	13.5%

What is it?

A dry red wine made from the Pinot Noir grape grown in Monterey, California. Aged in French oak (20% new) for 7 months.

What does it taste like?

Good complexity here, with red plum, red cherry and mocha flavors and a hint of damp earth. The texture is silky and the finish clean and pure.

If you like this, then try with confidence . . .

Greater quality, greater intensity

La Bauge au Dessus and other Pinot Noir from Au Bon Climat in Santa Barbara, California, or Le Grand Clos Pinot Noir from Le Clos Jordanne in Niagara, Canada

Greater quality, less intensity

The more elegant Oregon Pinot Noir, starting with Adelsheim, Bethel Heights and Rex Hill

Try something completely different

Fruit-driven Nebbiolo, such as Cascina Adelaide di Amabile Drocco Barolo Fossati, Aldo Conterno Barolo Cicala, Parusso Barolo Le Coste-Mosconi or G. D. Vajra Barolo Albe

LaMarca Prosecco

Recommended	$$	11.5%

What is it?

An off-dry sparkling white wine made from the Glera grape grown in the Prosecco region of Italy. Made using the tank-fermented method.

What does it taste like?

Floral and feminine, and just a touch sweet, with soft peach and melon flavors

If you like this, then try with confidence . . .

Greater quality, greater intensity

Champagne Mumm Demi-Sec

Greater quality, less intensity

Champagne De Venoge Vin du Paradis

Try something completely different

Veuve Clicquot Vintage Rich

Lan Rioja, *see* Bodegas Lan Rioja

Lanson Black Label NV Brut

Highly Recommended	**$$$**	**12.5%**

What is it?

A dry sparkling wine made from a blend of grapes (35% Chardonnay, 50% Pinot Noir, 15% Meunier) grown in Champagne, France. Traditional Method with lees aging for at least 3 years.

What does it taste like?

Rich and full-bodied, with clearly defined aromas of biscuit, honeyed toast and ripe red apple

If you like this, then try with confidence . . .

Greater quality, greater intensity
Lanson Vintage Gold Label
Greater quality, less intensity
Lanson Extra Age, then Lanson Noble Cuvée

Try something completely different

The top sparkling wines from England (Camel Valley, Henners, Herbert Hall, Nyetimber, Ridgeview) and Tasmania (Bay of Fires, Clover Hill, Jansz, Stefano Lubiana, Pirie, Relbia)

Lanson NV Brut Rosé

Recommended	**$$$**	**12.5%**

What is it?

A dry sparkling wine made from a blend of grapes (32% Chardonnay, 53% Pinot Noir, 15% Meunier) grown in Champagne, France. Traditional Method with lees aging for at least 3 years.

What does it taste like?

Light strawberry and red cherry aromas, with a medium-bodied, mouthwatering texture

If you like this, then try with confidence . . .

Greater quality, greater intensity
Krug Rosé
Greater quality, less intensity
Lanson Noble Cuvée

Try something completely different

Camel Valley Pinot Noir Brut

Lapostolle Casa Chardonnay

Highly Recommended	$	14%

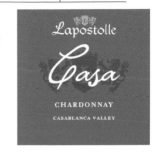

What is it?
A dry white wine made from the Chardonnay grape grown in Casablanca Valley, Chile. Just 1% was aged in used French oak barrels for 5 months. No malolactic fermentation.

What does it taste like?
Very much fruit-driven, the nose and palate have notes of lime, mango, pineapple and peaches, with a hint of sweet spice on its long, lingering finish.

If you like this, then try with confidence . . .
Greater quality, greater intensity
Any white Burgundy from Domaine (not Olivier) Leflaive
Greater quality, less intensity
The very best from the basic Mâcon-Villages appellation, such as Mâcon Solutré Clos des Bertillones Denogent

Try something completely different
White wines from cru classé châteaux in Pessac-Léognan

Lapostolle Cuvée Alexandre Cabernet Sauvignon

Highly Recommended	$$	14%

What is it?
A dry red wine made from the Cabernet Sauvignon grape grown in Colchagua Valley, Chile. Fermented with native yeasts then aged in small French oak barrels (one-third new) for 12 months.

What does it taste like?
Fresh and full-bodied, with high levels of tannin, but balanced with the very ripe fruit, including black currant, blackberry, and black cherry jam.

If you like this, then try with confidence . . .
Greater quality, greater intensity
Ventisquero Queulat Single Vineyard Cabernet Sauvignon
Greater quality, less intensity
Louis Filipe Edwards Pupilla Cabernet Sauvignon

Try something completely different
Washington Merlot from the best producers, such as L'Ecole No. 41, Leonetti, Seven Hills and Woodward Canyon

Lapostolle Cuvée Alexandre Carmenère

Recommended	$$	14.5%

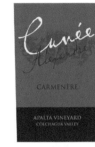

What is it?
A dry red wine made from the Carmenère grape grown in
Colchagua Valley, Chile. Fermented with native yeasts then aged
in small French oak barrels (one-third new) for 12 months.

What does it taste like?
Currant bush notes with very dark black fruit, full body, fine
tannins and a bit of heat on the finish

If you like this, then try with confidence . . .
Greater quality, greater intensity
Concha y Toro Terrunyo Carmenère
Greater quality, less intensity
Anakena Carmenère Single Vineyard

Try something completely different
Chilean Merlot or Cabernet Franc from Franciacorta in Italy

Lapostolle Cuvée Alexandre Chardonnay

Highly Recommended	$$	14.5%

What is it?
A dry white wine made from the Chardonnay grape grown
in Casablanca Valley, Chile. Two thirds of the wine was
fermented and aged in new and used French oak barrels
for 10 months, 20% of the wine undergoing malolactic
fermentation.

What does it taste like?
Aromas of butterscotch, sweet spice, ripe golden apple and
ripe peach. Fresh acidity to balance the intense fruit and oak.
Good length.

If you like this, then try with confidence . . .
Greater quality, greater intensity
Any white Burgundy from Domaine (not Olivier) Leflaive
Greater quality, less intensity
The very best from the basic Mâcon-Villages appellation,
such as Mâcon Solutré Clos des Bertillones Denogent

Try something completely different
White wines from cru classé châteaux in Pessac-Léognan

Lapostolle Cuvée Alexandre Merlot

Highly Recommended	$$	15%

What is it?

A dry red wine made from the Merlot grape grown in Colchagua Valley, Chile. Fermented with native yeasts in French oak vats then aged in small French oak barrels (one-third new) for 12 months.

What does it taste like?

Deep in color, with a classic Merlot nose of chocolate, ripe black plums and black cherries and bold tannins

If you like this, then try with confidence . . .

Greater quality, greater intensity

Great Merlot from California (Pahlmeyer, Paloma and Pride) or Washington (L'Ecole No. 41, Leonetti, Seven Hills and Woodward Canyon)

Greater quality, less intensity

Raphael Rosé of Merlot from Long Island

Try something completely different

Great Merlot-dominated blends from Pomerol, such as châteaux L'Evangile, La Fleur-Pétrus, Latour à Pomerol, Petit-Village, Trotanoy and, if you can afford them, Pétrus and Le Pin

Latour, *see* Louis Latour

Lindeman's Bin 50 Shiraz

Recommended	$	13.5%

What is it?

A dry red wine made from the Shiraz grape grown in Southeastern Australia. A portion is aged in American oak for 6 months.

What does it taste like?

Bramble, clove and smoke with structure provided by firm tannins and a juicy finish

If you like this, then try with confidence . . .

Greater quality, greater intensity
Penfolds St Henri and various Bin numbers (28, 128, 150, 389), culminating in RWT and Grange or Henschke Hill of Grace
Greater quality, less intensity
Clonakilla Shiraz-Viognier

Try something completely different

Zinfandel (especially those by Ridge), Petite Syrah (Ridge Vineyards Dynamite Hill, Rosenblum Rockpile, Turley Cellars Hayne Vineyard or Lava Cap Grand Hill) or even an Australian Zinfandel (such as Cape Mentelle)

Lindeman's Bin 65 Chardonnay

Recommended	$	13.5%

What is it?

A dry white wine made from the Chardonnay grape grown in Southeastern Australia with subtle oak influence

What does it taste like?

Slightly off-dry and fruity with flavors of bananas and baked apples plus butter and vanilla spice oak on the finish

If you like this, then try with confidence . . .

Greater quality, greater intensity
Penfolds Reserve Bin A Chardonnay
Greater quality, less intensity
Penfolds Yattarna Chardonnay

Try something completely different

Fabulous Australian Marsanne, Roussanne and Marsanne-Roussanne blends from Yeringberg

Loosen, *see* Dr.

Louis Latour Aloxe-Corton 1er Cru Les Chaillots

Recommended	$$$	13%

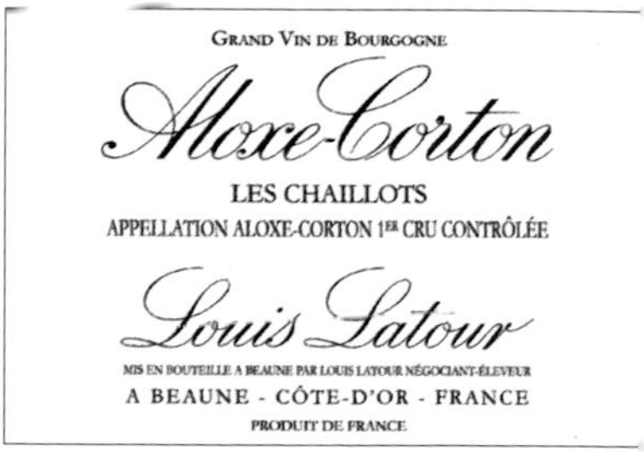

What is it?

A dry red wine made from the Pinot Noir grape grown in Aloxe-Corton, Burgundy, France. Aged in French oak barrels (25% new) for 10–12 months.

What does it taste like?

Young, vibrant fruit rounded out with vanilla oak. Tightly wound, with a long finish

GRAND VIN DE BOURGOGNE

Aloxe-Corton

LES CHAILLOTS
APPELLATION ALOXE-CORTON 1ᴱᴿ CRU CONTRÔLÉE

Louis Latour

MIS EN BOUTEILLE A BEAUNE PAR LOUIS LATOUR NÉGOCIANT-ÉLEVEUR
A BEAUNE - CÔTE-D'OR - FRANCE
PRODUIT DE FRANCE

If you like this, then try with confidence . . .

Greater quality, greater intensity

Aloxe-Corton from Tollot-Beaut

Greater quality, less intensity

Chorey-lès-Beaune from Tollot-Beaut

Try something completely different

Fruit-driven Nebbiolo, such as Cascina Adelaide di Amabile Drocco Barolo Fossati, Aldo Conterno Barolo Cicala, Parusso Barolo Le Coste-Mosconi or G. D. Vajra Barolo Albe

Louis Latour Chassagne-Montrachet

Highly Recommended | $$$ | 13.5%

What is it?
A dry white wine made from the Chardonnay grape grown in Chassagne-Montrachet, Burgundy, France. The wine was fermented in French oak barrels and went through malolactic fermentation.

What does it taste like?
Chalky aromas with light toast nuances, plus pear and golden apple with yeasty textural influence and bright acidity

If you like this, then try with confidence . . .
Greater quality, greater intensity
Louis Jadot Puligny-Montrachet Premier Cru La Garenne, then Domaine Leflaive Montrachet Grand Cru
Greater quality, less intensity
The very best from the basic Mâcon-Villages appellation, such as Mâcon Solutré Clos des Bertillones Denogent

Try something completely different
Top-end Australian Semillon or oaked white Bordeaux Pessac-Léognan, such as Château de Chevalier or its reliable second wine Esprit de Chevalier

Louis Latour Domaine de Valmoissine Pinot Noir

Recommended | $$ | 13.5%

What is it?
A dry red wine made from the Pinot Noir grape grown in Côtes de Verdon, Provence, France, with no oak influence

What does it taste like?
Nice Pinot character with density of pretty red fruit and a pleasant finish

If you like this, then try with confidence . . .
Greater quality, greater intensity
A soft Santenay Premier Cru from Françoise & Denis Clair or Bernard Morey
Greater quality, less intensity
A soft Santenay from Françoise & Denis Clair or Alain Gras

Try something completely different
Fruit-driven Nebbiolo, such as Cascina Adelaide di Amabile Drocco Barolo Fossati, Aldo Conterno Barolo Cicala, Parusso Barolo Le Coste-Mosconi or G. D. Vajra Barolo Albe

Louis Latour Duet Chardonnay-Viognier

Recommended	$$	13.5%

What is it?

A dry white wine made from a blend of grapes (Chardonnay and Viognier) grown in Coteaux de L'Ardèche, Southern Rhône, France

What does it taste like?

Floral nose of honeysuckle and ripe peaches, with a good balance between ample body and just enough acidity

If you like this, then try with confidence . . .

Greater quality, greater intensity

Any white Burgundy from Domaine (not Olivier) Leflaive

Greater quality, less intensity

The very best from the basic Mâcon-Villages appellation, such as Mâcon Solutré Clos des Bertillones Denogent

Try something completely different

The best Pinot Blanc from Alsace, starting with Domaine Weinbach or Collio Pinot Blanco from Schiopetto from Veneto in Italy

Louis Latour Grand Ardèche Chardonnay

Highly Recommended	$$	13.5%

What is it?

A dry white wine made from the Chardonnay grape grown in Coteaux de L'Ardèche, Southern Rhône, France. Fermented and aged in large, used French oak barrels. 100% of the wine underwent malolactic fermentation.

What does it taste like?

Great Chardonnay character, with baked apples and fresh pear and a toasty, spicy oak hint. Rich mid-palate with uplifting acidity.

If you like this, then try with confidence . . .

Greater quality, greater intensity

Any white Burgundy from Domaine (not Olivier) Leflaive

Greater quality, less intensity

The very best from the basic Mâcon-Villages appellation, such as Mâcon Solutré Clos des Bertillones Denogent

Try something completely different

The best Pinot Blanc from Alsace, starting with Domaine Weinbach or Collio Pinot Blanco from Schiopetto from Veneto in Italy

Louis Latour Marsannay

Highly Recommended	$$	13%

What is it?

A dry red wine made from the Pinot Noir grape grown in Marsannay, Burgundy, France with no oak influence

What does it taste like?

Good, round, satiny mouthfeel, juicy dark cherry and earth, long, penetrating finish. Very nice.

If you like this, then try with confidence . . .

Greater quality, greater intensity

Marsannay Les Longeroies from Denis Mortet or Marsannay Champ Pedrix from Géantet Pansiot

Greater quality, less intensity

Domaine Clair-Daü Rosé de Marsannay from Louis Jadot

Try something completely different

Fruit-driven Nebbiolo, such as Cascina Adelaide di Amabile Drocco Barolo Fossati, Aldo Conterno Barolo Cicala, Parusso Barolo Le Coste-Mosconi or G. D. Vajra Barolo Albe

Louis Latour Meursault

Recommended	$$$	13.5%

What is it?

A dry white wine made from the Chardonnay grape grown in Meursault, Burgundy, France. The wine was fermented in French oak barrels and went through malolactic fermentation.

What does it taste like?

Buttery, with ripe mango and red apple flavors and a soft texture

If you like this, then try with confidence . . .

Greater quality, greater intensity

Louis Jadot Puligny-Montrachet Premier Cru La Garenne, then Domaine Leflaive Montrachet Grand Cru

Greater quality, less intensity

The very best from the basic Mâcon-Villages appellation, such as Mâcon Solutré Clos des Bertillones Denogent

Try something completely different

Top-end Australian Semillon or oaked white Bordeaux Pessac-Léognan, such as Château de Chevalier or its reliable second wine Esprit de Chevalier

Louis Latour Pinot Noir Bourgogne

| Recommended | $$ | 13% |

What is it?

A dry red wine made from the Pinot Noir grape grown in Burgundy, France, with no oak influence

What does it taste like?

Fresh and uplifted, a good value Bourgogne with structure and grace

If you like this, then try with confidence . . .

Greater quality, greater intensity

A soft Santenay Premier Cru from Françoise & Denis Clair or Bernard Morey

Greater quality, less intensity

A soft Santenay from Françoise & Denis Clair or Alain Gras

Try something completely different

Fruit-driven Nebbiolo, such as Cascina Adelaide di Amabile Drocco Barolo Fossati, Aldo Conterno Barolo Cicala, Parusso Barolo Le Coste-Mosconi or G. D. Vajra Barolo Albe

---

Louis Latour Pommard

| Recommended | $$$ | 13.5% |

What is it?

A dry red wine made from the Pinot Noir grape grown in Pommard, Burgundy, France. Aged in French oak barrels for 10–12 months.

What does it taste like?

Dark plum, cherry and vanilla and a powerful structure

If you like this, then try with confidence . . .

Greater quality, greater intensity

Pommard Premier Cru from Courcel, then Comte Armand

Greater quality, less intensity

A soft Santenay Premier Cru from Françoise & Denis Clair or Bernard Morey

Try something completely different

Fruit-driven Nebbiolo, such as Cascina Adelaide di Amabile Drocco Barolo Fossati, Aldo Conterno Barolo Cicala, Parusso Barolo Le Coste-Mosconi or G. D. Vajra Barolo Albe

Louis Latour Pouilly-Fuissé

Recommended	$$	13%

What is it?

A dry white wine made from the Chardonnay grape grown in Pouilly-Fuissé, Burgundy, France. 100% of the wine went through malolactic fermentation.

What does it taste like?

Pure golden apple and pear flavors on a medium-bodied, creamy frame with refreshing acidity

If you like this, then try with confidence . . .

Greater quality, greater intensity

Pouilly-Fuissé from Guffens-Heyen or Château-Fuissé Vieilles Vignes

Greater quality, less intensity

The very best from the basic Mâcon-Villages appellation, such as Mâcon Solutré Clos des Bertillones Denogent

Try something completely different

White wines from cru classé châteaux in Pessac-Léognan

Louis Latour Puligny-Montrachet

Recommended	$$$	13.5%

What is it?

A dry white wine made from the Chardonnay grape grown in Puligny-Montrachet, Burgundy, France. The wine was fermented in French oak barrels and went through malolactic fermentation.

What does it taste like?

Lemon and light butterscotch with a round texture and elegant mineral finish

If you like this, then try with confidence . . .

Greater quality, greater intensity

Louis Jadot Puligny-Montrachet Premier Cru La Garenne, then Domaine Leflaive Montrachet Grand Cru

Greater quality, less intensity

The very best from the basic Mâcon-Villages appellation, such as Mâcon Solutré Clos des Bertillones Denogent

Try something completely different

White wines from cru classé châteaux in Pessac-Léognan

Louis M. Martini Sonoma Cabernet Sauvignon

Recommended	$$	13.5%

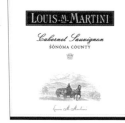

What is it?

A dry red wine—made from Cabernet Sauvignon with Petite Sirah—grown in California. The wine was matured in small oak barrels.

What does it taste like?

Tangy red currant and red cherry flavors, with medium body and supportive yet silky tannins

If you like this, then try with confidence . . .

Greater quality, greater intensity

Caymus Special Selection Cabernet Sauvignon or Dunn Vineyards Howell Mountain Cabernet Sauvignon

Greater quality, less intensity

Stag's Leap Cask 23 Estate Cabernet Sauvignon

Try something completely different

For a classic Bordeaux to match the intensity and voluptuousness of top California Cabernet Sauvignon, try a Merlot-dominated Pomerol such as châteaux L'Evangile, La Fleur-Pétrus, Latour à Pomerol, Petit-Village, Trotanoy and, if you can afford them, Pétrus and Le Pin

Louis Roederer NV Brut Premier

To Die For	$$$	12%

What is it?

A dry sparkling wine made from a blend of grapes (Pinot Noir, Chardonnay and Meunier) grown in Champagne, France. Traditional Method with lees aging for a minimum of 3 years.

What does it taste like?

Intense apple and citrus fruit with a touch of brioche, lively vibrant acidity and silky soft bubbles

If you like this, then try with confidence . . .

Greater quality, greater intensity

Louis Roederer Brut Vintage and Louis Roederer Blanc de Blancs

Greater quality, less intensity

Louis Roederer Cristal

Try something completely different

The top sparkling wines from England (Camel Valley, Henners, Herbert Hall, Nyetimber, Ridgeview), Tasmania (Bay of Fires, Clover Hill, Jansz, Stefano Lubiana, Pirie, Relbia) and, of course, California (Roederer Estate)

Luigi Bosca Malbec

Recommended	$$	14%

What is it?

A dry red wine made from the Malbec grape
grown in Mendoza, Argentina

What does it taste like?

Opaque purple, with aromas of blackberries, damsons
and coffee. Big but soft tannins, and very full-bodied.

If you like this, then try with confidence . . .

Greater quality, greater intensity

Luigi Bosca Vistalba Malbec and Nicolas Catena Zapata
Malbec Argentino, then Flichman Parcelo 26 for the
ultimate monster Malbec

Greater quality, less intensity

Colomé Malbec or Yacochuya Estate from Salta, Bodegas
Lagarde Agrelo and Terrazas Afincado single-vineyard
Malbecs

Try something completely different

Cahors from Clos Triguedina or Tannat Castel La Puebla Dayman
from Stagnari in Uruguay

M. Chapoutier Bila-Haut Côtes du Roussillon Villages

Highly Recommended	$$	14%

What is it?

A dry red wine made from a blend of grapes (65% Grenache, 35% Syrah) grown in Côtes du Roussillon Villages, Southern France. Aged in new French oak for 18 months.

What does it taste like?

Full-bodied with sweet spice, dark red fruit, savory pepper and a bright, juicy finish

If you like this, then try with confidence . . .

Greater quality, greater intensity
Domaine Pierre Usseglio Châteauneuf-du-Pape, then
Château Rayas
Greater quality, less intensity
E. Guigal Châteauneuf-du-Pape, then Domaine
du Vieux Télégraphe Châteauneuf-du-Pape

Try something completely different

Pure Grenache from Australia (Yalumba Bush Vine Grenache, Kilikanoon The Duke Clare Valley Grenache) or France (Mas Foulaquier Le Petit Duc)

M. Chapoutier La Ciboise Lubéron

Recommended	$$$	14%

What is it?

A dry red wine made from a blend of grapes (Grenache and Syrah) grown in Lubéron, Provence, France. Aged on fine lees in stainless steel vats for 9–12 months.

What does it taste like?

Soft and drinkable, with raspberry jam, white pepper and dark cherry notes

If you like this, then try with confidence . . .

Greater quality, greater intensity
Domaine Pierre Usseglio Châteauneuf-du-Pape, then Château Rayas
Greatert quality, less intensity
E. Guigal Châteauneuf-du Pape, then Domaine du Vieux Télégraphe Châteauneuf-du-Pape

Try something completely different

Pure Grenache from Australia (Yalumba Bush Vine Grenache, Kilikanoon The Duke Clare Valley Grenache) or France (Mas Foulaquier Le Petit Duc)

M. Chapoutier Belleruche Côtes-du-Rhône

Recommended	$	14%

What is it?

A dry red wine made from a blend of grapes (Grenache and Syrah) grown in Côtes-du-Rhône, France. Aged on the lees in stainless steel vats for 6 months.

What does it taste like?

Medium-bodied and smooth, with smoky meat and red berry flavors

If you like this, then try with confidence . . .

Greater quality, greater intensity
Yalumba Bush Vine Grenache
Greater quality, less intensity
E. Guigal Côtes-du-Rhône

Try something completely different

Pure Grenache from Australia (Yalumba Bush Vine Grenache, Kilikanoon The Duke Clare Valley Grenache) or France (Mas Foulaquier Le Petit Duc)

Macie, *see* Rocca delle Macie

MacMurray Ranch Sonoma Coast Pinot Noir

Recommended	$$	14%

What is it?

A dry red wine made from the Pinot Noir grape grown in Sonoma Coast, California. The fruit has a cold pre-ferment maceration, and the wine is matured for 6–9 months in a mix of French, European and American small oak.

What does it taste like?

Effusive and pure red fruit character with an herbal spicy note. A fuller style of Pinot, with good weight and structure.

If you like this, then try with confidence . . .

Greater quality, greater intensity

La Bauge au Dessus and other Pinot Noir from Au Bon Climat in Santa Barbara, California, or Le Grand Clos Pinot Noir from Le Clos Jordanne in Niagara, Canada

Greater quality, less intensity

The more elegant Oregon Pinot Noir, starting with Adelsheim, Bethel Heights and Rex Hill

Try something completely different

Fruit-driven Nebbiolo, such as Cascina Adelaide di Amabile Drocco Barolo Fossati, Aldo Conterno Barolo Cicala, Parusso Barolo Le Coste-Mosconi or G. D. Vajra Barolo Albe

Maculan Brentino

Recommended	$$	13.5%

What is it?

A dry red wine made from a blend of grapes (55% Merlot, 45% Cabernet Sauvignon) grown in Veneto, Italy. Half the wine is aged in small oak barrels.

What does it taste like?

An aromatic and fruit-driven red, with smooth notes of oak and supple tannins on the finish

If you like this, then try with confidence . . .

Greater quality, greater intensity

Château La Conseillante Pomerol

Greater quality, less intensity

Château d'Aiguilhe Côtes de Castillon

Try something completely different

Pure Merlot, such as Clos du Val Merlot from California or Woodward Canyon from Washington

Marqués de Cáceres Rioja Crianza

Recommended	$$	13%

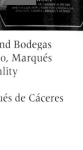

What is it?

A dry red wine made from a blend of grape varieties (85% Tempranillo, 15% Garnacha and Graciano), aged in small oak for 12 months and then a further 14 months in bottle before release

What does it taste like?

Bold strawberry and red plum fruit with prominent spicy oak.

If you like this, then try with confidence . . .

Greater quality, greater intensity

Rioja from Finca Allende, Artadi, Lealtanza, Manzanos, Marqués de Griñon, Nekeas, Palacios Remondo, La Rioja Alta, San Vicente and Bodegas Ysios, then the very best wines of Barón de Ley, Luis Canas, Contino, Marqués de Murrieta, Marqués de Riscal and Bodegas Muga for ultimate quality

Greater quality, less intensity

Reserva and Gran Reserva from La Rioja Alta Viña Ardanza, Marqués de Cáceres and Viña Tondonia Rioja or any rosado from a top Rioja producer

Try something completely different

Numanthia Termes then Numanthia Termanthia from Toro

Marqués de Cáceres Rioja Reserva

Recommended	$$	14%

What is it?

A dry red wine made from a blend of grape varieties (85% Tempranillo, 15% Garnacha and Graciano), aged in small French oak for 22 months and then a further 2 years in bottle before release

What does it taste like?

Developed plum and prune, with some floral and spicy notes. The palate is soft-textured and savory.

If you like this, then try with confidence . . .

Greater quality, greater intensity

Rioja from Finca Allende, Artadi, Lealtanza, Manzanos, Marqués de Griñon, Nekeas, Palacios Remondo, La Rioja Alta, San Vicente and Bodegas Ysios, then the very best wines of Barón de Ley, Luis Canas, Contino, Marqués de Murrieta, Marqués de Riscal and Bodegas Muga for ultimate quality

Greater quality, less intensity

Reserva and Gran Reserva from La Rioja Alta Viña Ardanza, Marqués de Cáceres and Viña Tondonia Rioja or any rosado from a top Rioja producer

Try something completely different

Numanthia Termes then Numanthia Termanthia from Toro

Marqués de Riscal Rioja Gran Reserva

Highly Recommended	$$	14.5%

What is it?

A dry red wine made from a blend of grape varieties (Tempranillo, Graciano, Mazuelo) grown in Rioja, Spain. The wine is matured for 32 months in small oak.

What does it taste like?

Fully mature red, with complex savory flavors of coffee, spices and leather as well as baked strawberry fruit and toasty oak. Very soft tannins, and very gentle and fragrant.

If you like this, then try with confidence . . .

Greater quality, greater intensity

Rioja from Finca Allende, Artadi, Lealtanza, Manzanos, Marqués de Griñon, Nekeas, Palacios Remondo, La Rioja Alta, San Vicente and Bodegas Ysios, then the very best wines of Barón de Ley, Luis Canas, Contino, Marqués de Murrieta, Marqués de Riscal and Bodegas Muga for ultimate quality

Greater quality, less intensity

Reserva and Gran Reserva from La Rioja Alta Viña Ardanza, Marqués de Cáceres and Viña Tondonia Rioja or any rosado from a top Rioja producer

Try something completely different

Numanthia Termes then Numanthia Termanthia from Toro

Marqués de Riscal Rioja Reserva

Highly Recommended	$$	14%

What is it?

A dry red wine made from a blend of grape varieties (90% Tempranillo, 10% Graciano and Mazuelo) grown in Rioja, Spain

What does it taste like?

Complex, aged red showing ripe strawberry fruit, with savory leather and earthy notes. Soft, silky tannins and lingering complex flavors.

If you like this, then try with confidence . . .

Greater quality, greater intensity

Rioja from Finca Allende, Artadi, Lealtanza, Manzanos, Marqués de Griñon, Nekeas, Palacios Remondo, La Rioja Alta, San Vicente and Bodegas Ysios, then the very best wines of Barón de Ley, Luis Canas, Contino, Marqués de Murrieta, Marqués de Riscal and Bodegas Muga for ultimate quality

Greater quality, less intensity

Reserva and Gran Reserva from La Rioja Alta Viña Ardanza, Marqués de Cáceres and Viña Tondonia Rioja or any rosado from a top Rioja producer

Try something completely different

Numanthia Termes then Numanthia Termanthia from Toro

Martín Códax Albariño

Recommended   **$$**   **13%**

What is it?
A dry white wine made from the Albariño grape grown in Rías Baixas, Spain

What does it taste like?
Light flavors of citrus and peas with a clean finish

If you like this, then try with confidence . . .
Greater quality, greater intensity
Albariño Organistrum
Greater quality, less intensity
Burgáns Albariño

Try something completely different
Hugel and Trimbach Riesling from Alsace or Grüner Veltliner from Austria, starting with Pfaffl in the Weinviertel, then Brundlmayer (Kamtal), and Knoll, F X Pichler, Prager and Hirzberger (Wachau)

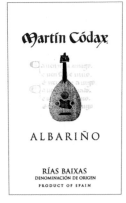

(Martín Códax

ALBARIÑO

RÍAS BAIXAS
DENOMINACIÓN DE ORIGEN
PRODUCT OF SPAIN

Martini, *see* Louis M. Martini

Maso Canali Pinot Grigio

Recommended | **$$** | **13%**

What is it?

A dry white wine made from a blend of grapes (Pinot Grigio, Chardonnay) in the Matua Valley, northwest Auckland, New Zealand. The small portion of Chardonnay grapes underwent passito drying to concentrate flavors and sugars, and add viscosity and mouthfeel to the final blend.

What does it taste like?

Quite rich and ripe lemon and melon fruit, with a gentle waxy richness on the palate

If you like this, then try with confidence . . .

Greater quality, greater intensity
JosMeyer Pinot Gris 1854 Fondation or Trimbach Pinot Gris Réserve with a few years additional bottle-age

Greater quality, less intensity
JosMeyer Pinot Blanc Les Lutins or Domaine Weinbach Pinot Blanc

Try something completely different

A good Soave such as Pieropan or Inama, perhaps even Chasselas from Blaise Duboux in Switzerland or, for the very adventurous, a super-soft Koshu from Japan, such as Misawa Private Reserve from Grace

Matua Valley Paretai Sauvignon Blanc

Highly Recommended	$$	13.5%

What is it?

A dry white wine made from the Sauvignon Blanc grape grown in Marlborough, New Zealand

What does it taste like?

Fresh and long, with intense and complex aromas of smoke, peas, asparagus, passion fruit and chives

If you like this, then try with confidence . . .

Greater quality, greater intensity

Iconic Marlborough Sauvignon Blanc, such as Cloudy Bay, Craggy Range Avery Vineyard, Hunter's, Isabel Estate, Koura Whaleback, Nobilo Icon and Palliser Estate

Greater quality, less intensity

The finest, most elegant Pouilly-Fumé, such as Didier Dagueneau Silex and Pur Sang

Try something completely different

Lean, linear Riesling from Alsace (Trimbach Clos Ste Hune or JosMeyer Grand Cru Hengst) and Mosel (Maximin Grünhaus Abtsberg Alte Reben Trocken)

Matua Valley Pinot Noir

Recommended   **$$** | **13.5%**

What is it?

A dry red wine made from the Pinot Noir grape grown in
Marlborough, New Zealand. Aged 8 months in French oak.

What does it taste like?

Pale in color, with light red fruit and vanilla nuances and a satiny texture

If you like this, then try with confidence . . .

Greater quality, greater intensity

Pinot Noir from Akarua, Ata Rangi, Craggy Range
Te Muna, Felton Road and Twin Paddocks

Greater quality, less intensity

Kim Crawford Marlborough New Zealand
Pansy Rosé

Try something completely different

Fruit-driven Nebbiolo, such as Cascina Adelaide
di Amabile Drocco Barolo Fossati, Aldo Conterno
Barolo Cicala, Parusso Barolo Le Coste-Mosconi
or G. D. Vajra Barolo Albe

Matua Valley Sauvignon Blanc

Recommended	$$	13%

What is it?

A dry white wine made from the Sauvignon Blanc grape grown in Marlborough, New Zealand

What does it taste like?

Quite zingy, with loads of kiwi fruit, and less herbaceousness than most of its kind

If you like this, then try with confidence . . .

Greater quality, greater intensity

Iconic Marlborough Sauvignon Blanc, such as Cloudy Bay, Craggy Range Avery Vineyard, Hunter's, Isabel Estate, Koura Whaleback, Nobilo Icon and Palliser Estate

Greater quality, less intensity

The finest, most elegant Pouilly-Fumé, such as Didier Dagueneau Silex and Pur Sang

Try something completely different

Lean, linear Riesling from Alsace (Trimbach Clos Ste Hune or JosMeyer Grand Cru Hengst) and Mosel (Maximin Grünhaus Abtsberg Alte Reben Trocken)

Michelle, *see* Chateau Ste Michelle

Mirassou Chardonnay

Recommended	$	13.5%

What is it?
A dry white wine made from the Chardonnay grape grown in California with subtle oak influence

What does it taste like?
Slightly off-dry, easy-drinking style. Clean, smooth, with a pleasant taste and finish.

If you like this, then try with confidence . . .
Greater quality, greater intensity
Jacob's Creek Chardonnay Adelaide Hills
Greater quality, less intensity
The very best from the basic Mâcon-Villages appellation, such as Mâcon Solutré Clos des Bertillones Denogent

Try something completely different
The best Pinot Blanc from Alsace, starting with Domaine Weinbach or Collio Pinot Blanco from Schiopetto from Veneto in Italy

Mirassou Moscato

Recommended	$	8%

What is it?
A medium-dry white wine made from the Moscato grape grown in California

What does it taste like?
Sweet, straightforward fruit in a soft, easy style

If you like this, then try with confidence . . .
Greater quality, greater intensity
Richer, fully sparkling Asti from the very finest producers, such as Romano Dogliotti Asti La Selvatica or Cerutti Asti Cesare
Greater quality, less intensity
Silvan Ridge Semi-Sparkling Early Muscat

Try something completely different
The light-as-a-dime fortified Muscat de Beaumes-de-Venise from top producers such as Domaine des Bernardins or Durban

Mirassou Pinot Noir

Recommended	$	13%

What is it?
A dry red wine made from the Pinot Noir grape grown in California with subtle oak influence

What does it taste like?
Upfront sweet, dark red fruits and a creamy texture

If you like this, then try with confidence . . .
Greater quality, greater intensity
La Bauge au Dessus and other Pinot Noir from Au Bon Climat in Santa Barbara, California, or Le Grand Clos Pinot Noir from Le Clos Jordanne in Niagara, Canada

Greater quality, less intensity
The more elegant Oregon Pinot Noir, starting with Adelsheim, Bethel Heights and Rex Hill

Try something completely different
Fruit-driven Nebbiolo, such as Cascina Adelaide di Amabile Drocco Barolo Fossati, Aldo Conterno Barolo Cicala, Parusso Barolo Le Coste-Mosconi or G. D. Vajra Barolo Albe

Mirassou Riesling

Recommended	$	12.5%

What is it?
An off-dry white wine made from the Riesling grape grown in California

What does it taste like?
Medium-sweet, with juicy ripe apple, lemon and peach flavors. Made in a crowd-pleasing, quaffable style.

If you like this, then try with confidence . . .
Greater quality, greater intensity
Chateau Ste Michelle Riesling Eroica
Greater quality, less intensity
Uncompromising Riesling wines of Heyman-Löwenstein

Try something completely different
Dry Australian Semillon, particularly from the Hunter Valley, with several years bottle-age

Mirassou Sauvignon Blanc

Recommended	$	13.5%

What is it?

A dry white wine made from the Sauvignon Blanc grape grown in California

What does it taste like?

Off-dry with subtle bruised apple, baking spice and vanilla oak flavors

If you like this, then try with confidence . . .

Greater quality, greater intensity

Iconic Marlborough Sauvignon Blanc, such as Cloudy Bay, Craggy Range Avery Vineyard, Hunter's, Isabel Estate, Koura Whaleback, Nobilo Icon and Palliser Estate

Greater quality, less intensity

The finest, most elegant Pouilly-Fumé, such as Didier Dagueneau Silex and Pur Sang

Try something completely different

Lean, linear Riesling from Alsace (Trimbach Clos Ste Hune or JosMeyer Grand Cru Hengst) and Mosel (Maximin Grünhaus Abtsberg Alte Reben Trocken)

Moët & Chandon NV Brut Impérial

Recommended	$$$	12%

What is it?

A dry sparkling wine made from a blend of grapes (Pinot Noir, Chardonnay and Meunier) grown in Champagne, France. Traditional Method with lees aging for a minimum of 3 years.

What does it taste like?

Fresh red apple fruitiness and attractive pastry notes, lively exuberant bubbles. The quality of the world's most popular Champagne has soared since 2005.

If you like this, then try with confidence . . .

Greater quality, greater intensity

Moët & Chandon Grand Vintage

Greater quality, less intensity

Dom Pérignon

Try something completely different

The top sparkling wines from England (Camel Valley, Henners, Herbert Hall, Nyetimber, Ridgeview) and Tasmania (Bay of Fires, Clover Hill, Jansz, Stefano Lubiana, Pirie, Relbia)

MontGras Reserva Cabernet Sauvignon

Highly Recommended	**$$**	**14%**

What is it?

A dry red wine made from the Cabernet Sauvignon grape grown in Colchagua Valley, Chile. Half of the wine was aged in new French and American oak barrels.

What does it taste like?

Minty, smoky, mouth-filling style with good integration of oak, intensity of ripe blackberry fruit and velvety tannins

If you like this, then try with confidence . . .

Greater quality, greater intensity

Ventisquero Queulat Single Vineyard Cabernet Sauvignon

Greater quality, less intensity

Louis Filipe Edwards Pupilla Cabernet Sauvignon

Try something completely different

Washington Merlot from the best producers, such as L'Ecole No. 41, Leonetti, Seven Hills and Woodward Canyon

MontGras Reserva Carmenère

Recommended	$$	14.5%

What is it?

A dry red wine made from the Carmenère grape grown in Colchagua Valley, Chile. 75% of the wine was aged in a combination of French and American oak barrels.

What does it taste like?

Extracted, with brambly, sweet dark red and blackberry fruit on a full-bodied frame with low acidity and firm tannins

If you like this, then try with confidence . . .

Greater quality, greater intensity
Concha y Toro Terrunyo Carmenère
Greater quality, less intensity
Anakena Carmenère Single Vineyard

Try something completely different

Chilean Merlot or Cabernet Franc from Franciacorta in Italy

MontGras Reserva Sauvignon Blanc

Recommended	$$	14%

What is it?

A dry wine made from the Sauvignon Blanc grape grown in San Antonio Valley, Chile

What does it taste like?

Effusive nose of gooseberry and elderflower that turn to ripe melon on the palate. A round, rich style, with lower acidity than most Chilean Sauvignon Blanc.

If you like this, then try with confidence . . .

Greater quality, greater intensity
Iconic Marlborough Sauvignon Blanc, such as Cloudy Bay, Craggy Range Avery Vineyard, Hunter's, Isabel Estate, Koura Whaleback, Nobilo Icon and Palliser Estate
Greater quality, less intensity
The finest, most elegant Pouilly-Fumé, such as Didier Dagueneau Silex and Pur Sang

Try something completely different

Lean, linear Riesling from Alsace (Trimbach Clos Ste Hune or JosMeyer Grand Cru Hengst) and Mosel (Maximin Grünhaus Abtsberg Alte Reben Trocken)

Mouton Cadet Bordeaux Blanc

Recommended	$	13%

What is it?

A dry white wine made from a blend of grape varieties (65% Sauvignon Blanc, 30% Semillon, 5% Muscadelle) grown in Bordeaux, France. Matured in oak for 4 months.

What does it taste like?

Fresh grapefruit and newly cut grass, light, crisp and fresh

If you like this, then try with confidence . . .

Greater quality, greater intensity

Check out cru classé Graves from Pessac-Léognan, culminating in Domaine de Chevalier

Greater quality, less intensity

Château Bonnet Blanc Entre-Deux-Mers

Try something completely different

Riesling, starting with Alsace (Hugel, Trimbach) but also dry Rieslings from Von Bühl and Bassermann Jordan (Pfalz, Germany)

Mouton Cadet Bordeaux Rouge

Recommended	$	13.5%

What is it?

A dry red wine made from a blend of grape varieties (65% Merlot, 20% Cabernet Sauvignon, 15% Cabernet Franc) grown in Bordeaux, France. Matured in vats for 6 months.

What does it taste like?

Expressive black currant and cedar, firm ripe tannins and a touch of oaky spiciness

If you like this, then try with confidence . . .

Greater quality, greater intensity

Château La Conseillante Pomerol

Greater quality, less intensity

Château d'Aiguilhe Côtes de Castillon

Try something completely different

Pure Merlot, such as Clos du Val Merlot from California or Woodward Canyon from Washington

Mumm Napa Blanc de Blancs

Highly Recommended	$$$	12.5%

What is it?

A dry white sparkling wine made from a blend of grapes (90% Chardonnay and 10% Pinot Gris), grown in Napa Valley, California. A small proportion of the blend is aged in French oak. Traditional Method with at least 36 months on yeast lees.

What does it taste like?

Beautifully focused, crisp citrus fruits and a long, elegant finish. Well worth the premium.

If you like this, then try with confidence . . .

Greater quality, greater intensity

Champagne Perrier-Jouët Belle Epoque (Flower Bottle) Blanc de Blancs

Greater quality, less intensity

Champagne Mumm de Cramant

Try something completely different

The best American sparkling wines beyond California, such as Argyle in Oregon, Mountain Dome in Washington, L. Mawby in Michigan and Lamoreaux Landing in New York

Mumm Napa DVX Brut

| **Highly Recommended** | **$$$** | **12.5%** |

What is it?

A dry white sparkling wine made from a blend of grapes (50% Chardonnay and 50% Pinot Noir) grown in Napa Valley, California. A portion of the wine is fermented in French oak. Traditional Method with at least 60 months on yeast lees.

What does it taste like?

Rich and crisp, with lots of bready-biscuity yeast-complexed flavors layering on the finish

If you like this, then try with confidence . . .

Greater quality, greater intensity

Champagne Mumm Cuvée R. Lalou

Greater quality, less intensity

Champagne Mumm de Cramant

Try something completely different

The best American sparkling wines beyond California, such as Argyle in Oregon, Mountain Dome in Washington, L. Mawby in Michigan, and Lamoreaux Landing in New York

Mumm Napa NV Brut Prestige

Recommended	$$	12.5%

What is it?
A dry white sparkling wine made from a blend of grapes (Chardonnay and Pinot Noir) grown in Napa Valley, California. Traditional Method with at least 18 months on yeast lees.

What does it taste like?
Consistently fresh and elegant, with spiced apple, melon and citrus fruits on the palate, and a soft, creamy mousse

If you like this, then try with confidence . . .
Greater quality, greater intensity
Champagne Mumm Cuvée R. Lalou
Greater quality, less intensity
Champagne Mumm de Cramant

Try something completely different
The best American sparkling wines beyond California, such as Argyle in Oregon, Mountain Dome in Washington, L. Mawby in Michigan, and Lamoreaux Landing in New York

Mumm NV Cordon Rouge Brut

Highly Recommended	$$$	12%

What is it?
A dry sparkling wine made from a blend of grapes (Pinot Noir, Chardonnay and Meunier) grown in Champagne, France. Traditional Method with lees aging for a minimum of 3 years.

What does it taste like?
Lean, refreshing style with yeast-complexed, golden apple flavors and excellent persistence

If you like this, then try with confidence . . .
Greater quality, greater intensity
Mumm Vintage, then Mumm Cuvée R. Lalou
Greater quality, less intensity
Champagne Mumm de Cramant

Try something completely different
The top sparkling wines from England (Camel Valley, Henners, Herbert Hall, Nyetimber, Ridgeview) and Tasmania (Bay of Fires, Clover Hill, Jansz, Stefano Lubiana, Pirie, Relbia)

Nederburg Winemaster's Reserve Sauvignon Blanc

Highly Recommended	$$	13.5%

What is it?

A dry white wine made from the Sauvignon Blanc grape grown in the Western Cape, South Africa

What does it taste like?

An unusual yet elegant style, with complex blossom and smoke elements on a medium-bodied, crisp frame

If you like this, then try with confidence . . .

Greater quality, greater intensity

Iconic Marlborough Sauvignon Blanc, such as Cloudy Bay, Craggy Range Avery Vineyard, Hunter's, Isabel Estate, Koura Whaleback, Nobilo Icon and Palliser Estate

Greater quality, less intensity

The finest, most elegant Pouilly-Fumé, such as Didier Dagueneau Silex and Pur Sang

Try something completely different

Lean, linear Riesling from Alsace (Trimbach Clos Ste Hune or JosMeyer Grand Cru Hengst) and Mosel (Maximin Grünhaus Abtsberg Alte Reben Trocken)

Nederburg Winemaster's Reserve Shiraz

Recommended	$$	14.5%

What is it?

A dry red wine made from the Shiraz grape grown in Western Cape, South Africa. Aged in a combination of new and used French oak barrels for 12–18 months.

What does it taste like?

Ripe and thick, with jammy fruit and a hint of tar with a smooth finish

If you like this, then try with confidence . . .

Greater quality, greater intensity

Penfolds St Henri and various Bin numbers (28, 128, 150, 389), culminating in RWT and Grange or Henschke Hill of Grace

Greater quality, less intensity

Clonakilla Shiraz-Viognier

Try something completely different

Zinfandel (especially those by Ridge), Petite Syrah (Ridge Vineyards Dynamite Hill, Rosenblum Rockpile, Turley Cellars Hayne Vineyard or Lava Cap Grand Hill) or even an Australian Zinfandel (such as Cape Mentelle)

WINEMASTER'S
RESERVE

SHIRAZ
WINE OF SOUTH AFRICA

Nicolas Potel Bourgogne Pinot Noir

Highly Recommended	$$	12.5%

What is it?

A dry red wine made from the Pinot Noir grape grown in Burgundy, France. Aged in large, used French oak for at least 6 months.

What does it taste like?

Light, fresh and juicy, with good expression of red Pinot fruit and a soft texture

If you like this, then try with confidence . . .

Greater quality, greater intensity

Nicolas Potel Volnay Vieilles Vignes

Greater quality, less intensity

A soft Santenay Premier Cru from Françoise & Denis Clair or Bernard Morey

Try something completely different

Fruit-driven Nebbiolo, such as Cascina Adelaide di Amabile Drocco Barolo Fossati, Aldo Conterno Barolo Cicala, Parusso Barolo Le Coste-Mosconi or G. D. Vajra Barolo Albe

Nino Franco Grave di Stecca Prosecco

Highly Recommended	$$$	11.5%

What is it?

A dry, brut-style sparkling white wine made from the Glera grape grown in a single vineyard on the slopes of Prealpi mountains in Prosecco, part of the Veneto region of northeastern Italy. Charmat method with no lees aging to retain fresh fruit character.

What does it taste like?

The balance between intensity of flavor and elegance of style make this one of the best brut-style Proseccos available

If you like this, then try with confidence . . .

Greater quality, greater intensity
Champagne Pol Roger Blanc de Blancs
Greater quality, less intensity
Champagne Duval-Leroy Blanc de Blancs

Try something completely different
Ridgeview Grosvenor

GRAVE DI STECCA

Nino Franco Primo Prosecco

Highly Recommended	$$	11.5%

What is it?

An off-dry sparkling white wine made from the Glera grape grown in Prosecco, in the Veneto region of northeastern Italy. Charmat method with no lees aging to retain fresh fruit character.

What does it taste like?

Deliciously rich floral aromas with creamy orchard fruits on the palate

If you like this, then try with confidence . . .

Greater quality, greater intensity
Champagne Mumm Demi-Sec
Greater quality, less intensity
Champagne De Venoge Vin du Paradis

Try something completely different
Veuve Clicquot Vintage Rich

Nino Franco Rustico Prosecco

Recommended	$$	11.5%

What is it?
A dry, brut-style sparkling white wine made from the Glera grape grown in Prosecco, in the Veneto region of northeastern Italy. Charmat method with no lees aging to retain fresh fruit character.

Nino Franco

What does it taste like?
A touch of peachy richness sets this apart from most other Prosecco.

If you like this, then try with confidence . . .
Greater quality, greater intensity
Champagne Pol Roger Blanc de Blancs
Greater quality, less intensity
Champagne Duval-Leroy Blanc de Blancs

Try something completely different
Ridgeview Grosvenor

Nobilo Icon Sauvignon Blanc

Recommended	$$	14%

What is it?
A dry white wine made from the Sauvignon Blanc grape grown in Marlborough, New Zealand

What does it taste like?
Very ripe style, with pronounced green pepper, ripe melon and peach aromas, moderate acidity and full body

If you like this, then try with confidence . . .
Greater quality, greater intensity
Iconic Marlborough Sauvignon Blanc, such as Cloudy Bay, Craggy Range Avery Vineyard, Hunter's, Isabel Estate, Koura Whaleback, Nobilo Icon and Palliser Estate
Greater quality, less intensity
The finest, most elegant Pouilly-Fumé, such as Didier Dagueneau Silex and Pur Sang

Try something completely different
Lean, linear Riesling from Alsace (Trimbach Clos Ste Hune or JosMeyer Grand Cru Hengst) and Mosel (Maximin Grünhaus Abtsberg Alte Reben Trocken)

Nobilo Sauvignon Blanc

Highly Recommended $$ 13%

What is it?

A dry white wine made from the Sauvignon Blanc grape grown in Marlborough, New Zealand

What does it taste like?

Shows excellent typicity, with intense gooseberry, passion fruit and chive notes with good persistence

If you like this, then try with confidence . . .

Greater quality, greater intensity

Iconic Marlborough Sauvignon Blanc, such as Cloudy Bay, Craggy Range Avery Vineyard, Hunter's, Isabel Estate, Koura Whaleback, Nobilo Icon and Palliser Estate

Greater quality, less intensity

The finest, most elegant Pouilly-Fumé, such as Didier Dagueneau Silex and Pur Sang

Try something completely different

Lean, linear Riesling from Alsace (Trimbach Clos Ste Hune or JosMeyer Grand Cru Hengst) and Mosel (Maximin Grünhaus Abtsberg Alte Reben Trocken)

Norton, *see* **Bodega Norton**

O. Fournier B Crux Sauvignon Blanc

Recommended	$$	12%

What is it?

A dry white wine made from the Sauvignon Blanc grape grown in Uco Valley, Mendoza, Argentina

What does it taste like?

Round style with elderflower, melon and passion fruit, backed by fresh acidity

If you like this, then try with confidence . . .

Greater quality, greater intensity

Iconic Marlborough Sauvignon Blanc, such as Cloudy Bay, Craggy Range Avery Vineyard, Hunter's, Isabel Estate, Koura Whaleback, Nobilo Icon and Palliser Estate

Greater quality, less intensity

The finest, most elegant Pouilly-Fumé, such as Didier Dagueneau Silex and Pur Sang

Try something completely different

Lean, linear Riesling from Alsace (Trimbach Clos Ste Hune or JosMeyer Grand Cru Hengst) and Mosel (Maximin Grünhaus Abtsberg Alte Reben Trocken)

O. Fournier Centauri Sauvignon Blanc

Recommended   **$$**   **12.5%**

What is it?
A dry white wine made from the Sauvignon Blanc grape grown in
Leyda Valley, Chile. 15% of the wine was fermented in large, used
French oak barrels.

What does it taste like?
Light-bodied and tangy with pronounced grass and lime zest notes

If you like this, then try with confidence . . .
Greater quality, greater intensity
Iconic Marlborough Sauvignon Blanc, such as Cloudy Bay, Craggy
Range Avery Vineyard, Hunter's, Isabel Estate, Koura Whaleback,
Nobilo Icon and Palliser Estate

Greater quality, less intensity
The finest, most elegant Pouilly-Fumé, such as Didier Dagueneau
Silex and Pur Sang

Try something completely different
Lean, linear Riesling from Alsace (Trimbach Clos Ste Hune or JosMeyer Grand
Cru Hengst) and Mosel (Maximin Grünhaus Abtsberg Alte Reben Trocken)

O. Fournier Spiga

Highly Recommended   **$$$**   **14.5%**

What is it?
A dry red wine made from the Tempranillo
grape grown in Ribera del Duero, Spain. Aged in
French oak barrels (50% new) for 13 months.

What does it taste like?
Modern, polished style with berry compote,
savory spice and dried herb flavors, a fine tannin
structure and moderate acidity

If you like this, then try with confidence . . .
Greater quality, greater intensity
Other top-class, pure Tempranillos from Ribera
del Duero include Pesquera, Alonso del Yerro María and, if you can afford it,
Dominio de Pingus.

Greater quality, less intensity
Cillar de Silos Rosado from Ribera de Duero

Try something completely different
O Fournier's wines from Argentina and Chile, or other top producers in different
parts of Spain, such as Rioja, Navarre and Toro

Olivier Leflaive Chassagne-Montrachet

To Die For	$$$	13.5%

What is it?

A dry white wine made from the Chardonnay grape grown in Chassagne-Montrachet, Burgundy, France. Fermented and aged in French oak (20% new) for 15–18 months.

What does it taste like?

Perfumed, with a gorgeous texture and purity of fruit. Harmonious wine with fine acidity and notes of hazelnut on the finish.

If you like this, then try with confidence . . .

Greater quality, greater intensity

Louis Jadot Puligny-Montrachet Premier Cru La Garenne, then Domaine Leflaive Montrachet Grand Cru

Greater quality, less intensity

The very best from the basic Mâcon-Villages appellation, such as Mâcon Solutré Clos des Bertillones Denogent

Try something completely different

White wines from cru classé châteaux in Pessac-Léognan

Pascal Jolivet Sancerre

Recommended	$$	12.5%

What is it?

A dry white wine made from the Sauvignon Blanc grape grown in Sancerre, France

What does it taste like?

Quite peachy, light and fresh, with some herbal complexity

If you like this, then try with confidence . . .

Greater quality, greater intensity

Iconic Marlborough Sauvignon Blanc, such as Cloudy Bay, Craggy Range Avery Vineyard, Hunter's, Isabel Estate, Koura Whaleback, Nobilo Icon and Palliser Estate

Greater quality, less intensity

The finest, most elegant Pouilly-Fumé, such as Didier Dagueneau Silex and Pur Sang

Try something completely different

Lean, linear Riesling from Alsace (Trimbach Clos Ste Hune or JosMeyer Grand Cru Hengst) and Mosel (Maximin Grünhaus Abtsberg Alte Reben Trocken)

Paul Jaboulet Aîné Crozes Hermitage

Highly Recommended	$$	13%

What is it?

A dry red wine made from the Syrah grape grown in Crozes-Hermitage, Northern Rhône, France. Fermented and aged in used French oak barrels for 12 months.

What does it taste like?

Smooth yet characterful, with aromas of dark roses, blueberry and black pepper, with mild tannins and acidity

If you like this, then try with confidence . . .

Greater quality, greater intensity

Hermitage from Chapoutier (especially l'Ermite) and Marc Sorrel (Gréal), or fuller-style Côte Rôtie such as those by Guigal (Château d'Ampuis and the single-vineyard bottlings)

Greater quality, less intensity

René Rostaing and Yves Montez produce Côte Rôtie of exceptional quality in a more elegant style and emphasizing freshness and florality.

Try something completely different

California Petite Sirah, the very best of which include Rosenblum Rockpile, Turley Cellars Hayne Vineyard or Lava Cap Grand Hill

Paul Jaboulet Aîné Parallèle 45

Highly Recommended	$$	13.5%

What is it?

A dry red wine made from a blend of grapes (60% Grenache, 40% Syrah) grown in Côtes-du-Rhône, France

What does it taste like?

Soft and easy-drinking yet has interest, with complex flavors of spice, herb and tar plus fresh wild red berries

If you like this, then try with confidence . . .

Greater quality, greater intensity

Domaine Pierre Usseglio Châteauneuf-du-Pape, then Château Rayas

Greater quality, less intensity

E. Guigal Châteauneuf-du-Pape, then Domaine du Vieux Télégraphe Châteauneuf-du-Pape

Try something completely different

Pure Grenache from Australia (Yalumba Bush Vine Grenache, Kilikanoon The Duke Clare Valley Grenache) or France (Mas Foulaquier Le Petit Duc)

Penfolds Bin 28 Kalimna Shiraz

Highly Recommended $$$ 14.5%

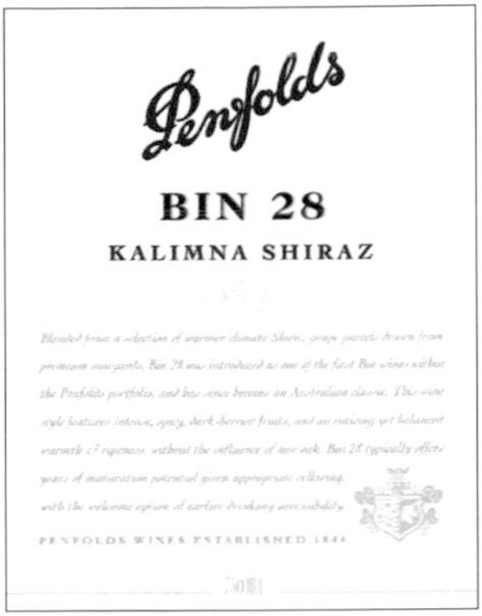

What is it?

A dry red wine made from the Shiraz grape grown in Barossa, South Australia. Aged in large, used American oak barrels for 12 months.

What does it taste like?

Full-bodied, with opulent fruit, roasted herbs and meat and well-integrated toasty oak. The finish is long with gripping tannins.

If you like this, then try with confidence . . .

Greater quality, greater intensity

Penfolds St Henri and various Bin numbers (128, 150, 389), culminating in RWT and Grange or Henschke Hill of Grace

Greater quality, less intensity

Clonakilla Shiraz-Viognier

Try something completely different

Zinfandel (especially those by Ridge), Petite Syrah (Ridge Vineyards Dynamite Hill, Rosenblum Rockpile, Turley Cellars Hayne Vineyard or Lava Cap Grand Hill) or even an Australian Zinfandel (such as Cape Mentelle)

Penfolds

BIN 28

KALIMNA SHIRAZ

PENFOLDS WINES ESTABLISHED 1844

Penfolds Koonunga Hill Chardonnay

Recommended	$	12%

What is it?

A dry white wine made from the Chardonnay grape grown in Southeastern Australia. A portion of the wine was aged in French oak for 8 months.

What does it taste like?

Perfectly ripe peach fruit with smoky complexity and a smooth finish

If you like this, then try with confidence . . .

Greater quality, greater intensity
Penfolds Reserve Bin A Chardonnay
Greater quality, less intensity
Penfolds Yattarna Chardonnay

Try something completely different

Fabulous Australian Marsanne, Roussanne and Marsanne-Roussanne blends from Yeringberg

Penfolds Koonunga Shiraz-Cabernet

Recommended	$	13.5%

What is it?

A dry red wine made from a blend of grapes (70% Shiraz, 30% Cabernet Sauvignon) grown in South Australia. The majority of the wine was aged in used French and American oak for 12 months.

What does it taste like?

Floral, dried herbs, juicy black currant and blackberry notes with smoky oak, and a full, rich texture

If you like this, then try with confidence . . .

Greater quality, greater intensity

Lindeman's Limestone Ridge Vineyard Shiraz Cabernet or Penfolds Koonunga Hill Seventy Six Shiraz Cabernet

Greater quality, less intensity

Hardy's Chronicle No. 1 Twice Lost Shiraz Cabernet Rosé

Try something completely different

Search out Sangiovese-dominated blends, such as The Mongrel from Hugh Hamilton in McLaren Vale

Penfolds RWT Shiraz

To Die For	$$$	14.5%

What is it?

A dry red wine made from the Shiraz grape grown in Barossa, South Australia. Aged in French oak (two-thirds new) for 14 months.

What does it taste like?

Penetrating aromas of mint, lavender and rosemary, with expressive, delineated blueberry, blackberry and cassis fruit. Bold and creamy-textured yet juicy with a floral, violet-tinged finish.

If you like this, then try with confidence . . .

Greater quality, greater intensity

Penfolds Grange or Henschke Hill of Grace

Greater quality, less intensity

Clonakilla Shiraz-Viognier

Try something completely different

Zinfandel (especially those by Ridge), Petite Syrah (Ridge Vineyards Dynamite Hill, Rosenblum Rockpile, Turley Cellars Hayne Vineyard or Lava Cap Grand Hill) or even an Australian Zinfandel (such as Cape Mentelle)

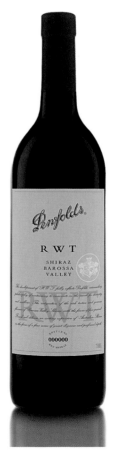

Pèppoli Chianti Classico Antinori

Highly Recommended	$$	13%

What is it?

A dry red wine made predominantly from the Sangiovese grape (includes 10% mixed Merlot and Syrah) grown in Chianti Classico in Tuscany, Italy. Aged for a minimum of 9 months in 90% large Slavonian oak and 10% small American oak.

What does it taste like?

A sleek and poised Chianti of some class, with cherries, plums and well-integrated oak

If you like this, then try with confidence . . .

Greater quality, greater intensity

The best, richest Chianti Classico (Castello di Ama, Poggio al Sole Casasilia, Querciabella) and Brunello di Montalcino (Casanova di Neri, Case Basse, Mastrojanne, Siro Pacenti)

Greater quality, less intensity

Lighter and fruitier with Yalumba Y Series Sangiovese Rosé or Mitolo Jester McLaren Vale Sangiovese Rosé

Try something completely different

Montepulciano d'Abruzzo (Valentini is best)

Perrier-Jouët NV Grand Brut

Recommended	$$$	12%

What is it?

A dry sparkling wine made from a blend of grapes (Pinot Noir, Chardonnay and Meunier) grown in Champagne, France. Traditional Method with lees aging for a minimum of 3 years.

What does it taste like?

Full, rich and biscuity, with integrated, harmonious flavors

If you like this, then try with confidence . . .

Greater quality, greater intensity

Perrier-Jouët no longer produces a straight Vintage, thus it has to be Perrier-Jouët Belle Epoque.

Greater quality, less intensity

Perrier-Jouët Belle Epoque Blanc de Blancs

Try something completely different

The top sparkling wines from England (Camel Valley, Henners, Herbert Hall, Nyetimber, Ridgeview) and Tasmania (Bay of Fires, Clover Hill, Jansz, Stefano Lubiana, Pirie, Relbia)

Pewsey Vale Riesling The Contours Museum Reserve

To Die For	$$$	13%

What is it?

A dry white wine made from the Riesling grape grown in Eden Valley, South Australia. The was aged in bottle for 5 years before release.

What does it taste like?

Dry, with an incredibly intense and perfumed nose featuring lime custard and green apple. A really stunning wine, with crisp acidity and a very long finish.

If you like this, then try with confidence . . .

Greater quality, greater intensity

Grosset Polish Hill or Pressing Matters (R0 or R9)

Greater quality, less intensity

Observatory Hill Vintner's Reserve or, for a leaner, more linear Riesling, Puddleduck from Tasmania

Try something completely different

Dry Australian Semillon, particularly from the Hunter Valley, with several years bottle-age

Piccini Chianti

Recommended | $ | 12.5%

What is it?

A dry red wine made predominantly from the Sangiovese grape grown in Chianti Classico in Tuscany, Italy. Distinctive orange label.

What does it taste like?

The sleek cherry fruit and supple tannins in this easy-drinking Chianti are ideal to wash down any meat pasta without pause for thought

If you like this, then try with confidence . . .

Greater quality, greater intensity

The best, richest Chianti Classico (Castello di Ama, Poggio al Sole Casasilia, Querciabella) and Brunello di Montalcino (Casanova di Neri, Case Basse, Mastrojanne, Siro Pacenti)

Greater quality, less intensity

Lighter and fruitier with Yalumba Y Series Sangiovese Rosé or Mitolo Jester McLaren Vale Sangiovese Rosé

Try something completely different

Montepulciano d'Abruzzo (Valentini is best)

Planeta La Segreta Blanca

Highly Recommended	$	13.5%

What is it?

A dry white wine made from a blend of grapes (50% Grecanico, 30% Chardonnay, 10% Viognier, 10% Fiano) grown in Sicily, Italy, with no oak influence

What does it taste like?

Aromas of honey, ripe pear, apple blossom, with additional notes of peach on the palate. Lovely taste, texture and excellent fruit concentration with a bright finish.

If you like this, then try with confidence . . .

Greater quality, greater intensity

The Greciano is the same variety as the Garganega, the principal grape in Soave, and the best Soave Classico, such as Inama Vigneto du Lot and Pieropan Vigneto Calvarino or Vigneto la Rocca have a tad more intensity than Planeta La Segreta Blanca

Greater quality, less intensity

Filippi Castelcerino Soave Colli Scaliger

Try something completely different

Good Chasselas from Blaise Duboux in Switzerland or, for the very adventurous, a super-soft Koshu from Japan, such as Misawa Private Reserve from Grace Vineyards in Yamanashi

Planeta La Segreta Rosso

Recommended	$	13.5%

What is it?

A dry red wine made from a blend of grapes (50% Nero d'Avola, 25% Merlot, 20% Syrah, 5% Cabernet Franc) grown in Sicily, Italy

What does it taste like?

Medium-bodied, with juicy, ripe red and black plums and a hint of tar. The finish is clean and smooth.

If you like this, then try with confidence . . .

Greater quality, greater intensity

Planeta Cerasuolo di Vittoria, then their Dorilli

Greater quality, less intensity

Mastroberardino Taurasi Radici

Try something completely different

For other intense, spicy reds, look at Portugal, e.g. Dow's Vale do Bomfim

Pol Roger NV Reserve Brut

Highly Recommended   **$$$**   **12.5%**

What is it?

A dry sparkling wine made from a blend of grapes (Pinot Noir, Chardonnay and Meunier) grown in Champagne, France. Traditional Method with lees aging a minimum of 3 years. Dosage 12 g/l.

What does it taste like?

Full and creamy, with a bracing backbone of acidity. Fresh lemon, crisp green apple and toast flavors with a long finish.

If you like this, then try with confidence . . .

Greater quality, greater intensity

Pol Roger Vintage, then Cuvée Winston Churchill

Greater quality, less intensity

Although not less intense, Pol Roger Blanc de Blancs certainly has more finesse.

Try something completely different

The top sparkling wines from England (Camel Valley, Henners, Herbert Hall, Nyetimber, Ridgeview) and Tasmania (Bay of Fires, Clover Hill, Jansz, Stefano Lubiana, Pirie, Relbia)

Potel, *see* Nicolas Potel

Ravenswood Zinfandel Vintners Blend

Highly Recommended	$	13.5%

What is it?

A dry red wine made from the Zinfandel grape grown in Lodi, California. Aged 12 months in French Oak (25% new).

What does it taste like?

Good concentration of dark raspberry, raisin and fig flavors, well-integrated oak, medium-full body and a long, pleasant finish

If you like this, then try with confidence . . .

Greater quality, greater intensity
Ravenswood Lodi Old Vine Zinfandel, then single-vineyard Zinfandels from Ravenswood or Rosenblum
Greater quality, less intensity
Kendall Jackson Zinfandel Vintners Reserve, then single-vineyard Zinfandels by Ridge

Try something completely different

Zinfandel is a Croatian grape variety (Tribidrag, aka Crljenak Kastelanski) that is also grown in Puglia, Italy (as Primitivo), producing intensely ripe, full-bodied red wines at moderate prices

Redwood Creek Cabernet Sauvignon

Recommended	$	13%

What is it?

A dry red wine made from the Cabernet Sauvignon grape grown in California with subtle oak influence

What does it taste like?

Straightforward and juicy, with black cherry and plum flavors and a hint of vanilla on the clean finish

If you like this, then try with confidence . . .

Greater quality, greater intensity
Caymus Special Selection Cabernet Sauvignon or Dunn Vineyards Howell Mountain Cabernet Sauvignon
Greater quality, less intensity
Stag's Leap Cask 23 Estate Cabernet Sauvignon

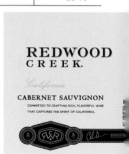

Try something completely different

For a classic Bordeaux to match the intensity and voluptuousness of top California Cabernet Sauvignon, try a Merlot-dominated Pomerol such as châteaux L'Evangile, La Fleur-Pétrus, Latour à Pomerol, Petit-Village, Trotanoy and, if you can afford them, Pétrus and Le Pin

Redwood Creek Chardonnay

Recommended	$	13.5%

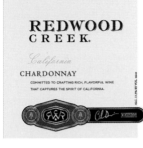

What is it?

A dry white wine made from the Chardonnay grape grown in California with subtle oak influence

What does it taste like?

Fruity, light-bodied, with hints of toasty oak and ripe pear

If you like this, then try with confidence . . .

Greater quality, greater intensity

Jacob's Creek Chardonnay Adelaide Hills

Greater quality, less intensity

The very best from the basic Mâcon-Villages appellation, such as Mâcon Solutré Clos des Bertilloncs Denogent

Try something completely different

The best Pinot Blanc from Alsace, starting with Domaine Weinbach or Collio Pinot Blanco from Schiopetto from Veneto in Italy

Redwood Creek Merlot

Recommended	$	13.5%

What is it?

A dry red wine made from the Merlot grape grown in California with subtle oak influence

What does it taste like?

Smooth and pleasant, with black cherry, plum, vanilla and a hint of green pepper

If you like this, then try with confidence . . .

Greater quality, greater intensity

Great Merlot from California (Pahlmeyer, Paloma and Pride) or Washington (L'Ecole No. 41, Leonetti, Seven Hills and Woodward Canyon)

Greater quality, less intensity

Raphael Rosé of Merlot from Long Island

Try something completely different

Great Merlot-dominated blends from Pomerol, such as châteaux L'Evangile, La Fleur-Pétrus, Latour à Pomerol, Petit-Village, Trotanoy and, if you can afford them, Pétrus and Le Pin

Redwood Creek Pinot Noir

Recommended	$	13.5%

What is it?

A dry red wine made from the Pinot Noir grape grown in California with subtle oak influence

What does it taste like?

Good persistence with chocolate, cherry and mild acidity

If you like this, then try with confidence . . .

Greater quality, greater intensity

La Bauge au Dessus and other Pinot Noir from Au Bon Climat in Santa Barbara, California, or Le Grand Clos Pinot Noir from Le Clos Jordanne in Niagara, Canada

Greater quality, less intensity

The more elegant Oregon Pinot Noir, starting with Adelsheim, Bethel Heights and Rex Hill

Try something completely different

Fruit-driven Nebbiolo, such as Cascina Adelaide di Amabile Drocco Barolo Fossati, Aldo Conterno Barolo Cicala, Parusso Barolo Le Coste-Mosconi or G. D. Vajra Barolo Albe

Remy Pannier Chinon

Highly Recommended	$$	13%

What is it?

A dry red wine made from the Cabernet Franc grape grown in Chinon, Loire, France

What does it taste like?

Full of character, with structured young, fresh, vibrant red fruit and violets with a touch of herbs. Very smooth and consumer-friendly.

If you like this, then try with confidence . . .

Greater quality, greater intensity

Alliet Chinon Vieilles Vignes

Greater quality, less intensity

Bernard Baudry Chinon Les Granges

Try something completely different

Other fresh, crisp reds with grippy tannins, such as Lagrein from the South Tyrol, Italy

Remy Pannier Vouvray

Recommended	$$	11.5%

What is it?
An off-dry white wine made from the
Chenin Blanc grape grown in Vouvray,
Loire, France

What does it taste like?
Off-dry style with friendly, soft peach,
apricot and orange blossom flavors

If you like this, then try with confidence . . .
Greater quality, greater intensity
Vouvray Demi-Sec from Domaine Huet
Greater quality, less intensity
Vouvray Demi-Sec from Domaine du Clos Naudin by Philippe Foreau

Try something completely different
If you love Vouvray Demi-Sec, you will be in heaven with any fine Mosel
Riesling Kabinett or Spätlese

Rex-Goliath Merlot

Highly Recommended	$	13.5%

What is it?
An off-dry red wine made from the Merlot grape grown
in various areas of California. Aged in American oak.

What does it taste like?
A gluggy red full of soft, sapid, expansive fruit with
a whisper of spiced oak on the finish. Best consumed
on day of opening.

If you like this, then try with confidence . . .
Greater quality, greater intensity
Great Merlot from California (Pahlmeyer, Paloma
and Pride) or Washington (L'Ecole No. 41, Leonetti, Seven
Hills and Woodward Canyon)
Greater quality, less intensity
Raphael Rosé of Merlot from Long Island

Try something completely different
Great Merlot-dominated blends from Pomerol, such as châteaux L'Evangile,
La Fleur-Pétrus, Latour à Pomerol, Petit-Village, Trotanoy and, if you can
afford them, Pétrus and Le Pin

Rex-Goliath Zinfandel

Recommended	$	13.5%

What is it?

An off-dry red wine made from the Merlot grape grown in various areas of California. Aged in French and American oak

What does it taste like?

Violet-floral aromas, cherry and berry fruit, with a hint of smooth oak finish. Drinks even better on the second day.

If you like this, then try with confidence . . .

Greater quality, greater intensity

Ravenswood Lodi Old Vine Zinfandel, then single-vineyard Zinfandels from Ravenswood or Rosenblum

Greater quality, less intensity

Kendall Jackson Zinfandel Vintners Reserve, then single-vineyard Zinfandels by Ridge

Try something completely different

Zinfandel is a Croatian grape variety (Tribidrag, aka Crljenak Kastelanski) that is also grown in Puglia, Italy (as Primitivo), producing intensely ripe, full-bodied red wines at moderate prices

Riscal, *see* Marqués de Riscal

Rita, *see* Santa Rita

Robert Mondavi Private Selection Cabernet Sauvignon

Recommended	$	13.5%

What is it?
A dry red wine made from the Cabernet Sauvignon grape grown in California. Aged 12 months in American and French oak.

What does it taste like?
Medium-bodied with smooth tannins and flavors of black cherry jam with a hint of vanilla

If you like this, then try with confidence . . .
Greater quality, greater intensity
Caymus Special Selection Cabernet Sauvignon or Dunn Vineyards Howell Mountain Cabernet Sauvignon
Greater quality, less intensity
Stag's Leap Cask 23 Estate Cabernet Sauvignon

ROBERT MONDAVI
PRIVATE SELECTION.

CABERNET SAUVIGNON
Central Coast

Try something completely different
For a classic Bordeaux to match the intensity and voluptuousness of top California Cabernet Sauvignon, try a Merlot-dominated Pomerol such as châteaux L'Evangile, La Fleur-Pétrus, Latour à Pomerol, Petit-Village, Trotanoy and, if you can afford them, Pétrus and Le Pin

Robert Mondavi Private Selection Chardonnay

Recommended	$	13.5%

What is it?
A dry white wine made from the Chardonnay grape grown in California. One third of the wine was fermented and aged in American and French oak and underwent malolactic fermentation.

What does it taste like?
Well balanced and pleasant, with baked red apples, sweet spice and vanilla flavors

ROBERT MONDAVI
PRIVATE SELECTION.

CHARDONNAY
Central Coast

If you like this, then try with confidence . . .
Greater quality, greater intensity
Jacob's Creek Chardonnay Adelaide Hills
Greater quality, less intensity
The very best from the basic Mâcon-Villages appellation, such as Mâcon Solutré Clos des Bertillones Denogent

Try something completely different
The best Pinot Blanc from Alsace, starting with Domaine Weinbach or Collio Pinot Blanco from Schiopetto from Veneto in Italy

Robert Mondavi Private Selection Merlot

Highly Recommended	$	13.5%

What is it?
A dry red wine made from the Merlot grape grown in California. Aged 10 months in American and French oak.

What does it taste like?
Lovely, supple texture with good definition of varietal fruit character (black plum, black cherry) and a whiff of vanilla. Very nicely balanced.

If you like this, then try with confidence . . .
Greater quality, greater intensity
Great Merlot from California (Pahlmeyer, Paloma and Pride) or Washington (L'Ecole No. 41, Leonetti, Seven Hills and Woodward Canyon)
Greater quality, less intensity
Raphael Rosé of Merlot from Long Island

Try something completely different
Great Merlot-dominated blends from Pomerol, such as châteaux L'Evangile, La Fleur-Pétrus, Latour à Pomerol, Petit-Village, Trotanoy and, if you can afford them, Pétrus and Le Pin

ROBERT MONDAVI
PRIVATE SELECTION.

MERLOT
Central Coast

Robert Mondavi Private Selection Pinot Grigio

Highly Recommended	$	12.5%

What is it?
A dry white wine made from the Pinot Grigio grape grown in California

What does it taste like?
Restrained stone fruits with hints of lemon; light-bodied with refreshing acidity

If you like this, then try with confidence . . .
Greater quality, greater intensity
JosMeyer Pinot Gris 1854 Fondation or Trimbach Pinot Gris Réserve with a few years additional bottle-age
Greater quality, less intensity
JosMeyer Pinot Blanc Les Lutins or Domaine Weinbach Pinot Blanc

Try something completely different
A good Soave such as Pieropan or Inama, perhaps even Chassela from Blaise Duboux in Switzerland or, for the very adventurous, a super-soft Koshu from Japan, such as Misawa Private Reserve from Grace

ROBERT MONDAVI
PRIVATE SELECTION.

PINOT GRIGIO
Central Coast

Robert Mondavi Private Selection Pinot Noir

| Highly Recommended | $ | 13.5% |

What is it?

A dry red wine made from the Pinot Noir grape grown in California. Aged 4 months in used American and French oak.

What does it taste like?

Delicate with pretty Pinot character; aromas of vanilla, red cherry and strawberry with a light and supple texture

ROBERT MONDAVI
PRIVATE SELECTION.
PINOT NOIR
California

If you like this, then try with confidence . . .

Greater quality, greater intensity

La Bauge au Dessus and other Pinot Noir from Au Bon Climat in Santa Barbara, California, or Le Grand Clos Pinot Noir from Le Clos Jordanne in Niagara, Canada

Greater quality, less intensity

The more elegant Oregon Pinot Noir, starting with Adelsheim, Bethel Heights and Rex Hill

Try something completely different

Fruit-driven Nebbiolo, such as Cascina Adelaide di Amabile Drocco Barolo Fossati, Aldo Conterno Barolo Cicala, Parusso Barolo Le Coste-Mosconi or G. D. Vajra Barolo Albe

Robert Mondavi Private Selection Zinfandel

| Recommended | $ | 13.5% |

What is it?

A dry red wine made from the Zinfandel grape grown in California. Aged 11 months in French and American oak.

What does it taste like?

Medium-bodied, with confected red fruit and a note of underbrush

If you like this, then try with confidence . . .

Greater quality, greater intensity

Ravenswood Lodi Old Vine Zinfandel, then single-vineyard Zinfandels from Ravenswood or Rosenblum

Greater quality, less intensity

Kendall Jackson Zinfandel Vintners Reserve, then single-vineyard Zinfandels by Ridge

ROBERT MONDAVI
PRIVATE SELECTION.
ZINFANDEL
California

Try something completely different

Zinfandel is a Croatian grape variety (Tribidrag, aka Crljenak Kastelanski) that is also grown in Puglia, Italy (as Primitivo), producing intensely ripe, full-bodied red wines at moderate prices

Robert Mondavi Sauvignon Blanc

Highly Recommended	$	12.5%

What is it?

A dry white wine made from the Sauvignon Blanc grape grown in California

What does it taste like?

Dry, with well-defined flavors of peach, lime and chive. Tangy and pleasant, with good length.

If you like this, then try with confidence . . .

Greater quality, greater intensity

ROBERT MONDAVI
PRIVATE SELECTION.

SAUVIGNON BLANC
Central Coast

Iconic Marlborough Sauvignon Blanc, such as Cloudy Bay, Craggy Range Avery Vineyard, Hunter's, Isabel Estate, Koura Whaleback, Nobilo Icon and Palliser Estate

Greater quality, less intensity

The finest, most elegant Pouilly-Fumé, such as Didier Dagueneau Silex and Pur Sang

Try something completely different

Lean, linear Riesling from Alsace (Trimbach Clos Ste Hune or JosMeyer Grand Cru Hengst) and Mosel (Maximin Grünhaus Abtsberg Alte Reben Trocken)

Rocca delle Macie Chianti Classico

Highly Recommended	$$	12.5%

What is it?

A dry red wine made predominantly from the Sangiovese grape grown in Chianti Classico in Tuscany, Italy. Aged 6–10 months in used Slavonian and French oak barrels.

What does it taste like?

Consumer-friendly yet beautiful example of Sangiovese, with balanced acidity and density of fruit

If you like this, then try with confidence . . .

Greater quality, greater intensity

The best, richest Chianti Classico (Castello di Ama, Poggio al Sole Casasilia, Querciabella) and Brunello di Montalcino (Casanova di Neri, Case Basse, Mastrojanne, Siro Pacenti)

Greater quality, less intensity

Lighter and fruitier with Yalumba Y Series Sangiovese Rosé or Mitolo Jester McLaren Vale Sangiovese Rosé

Try something completely different

Montepulciano d'Abruzzo (Valentini is best)

Rocca delle Macie Rubizzo Sangiovese di Toscana

Highly Recommended	$$	13.5%

What is it?

A dry red wine made from a blend of grapes (80% Sangiovese, 20% Cabernet Sauvignon) grown in Tuscany, Italy. Aged for 9–14 months in small, new French oak barrels.

What does it taste like?

Good structure, weight, intensity of red cherry and black plums

If you like this, then try with confidence . . .

Greater quality, greater intensity

The best, richest Chianti Classico (Castello di Ama, Poggio al Sole Casasilia, Querciabella) and Brunello di Montalcino (Casanova di Neri, Case Basse, Mastrojanne, Siro Pacenti)

Greater quality, less intensity

Lighter and fruitier with Yalumba Y Series Sangiovese Rosé or Mitolo Jester McLaren Vale Sangiovese Rosé

Try something completely different

Montepulciano d'Abruzzo (Valentini is best)

Rocca delle Macie SASYR

Recommended	$$	13.5%

What is it?

A dry red wine made from a blend of grapes (60% Sangiovese, 40% Syrah) grown in Tuscany, Italy. 15% of the Sangiovese was aged in small French oak barrels for 6 months.

What does it taste like?

Interesting mix of leather and confected blackberry and black cherry with chunky tannins

If you like this, then try with confidence . . .

Greater quality, greater intensity

The best, richest Chianti Classico (Castello di Ama, Poggio al Sole Casasilia, Querciabella) and Brunello di Montalcino (Casanova di Neri, Case Basse, Mastrojanne, Siro Pacenti)

Greater quality, less intensity

Lighter and fruitier with Yalumba Y Series Sangiovese Rosé or Mitolo Jester McLaren Vale Sangiovese Rosé

Try something completely different

Montepulciano d'Abruzzo (Valentini is best)

Rombauer Chardonnay

| **Highly Recommended** | **$$$** | **14.5%** |

What is it?

A dry white wine made from the Chardonnay grape grown in Carneros, California. The wine is matured for 10 months in small American and French oak.

What does it taste like?

The quintessential buttery Chardonnay. Aromas of banana, butterscotch and ripe pear, the creamy texture is balanced by just enough acidity to keep it fresh.

If you like this, then try with confidence . . .

Greater quality, greater intensity

Any white Burgundy from Domaine (not Olivier) Leflaive

Greater quality, less intensity

The very best from the basic Mâcon-Villages appellation, such as Mâcon Solutré Clos des Bertillones Denogent

Try something completely different

The best Pinot Blanc from Alsace, starting with Domaine Weinbach or Collio Pinot Blanco from Schiopetto from Veneto in Italy

Rosemount Cabernet Sauvignon

Recommended	$	13.5%

What is it?

A dry red wine made from the Cabernet Sauvignon grape grown in Southeastern Australia with subtle oak influence

What does it taste like?

Chocolate, coffee and vanilla aromas with a pleasant, well-structured palate

If you like this, then try with confidence . . .

Greater quality, greater intensity

Wolf Blass Gold Label Cabernet Sauvignon

Greater quality, less intensity

Jacob's Creek Cabernet Sauvignon Reserve
Coonawarra

Try something completely different

Washington Merlot from the best producers, such as L'Ecole No. 41, Leonetti, Seven Hills and Woodward Canyon

Rosemount Chardonnay

Recommended	$	13%

What is it?

A dry white wine made from the Chardonnay grape grown in Southeastern Australia with subtle oak influence

What does it taste like?

Round yet juicy, with ripe tropical and peach flavors, very light oak notes and nice length

If you like this, then try with confidence . . .

Greater quality, greater intensity

Penfolds Reserve Bin A Chardonnay

Greater quality, less intensity

Rosemount Estate Regional Showcase Robe Chardonnay

Try something completely different

Fabulous Australian Marsanne, Roussanne and Marsanne-Roussanne blends from Yeringberg

Rosemount Pinot Grigio

Recommended	$	12.5%

What is it?

A dry white wine made from the Pinot Grigio grape grown in Southeastern Australia

What does it taste like?

Nicely balanced, easy-drinking style with ripe melon and citrus flavors

If you like this, then try with confidence . . .

Greater quality, greater intensity

JosMeyer Pinot Gris 1854 Fondation or Trimbach Pinot Gris Réserve with a few years additional bottle-age

Greater quality, less intensity

JosMeyer Pinot Blanc Les Lutins or Domaine Weinbach Pinot Blanc

Try something completely different

A good Soave such as Pieropan or Inama, perhaps even Chasselas from Blaise Duboux in Switzerland or, for the very adventurous, a super-soft Koshu from Japan, such as Misawa Private Reserve from Grace

Rosemount Pinot Noir

Recommended	$	13.5%

What is it?

A dry red wine made from the Pinot Noir grape grown in Southeastern Australia with subtle oak influence

What does it taste like?

Soft and fruity with clean flavors of strawberry and red cherry

If you like this, then try with confidence . . .

Greater quality, greater intensity

Top Australian Pinot Noir from By Far, Farr Rising, Freycinet and Kooyong

Greater quality, less intensity

Yering Station ED Yarra Valley Pinot Noir Rosé or Shelmerdine Vineyards Yarra Valley Pinot Noir Rosé

Try something completely different

Fruit-driven Nebbiolo, such as Cascina Adelaide di Amabile Drocco Barolo Fossati, Aldo Conterno Barolo Cicala, Parusso Barolo Le Coste-Mosconi or G. D. Vajra Barolo Albe

Rosemount Sauvignon Blanc

Recommended	$	12%

What is it?

A dry white wine made from the Sauvignon Blanc grape grown in Southeastern Australia

What does it taste like?

Dry, with pungent grass and lime zest flavors that linger nicely

If you like this, then try with confidence . . .

Greater quality, greater intensity

Iconic Marlborough Sauvignon Blanc, such as Cloudy Bay, Craggy Range Avery Vineyard, Hunter's, Isabel Estate, Koura Whaleback, Nobilo Icon and Palliser Estate

Greater quality, less intensity

The finest, most elegant Pouilly-Fumé, such as Didier Dagueneau Silex and Pur Sang

Try something completely different

Lean, linear Riesling from Alsace (Trimbach Clos Ste Hune or JosMeyer Grand Cru Hengst) and Mosel (Maximin Grünhaus Abtsberg Alte Reben Trocken)

Rosemount Traminer Riesling

Recommended	$	9%

What is it?

An off-dry white wine made from a blend of grapes (Traminer and Riesling) grown in Southeastern Australia

What does it taste like?

Aromatic, featuring white flowers, lychees, grapes and white peaches, in a medium-dry, clean style

If you like this, then try with confidence . . .

Greater quality, greater intensity

Angove Family Winemakers Butterfly Ridge Riesling Gewürztraminer or the drier K1 by Geoff Hardy Silver Label Riesling Gewürztraminer

Greater quality, less intensity

Hugel Gentil or Rolly-Gassmann Terroirs des Châteaux Forts

Try something completely different

Look to the Pfalz for Kabinett rendering of aromatic varieties such as Scheurebe and Muskateller

Ruffino Chianti Classico Riserva Ducale Oro

Highly Recommended	$$	13.5%

What is it?

A dry red wine made primarily from the Sangiovese grape grown in Chianti Classico in Tuscany, Italy. A portion of the wine was aged in large oak barrels for 48 months.

What does it taste like?

Richer and weightier than the standard Riserva Ducale, Oro boasts an elegant core of fruit with delicate spicy-floral notes on the finish

If you like this, then try with confidence . . .

Greater quality, greater intensity

The best, richest Chianti Classico (Castello di Ama, Poggio al Sole Casasilia, Querciabella) and Brunello di Montalcino (Casanova di Neri, Case Basse, Mastrojanni, Siro Pacenti)

Greater quality, less intensity

Lighter and fruitier with Yalumba Y Series Sangiovese Rosé or Mitolo Jester McLaren Vale Sangiovese Rosé

Try something completely different

Montepulciano d'Abruzzo (Valentini is best)

Ruffino Chianti Classico Riserva Ducale

Highly Recommended	$	13.5%

What is it?

A dry red wine made primarily from the Sangiovese grape grown in Chianti Classico in Tuscany, Italy. A portion of the wine was aged in large oak barrels for 24 months.

What does it taste like?

Surprisingly full-bodied and powerful, with Barolo-like notes of tar and roses threading their way through the cherry fruit of the Sangiovese grape

If you like this, then try with confidence . . .

Greater quality, greater intensity

The best, richest Chianti Classico (Castello di Ama, Poggio al Sole Casasilia, Querciabella) and Brunello di Montalcino (Casanova di Neri, Case Basse, Mastrojanne, Siro Pacenti)

Greater quality, less intensity

Lighter and fruitier with Yalumba Y Series Sangiovese Rosé or Mitolo Jester McLaren Vale Sangiovese Rosé

Try something completely different

Montepulciano d'Abruzzo (Valentini is best)

Ruffino Chianti

Recommended	$	12.5%

What is it?

A dry red wine made predominantly from the Sangiovese grape grown in Chianti in Tuscany, Italy with no oak influence

What does it taste like?

Very clean, light and fragrant. Good acidity balanced with light cherry fruit and a touch of earthy complexity.

If you like this, then try with confidence . . .

Greater quality, greater intensity

The best, richest Chianti Classico (Castello di Ama, Poggio al Sole Casasilia, Querciabella) and Brunello di Montalcino (Casanova di Neri, Case Basse, Mastrojanne, Siro Pacenti)

Greater quality, less intensity

Lighter and fruitier with Yalumba Y Series Sangiovese Rosé or Mitolo Jester McLaren Vale Sangiovese Rosé

Try something completely different

Montepulciano d'Abruzzo (Valentini is best)

Ruffino Pinot Grigio

Recommended	$	12%

What is it?

A dry white wine made from the Pinot Grigio grape grown in Friuli-Venezia Giulia, northeastern Italy

What does it taste like?

Very light and lean, with crisp lemon and unripe apple flavors

If you like this, then try with confidence . . .

Greater quality, greater intensity

JosMeyer Pinot Gris 1854 Fondation or Trimbach Pinot Gris Réserve with a few years additional bottle-age

Greater quality, less intensity

JosMeyer Pinot Blanc Les Lutins or Domaine Weinbach Pinot Blanc

Try something completely different

A good Soave such as Pieropan or Inama, perhaps even Chasselas from Blaise Duboux in Switzerland or, for the very adventurous, a super-soft Koshu from Japan, such as Misawa Private Reserve from Grace

Ruiz, *see* **Santiago Ruiz**

Sandeman Founders Reserve

Recommended	$$	20%

What is it?

A sweet fortified red wine made from a blend of grapes (Touriga Franca, Tinta Roriz, Tinta Amarela, Tinta Barroca, Tinto Cão) grown in Douro, Portugal. Aged 5 years prior to release.

What does it taste like?

Sweet with warm, elegant, spicy fruit

If you like this, then try with confidence . . .

Greater quality, greater intensity

The finest quality, most intense ruby-style wines such as Vintage Ports from Taylor's, Graham's and Fonseca

Greater quality, less intensity

The finest quality, least intense ruby style is Ferreira's Vintage Port, but try also single-quinta Ports and, the lightest of all, "pink" Port from Croft, Porto Cruz and Quinta & Vineyard

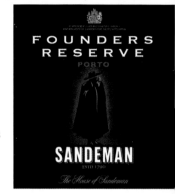

Try something completely different

Other sweet, ruby-style fortified wines, such as Banyuls from France or Australian Ruby and Australian Vintage (both formerly known as Australian Liqueur Port)

Sandeman Late Bottled Vintage

Recommended	$$	20.5%

What is it?

A sweet fortified red wine made from a blend of grapes (Touriga Franca, Tinta Roriz, Tinta Amarela, Tinta Barroca, Tinto Cão) grown in Douro, Portugal. Aged 5 years prior to release.

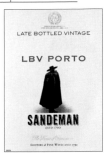

What does it taste like?

Sweet, accessible, spiced molasses and fruit, with supple tannin structure

If you like this, then try with confidence . . .

Greater quality, greater intensity

The finest quality, most intense ruby-style wines such as Vintage Ports from Taylor's, Graham's and Fonseca

Greater quality, less intensity

The finest quality, least intense ruby style is Ferreira's Vintage Port, but try also single-quinta Ports and, the lightest of all, "pink" Port from Croft, Porto Cruz and Quinta & Vineyard

Try something completely different

Other sweet, ruby-style fortified wines, such as Banyuls from France or Australian Ruby and Australian Vintage (both formerly known as Australian Liqueur Port)

Sandeman Ten Years Old Tawny

Highly Recommended	$$$	20%

What is it?

A sweet fortified red wine made from a blend of grapes (Touriga Franca, Tinta Roriz, Tinta Amarela, Tinta Barroca, Tinto Cão) grown in Douro, Portugal. A blend of wines aged in wood for 9–12 years.

What does it taste like?

Deliciously rich, with fine depth of spiced molasses and fruit. Long and complex.

If you like this, then try with confidence . . .

Greater quality, greater intensity

Sandeman Twenty Years Old Tawny

Greater quality, less intensity

Sandeman Twenty Years Old Tawny

Try something completely different

The tawny-like Fondillón, a 15-year-old Monastrell, with a non-fortified 16% of alcohol from Casta Diva in Alicante, Spain, or Penfolds Club Reserve Classic Tawny, then the truly iconic Penfolds Grandfather and Great Grandfather Rare Tawnies

Sandeman Twenty Years Old Tawny

To Die For	$$$	20%

What is it?

A sweet fortified red wine made from a blend of grapes (Touriga Franca, Tinta Roriz, Tinta Amarela, Tinta Barroca, Tinto Cão) grown in Douro, Portugal. A blend of wines aged in wood for 15–40 years.

What does it taste like?

Decadently and deliciously rich, with a sultry, complex mix of molasses, spice, nuts and fruit on the nose and palate. Wonderful warmth and grip.

If you like this, then try with confidence . . .

Greater quality, greater intensity

The 20-Year-Old Tawny from Taylor Fladgate or the 30-Year-Old Tawny Ramos Pinto

Greater quality, less intensity

Ferreira Duque de Braganca 20 Year Old Tawny Port

Try something completely different

The tawny-like Fondillón, a 15-year-old Monastrell, with a non-fortified 16% of alcohol from Casta Diva in Alicante, Spain, or Penfolds Club Reserve Classic Tawny, then the truly iconic Penfolds Grandfather and Great Grandfather Rare Tawnies

Santa Cristina Chianti Superiore Antinori

Highly Recommended	$$	13%

What is it?

A dry red wine made from a blend of grapes (60% Sangiovese, plus 40% in total of Cabernet, Merlot and Syrah) grown in Tuscany, Italy

What does it taste like?

Delectably young and fresh in a soft, sleek, easy-drinking, fruit-driven style

If you like this, then try with confidence . . .

Greater quality, greater intensity

The best, richest Chianti Classico (Castello di Ama, Poggio al Sole Casasilia, Querciabella) and Brunello di Montalcino (Casanova di Neri, Case Basse, Mastrojanne, Siro Pacenti)

Greater quality, less intensity

Lighter and fruitier with Yalumba Y Series Sangiovese Rosé or Mitolo Jester McLaren Vale Sangiovese Rosé

Try something completely different

Montepulciano d'Abruzzo (Valentini is best)

Santa Cristina Toscana Antinori

Recommended	$	13%

What is it?

A dry red wine made from predominantly Sangiovese grapes (includes 10% Merlot) grown in Tuscany, Italy

What does it taste like?

Reminiscent of an honest, chunky, old-style Chianti that becomes smoother with food

If you like this, then try with confidence . . .

Greater quality, greater intensity

The best, richest Chianti Classico (Castello di Ama, Poggio al Sole Casasilia, Querciabella) and Brunello

di Montalcino (Casanova di Neri, Case Basse, Mastrojanne, Siro Pacenti)

Greater quality, less intensity

Lighter and fruitier with Yalumba Y Series Sangiovese Rosé or Mitolo Jester McLaren Vale Sangiovese Rosé

Try something completely different

Montepulciano d'Abruzzo (Valentini is best)

Santa Rita Cabernet Sauvignon 120

Recommended	$	13.5%

What is it?

A dry red wine made from the Cabernet Sauvignon grape grown in Valle Central, Chile. Aged 8 months in a combination of new and used French and American oak.

What does it taste like?

Rich and chunky with sweet spice, dark black fruits and pronounced vanilla cookie aromas

If you like this, then try with confidence . . .

Greater quality, greater intensity
Louis Filipe Edwards Family Selection Gran Reserve Cabernet Sauvignon
Greater quality, less intensity
Louis Filipe Edwards Pupilla Cabernet Sauvignon

Try something completely different

Washington Merlot from the best producers, such as L'Ecole No. 41, Leonetti, Seven Hills and Woodward Canyon

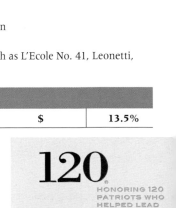

Santa Rita Sauvignon Blanc 120

Recommended	$	13.5%

What is it?

A dry white wine made from the Sauvignon Blanc grape grown in Valle Central, Chile

What does it taste like?

Dry, with straightforward flavors of nettles, limes and gooseberry with decent length

If you like this, then try with confidence . . .

Greater quality, greater intensity
Iconic Marlborough Sauvignon Blanc, such as Cloudy Bay, Craggy Range Avery Vineyard, Hunter's, Isabel Estate, Koura Whaleback, Nobilo Icon and Palliser Estate
Greater quality, less intensity
The finest, most elegant Pouilly-Fumé, such as Didier Dagueneau Silex and Pur Sang

Try something completely different

Lean, linear Riesling from Alsace (Trimbach Clos Ste Hune or JosMeyer Grand Cru Hengst) and Mosel (Maximin Grünhaus Abtsberg Alte Reben Trocken)

Santi Valpolicella Ripasso Classico Superiore Solane

Highly Recommended	$$	13.5%

What is it?

A dry red wine made from a blend of grapes (70% Corvina, 30% Rondinella) grown in Valpolicella, in the Veneto region of Italy. Aged in small French oak barrels for 3–5 months followed by 12 months in large used French oak barrels.

What does it taste like?

Spicy red licorice and plum fruit with herbal, perfumed complexity. Subtle vanilla and cedar oak give a structured impression on the palate.

If you like this, then try with confidence . . .

Greater quality, greater intensity

Allegrini Amarone della Valpolicella Classico

Greater quality, less intensity

Corte Sant'Alda Valpolicella Classico

Try something completely different

Margan Family Special Reserve Ripasso, a splendid Australian take on this classic wine

Santiago Ruiz Albariño

Highly Recommended	$$	12%

What is it?

A dry white wine made from the Albariño grape grown in Rías Baixas, Spain

What does it taste like?

Clean, crisp and appealing wine with a good core of citrus and stone fruit and juicy acidity

If you like this, then try with confidence . . .

Greater quality, greater intensity

Albariño Organistrum

Greater quality, less intensity

Burgáns Albariño

Try something completely different

Hugel and Trimbach Riesling from Alsace or Grüner Veltliner from Austria, starting with Pfaffl in the Weinviertel, then Brundlmayer (Kamtal), and Knoll, F X Pichler, Prager and Hirzberger (Wachau)

Segura Viudas Brut Reserva

Recommended	$	11.5%

What is it?

A dry sparkling wine made from a blend of grapes (50% Macabeo, 35% Parellada, 15% Xarel-lo) grown in Penedès, Spain. Traditional Method with lees aging for at least 15 months.

What does it taste like?

Surprisingly pronounced bready, yeast-complexed notes give some gravitas to this medium-bodied, apple and lemon-scented offering

If you like this, then try with confidence . . .

Greater quality, greater intensity

Charles Heidsieck NV Brut Réserve

Greater quality, less intensity

Pommery Cuvée Louise or, if you can afford it, Louis Roederer Cristal

Try something completely different

Ca'del Bosco Cuvée Annamaria Clementi after two or three years additional aging

Segura Viudas Heredad Brut Reserva

Highly Recommended	**$$**	12%

What is it?

A dry sparkling wine made from a blend of grapes (67% Macabeo, 33% Parellada) grown in Penedès, Spain. Traditional Method with lees aging for at least 30 months.

What does it taste like?

Perfumed, with nice flavor and intensity, a creamy texture and moderate acidity

If you like this, then try with confidence . . .

Greater quality, greater intensity
Charles Heidsieck NV Brut Réserve
Greater quality, less intensity
Pommery Cuvée Louise or, if you can afford it,
Louis Roederer Cristal

Try something completely different

Ca'del Bosco Cuvée Annamaria Clementi after two or three years additional aging

Silver Oak Alexander Valley Cabernet Sauvignon

| To Die For | $$$ | 14% |

What is it?

A dry red wine made from the Cabernet Sauvignon grape grown in the Anderson Valley, California. The wine was matured for 24 months in small American oak, followed by a further year in bottle prior to release

What does it taste like?

Very intense black currant and black cherry, with well-integrated spicy oak. Massive and powerful on the palate, with big soft tannins.

If you like this, then try with confidence . . .

Greater quality, greater intensity

Caymus Special Selection Cabernet Sauvignon or Dunn Vineyards Howell Mountain Cabernet Sauvignon

Greater quality, less intensity

Stag's Leap Cask 23 Estate Cabernet Sauvignon

Try something completely different

For a classic Bordeaux to match the intensity and voluptuousness of top California Cabernet Sauvignon, try a Merlot-dominated Pomerol such as châteaux L'Evangile, La Fleur-Pétrus, Latour à Pomerol, Petit-Village, Trotanoy and, if you can afford them, Pétrus and Le Pin

Simonnet-Fèbvre Chablis 1er Cru Vaillons

Recommended	$$	13.5%

What is it?

A dry white wine made from the Chardonnay grape grown in Chablis, Burgundy, France

What does it taste like?

Ripe style bordering on stone fruit with leesy richness and integrated acidity

If you like this, then try with confidence . . .

Greater quality, greater intensity

Premier, then Grand Cru Chablis from Michel Laroche

Greater quality, less intensity

The very best from the basic Mâcon-Villages appellation, such as Mâcon Solutré Clos des Bertillones Denogent

Try something completely different

The best Pinot Blanc from Alsace, starting with Domaine Weinbach or Collio Pinot Blanco from Schiopetto from Veneto in Italy

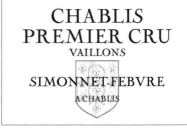

Simonnet-Fèbvre Chablis

Highly Recommended	$$	12.5%

What is it?

A dry white wine made from the Chardonnay grape grown in Chablis, Burgundy, France

What does it taste like?

Classic Chablis, with smoky, dried straw, green apple and lemon zest flavors. Light-bodied and fresh with a long finish.

If you like this, then try with confidence . . .

Greater quality, greater intensity

Premier, then Grand Cru Chablis from Michel Laroche

Greater quality, less intensity

The very best from the basic Mâcon-Villages appellation, such as Mâcon Solutré Clos des Bertillones Denogent

Try something completely different

The best Pinot Blanc from Alsace, starting with Domaine Weinbach or Collio Pinot Blanco from Schiopetto from Veneto in Italy

Simonnet-Fèbvre Crémant de Bourgogne Brut Rosé

Highly Recommended	$$	12%

What is it?

A dry sparkling rosé wine made from the Pinot Noir grape grown in Burgundy, France. Traditional Method with lees aging for at least 9 months.

What does it taste like?

Mouthfilling, creamy mousse, with pretty strawberry and red cherry flavors and a crisp, bright finish

If you like this, then try with confidence . . .

Greater quality, greater intensity

Top quality rosé Champagnes of richness and weight, such as Dom Pérignon Rosé, Dom Ruinart Rosé or Taittinger Comtes de Champagne Rosé

Greater quality, less intensity

Top-quality rosé Champagnes of lightness and elegance, such as Pommery Cuvée Louise Pommery Rosé or, if you can afford it, Louis Roederer Cristal Rosé

Try something completely different

Camel Valley Pinot Noir Brut

Simonnet-Fèbvre Crémant de Bourgogne Brut

Highly Recommended	$$	12%

What is it?

A dry sparkling wine made from a blend of grapes (60% Chardonnay, 40% Pinot Noir) grown in Burgundy, France. Traditional Method with lees aging for at least 9 months.

What does it taste like?

Medium-bodied with good mid-palate intensity, creamy mousse and a dry, clean finish

If you like this, then try with confidence . . .

Greater quality, greater intensity

Charles Heidsieck NV Brut Réserve

Greater quality, less intensity

Pommery Cuvée Louise or, if you can afford it, Louis Roederer Cristal

Try something completely different

Ca'del Bosco Cuvée Annamaria Clementi after two or three years additional aging

Simonsig Chenin Blanc

| Highly Recommended | $ | 14.5% |

What is it?

A dry white wine made from the Chenin Blanc grape grown in Stellenbosch, South Africa. Aged in stainless steel vats on the lees for 4–10 weeks to impart richer mouthfeel.

What does it taste like?

Bright, fresh and zesty, with lime, lemon and white peach flavors and a hint of honey. The palate is rich and round with a juicy, ripe red apple finish.

If you like this, then try with confidence . . .

Greater quality, greater intensity
Ken Forrester Old Vine Reserve Chenin Blanc
Greater quality, less intensity
Ken Forrester Petit Chenin Blanc

Try something completely different
Vidal-Fleury Condrieu or Voignier from Yalumba

Simonsig Pinotage Redhill Stellenbosch

| Recommended | $$ | 14.5% |

What is it?

A dry red wine made from the Pinotage grape grown in the Redhill Vineyard in Stellenbosch, South Africa. Aged 16 months in oak barrels (two-thirds French oak, one-third American oak, two-thirds new).

What does it taste like?

Deep black cherry, toast and vanilla aromas with meatiness on the palate. A very balanced and classy wine.

If you like this, then try with confidence . . .

Greater quality, greater intensity
Kaapzicht Pinotage, then their Steytler Pinotage
Greater quality, less intensity
Southern Right Pinotage

Try something completely different
Southern Italian reds made from Primitivo (a.k.a. Zinfandel) or Nero d'Avola

Simonsig Pinotage

Recommended	$$	14%

What is it?
A dry red wine made from the Pinotage grape grown in Stellenbosch, South Africa

What does it taste like?
Nice ripe red berry fruit with a hint of tar and smoked meat. Full-bodied and flavorful with good length.

If you like this, then try with confidence . . .
Greater quality, greater intensity
Kaapzicht Pinotage, then their Steytler Pinotage
Greater quality, less intensity
Southern Right Pinotage

Try something completely different
Southern Italian reds made from Primitivo (a.k.a. Zinfandel) or Nero d'Avola

Smith Woodhouse Late Bottled Vintage

To Die For	$$$	20%

What is it?
A sweet fortified red wine made from a blend of grapes (Tinta Barroca, Tinta Roriz, Touriga Franca, Touriga Nacional and other traditional Port varieties) grown in Douro, Portugal. Aged 4 years in barrels, followed by 4 years in bottle prior to release.

What does it taste like?
Pure, intense aromas and flavors of red licorice, chocolate, dried plums, clove and cranberry jelly. Extremely well-integrated tannins and a harmonious, long, very lovely finish.

If you like this, then try with confidence . . .
Greater quality, greater intensity
The finest quality, most intense ruby-style wines such as Vintage Ports from Taylor's, Graham's and Fonseca
Greater quality, less intensity
The finest quality, least intense ruby style is Ferreira's Vintage Port, but try also single-quinta Ports and, the lightest of all, "pink" Port from Croft, Porto Cruz and Quinta & Vineyard

Try something completely different
Other sweet, ruby-style fortified wines, such as Banyuls from France or Australian Ruby and Australian Vintage (both formerly known as Australian Liqueur Port)

Sonoma Cutrer Chardonnay

Recommended	$$	14%

What is it?

A dry white wine made from the Chardonnay grape grown in the Sonoma Coast, California. The wine was fermented in oak and completed malolactic fermentation.

What does it taste like?

Opulent pineapple and mango fruit, with coconut and ginger spices from oak, supported by a rich creamy-textured palate

If you like this, then try with confidence . . .

Greater quality, greater intensity

Any white Burgundy from Domaine (not Olivier) Leflaive

Greater quality, less intensity

The very best from the basic Mâcon-Villages appellation, such as Mâcon Solutré Clos des Bertillones Denogent

Try something completely different

The best Pinot Blanc from Alsace, starting with Domaine Weinbach or Collio Pinot Blanco from Schiopetto from Veneto in Italy

ESTATE BOTTLED

SONOMA-CUTRER

RUSSIAN RIVER RANCHES

Spy Valley Marlborough Pinot Gris

Highly Recommended	$$	14%

What is it?

An off-dry white wine made from the Pinot Gris grape grown in Marlborough, New Zealand. A portion of the wine was fermented in old oak casks and went through malolactic fermentation. Residual Sugar 9.6 g/l.

What does it taste like?

Full-bodied, off-dry style with delicious musky, apricot fruit, finishes very clean and pure

If you like this, then try with confidence . . .

Greater quality, greater intensity

JosMeyer Pinot Gris 1854 Fondation or Trimbach Pinot Gris Réserve with a few years additional bottle-age

Greater quality, less intensity

JosMeyer Pinot Blanc Les Lutins or Domaine Weinbach Pinot Blanc

Try something completely different

A good Soave such as Pieropan or Inama, perhaps even Chasselas from Blaise Duboux in Switzerland or, for the very adventurous, a super-soft Koshu from Japan, such as Misawa Private Reserve from Grace

Spy Valley Pinot Noir

Highly Recommended	$$	14%

What is it?

A dry red wine made from the Pinot Noir grape grown in Marlborough, New Zealand. Aged in French oak for 9 months.

What does it taste like?

Elegant style, with pretty red fruit aromas and a soft texture

If you like this, then try with confidence . . .

Greater quality, greater intensity

Pinot Noir from Akarua, Ata Rangi, Craggy Range Te Muna, Felton Road and Twin Paddocks

Greater quality, less intensity

Kim Crawford Marlborough New Zealand Pansy Rosé

Try something completely different

Fruit-driven Nebbiolo, such as Cascina Adelaide di Amabile Drocco Barolo Fossati, Aldo Conterno Barolo Cicala, Parusso Barolo Le Coste-Mosconi or G. D. Vajra Barolo Albe

SPY VALLEY

Pinot Noir

VINTAGE

MARLBOROUGH
NEW ZEALAND WINE

Spy Valley Riesling

Highly Recommended	$$	13%

What is it?

An off-dry white wine made from the Riesling grape grown in Marlborough, New Zealand. A portion of the wine was fermented in old oak casks. Residual Sugar 8.9 g/l.

What does it taste like?

Dry style, with refreshing, vibrant peach and green apple flavors

If you like this, then try with confidence . . .

Greater quality, greater intensity

Pressing Matters R0 from Tasmania

Greater quality, less intensity

Observatory Hill Vintner's Reserve or, for a leaner, more linear Riesling, Puddleduck from Tasmania

Try something completely different

Dry Australian Semillon, particularly from the Hunter Valley, with several years bottle-age

Spy Valley Sauvignon Blanc

Highly Recommended	$$	13.5%

What is it?

A dry white wine made from the Sauvignon Blanc grape grown in Marlborough, New Zealand

What does it taste like?

Classic, pungent, dry style with good weight, featuring grassy gooseberry and passion fruit flavors

If you like this, then try with confidence . . .

Greater quality, greater intensity

Iconic Marlborough Sauvignon Blanc, such as Cloudy Bay, Craggy Range Avery Vineyard, Hunter's, Isabel Estate, Koura Whaleback, Nobilo Icon and Palliser Estate

Greater quality, less intensity

The finest, most elegant Pouilly-Fumé, such as Didier Dagueneau Silex and Pur Sang

Try something completely different

Lean, linear Riesling from Alsace (Trimbach Clos Ste Hune or JosMeyer Grand Cru Hengst) and Mosel (Maximin Grünhaus Abtsberg Alte Reben Trocken)

Stag's Leap Wine Cellars Artemis Cabernet Sauvignon

Highly Recommended	$$$	14.5%

STAG'S LEAP WINE CELLARS

ARTEMIS

Cabernet Sauvignon
Napa Valley

What is it?

A dry red wine made predominantly from the Cabernet Sauvignon grape grown in Napa, California. Aged in new French oak (just under half new) for 18 months.

What does it taste like?

Chocolate, charred oak, additional deep flavors of cassis and coffee. Very rich and smooth with low acidity and big, ripe, refined tannins.

If you like this, then try with confidence . . .

Greater quality, greater intensity

Caymus Special Selection Cabernet Sauvignon or Dunn Vineyards Howell Mountain Cabernet Sauvignon

Greater quality, less intensity

Stag's Leap Cask 23 Estate Cabernet Sauvignon

Try something completely different

For a classic Bordeaux to match the intensity and voluptuousness of top California Cabernet Sauvignon, try a Merlot-dominated Pomerol such as châteaux L'Evangile, La Fleur-Pétrus, Latour à Pomerol, Petit-Village, Trotanoy and, if you can afford them, Pétrus and Le Pin

Starborough Sauvignon Blanc

Highly Recommended	$$	13.5%

STARBOROUGH

MARLBOROUGH
New Zealand

SAUVIGNON BLANC

What is it?

A dry white wine made from the Sauvignon Blanc grape grown in Marlborough, New Zealand

What does it taste like?

Tangy, with sweet gooseberry and white nectarine fruit along with green pea and green pepper. A crowd-pleaser.

If you like this, then try with confidence . . .

Greater quality, greater intensity

Iconic Marlborough Sauvignon Blanc, such as Cloudy Bay, Craggy Range Avery Vineyard, Hunter's, Isabel Estate, Koura Whaleback, Nobilo Icon and Palliser Estate

Greater quality, less intensity

The finest, most elegant Pouilly-Fumé, such as Didier Dagueneau Silex and Pur Sang

Try something completely different

Lean, linear Riesling from Alsace (Trimbach Clos Ste Hune or JosMeyer Grand Cru Hengst) and Mosel (Maximin Grünhaus Abtsberg Alte Reben Trocken)

Stoneleigh Sauvignon Blanc

Highly Recommended	$$	12.5%

What is it?
A dry white wine made from the Sauvignon Blanc grape grown in Marlborough, New Zealand

What does it taste like?
Pungent, with fresh grass, elderflower, passion fruit and gooseberry aromas. Light-bodied, with a refreshing, clean finish.

If you like this, then try with confidence . . .
Greater quality, greater intensity
Iconic Marlborough Sauvignon Blanc, such as Cloudy Bay, Craggy Range Avery Vineyard, Hunter's, Isabel Estate, Koura Whaleback, Nobilo Icon and Palliser Estate
Greater quality, less intensity
The finest, most elegant Pouilly-Fumé, such as Didier Dagueneau Silex and Pur Sang

Try something completely different
Lean, linear Riesling from Alsace (Trimbach Clos Ste Hune or JosMeyer Grand Cru Hengst) and Mosel (Maximin Grünhaus Abtsberg Alte Reben Trocken)

Sutter Home White Zinfandel

Recommended	$	10%

What is it?

A medium-sweet rosé wine made from the Zinfandel grape grown in California

What does it taste like?

Bursting with sweet strawberries and summer fruits. Sweet and easy-drinking.

If you like this, then try with confidence . . .

Greater quality, greater intensity

A Kir, but made from a fine Moscato d'Asti rather than a dry white Burgundy, and the tiniest possible dash of Cassis for color

Greater quality, less intensity

Chateau de la Varière Cabernet d'Anjou Demi-Sec or dry rosés such as E. Guigal Côtes-du-Rhône Rosé, or the fruitier Garnacha-based rosado of Navarra in Spain

Try something completely different

Riesling Kabinett or Spätlese from Germany

Taittinger NV Brut

Highly Recommended	$$$	12%

What is it?

A dry sparkling wine made from a blend of grapes (40% Chardonnay, 60% Pinot Noir and Meunier) grown in Champagne, France. Traditional Method with lees aging for a minimum of 3 years.

What does it taste like?

Fresh citrus, white flowers and bread aromas, very light and fluffy

If you like this, then try with confidence . . .

Greater quality, greater intensity

Taittinger Vintage

Greater quality, less intensity

Taittinger Comtes de Champagne Blanc de Blancs

Try something completely different

The top sparkling wines from England (Camel Valley, Henners, Herbert Hall, Nyetimber, Ridgeview) and Tasmania (Bay of Fires, Clover Hill, Jansz, Stefano Lubiano, Pirie, Relbia)

Taylor Fladgate 10 Year Tawny Port

To Die For	$$$	20%

What is it?

A sweet fortified red wine made from a blend of grapes (Tinta Barroca, Tinta Roriz, Touriga Franca, Touriga Nacional and other traditional Port varieties) and matured in large oak for many years, during which the wine gently oxidizes in a controlled way

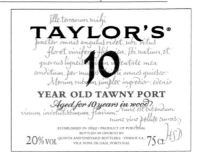

What does it taste like?

Sweet, with a lovely combination of dried cherry, prune, coffee and caramel

If you like this, then try with confidence . . .

Greater quality, greater intensity

This is arguably as good as it gets for a 10-Year Tawny, but Taylor Fladgate 20-Year Tawny is richer.

Greater quality, less intensity

Fonseca 20 Year Old Tawny Port and Sandeman Twenty Years Old Tawny Port. Both are intensely flavored, but more elegant, complex and harmonious.

Try something completely different

The tawny-like Fondillón, a 15-year-old Monastrell, with a non-fortified 16% of alcohol from Casta Diva in Alicante, Spain, or Penfolds Club Reserve Classic Tawny, then the truly iconic Penfolds Grandfather and Great Grandfather Rare Tawnies

Taylor Fladgate 20 Year Tawny Port

To Die For	$$$	20%

What is it?

A sweet fortified red wine made from a blend of grapes (Tinta Barroca, Tinta Roriz, Touriga Franca, Touriga Nacional and other traditional Port varieties) and matured in large oak for many years, during which the wine gently oxidizes in a controlled way

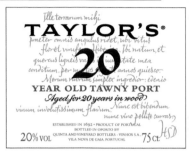

What does it taste like?

Lusciously sweet and immensely complex wine with flavors of fruitcake, toffee, coffee and caramel

If you like this, then try with confidence . . .

Greater quality, greater intensity

Taylor Fladgate 40-Year Tawny

Greater quality, less intensity

Older Tawny Ports are not necessarily better, and some can be rather tired, but the best (such as those from Quinta do Noval) are complex, retain sufficient freshness and show incredible harmony and elegance.

Try something completely different

The tawny-like Fondillón, a 15-year-old Monastrell, with a non-fortified 16% of alcohol from Casta Diva in Alicante, Spain, or Penfolds Club Reserve Classic Tawny, then the truly iconic Penfolds Grandfather and Great Grandfather Rare Tawnies

Terrazas de los Andes Reserva Malbec

Highly Recommended	$$	14%

What is it?

A dry red wine made from the Malbec grape grown in Mendoza, Argentina. The wine is matured for 12 months in a mix of old and new French and American small oak barrels.

What does it taste like?

Very deep plum and blueberry, full-bodied and spicy

If you like this, then try with confidence . . .

Greater quality, greater intensity

Luigi Bosca Vistalba Malbec and Nicolas Catena Zapata Malbec Argentino, then Flichman Parcelo 26 for the ultimate monster Malbec

Greater quality, less intensity

Colomé Malbec or Yacochuya Estate from Salta, Bodegas Lagarde Agrelo and Terrazas Afincado single-vineyard Malbecs.

Try something completely different

Cahors from Clos Triguedina or Tannat Castel La Puebla Dayman from Stagnari in Uruguay

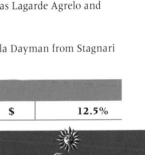

Torres Gran Viña Sol

Recommended	$	12.5%

What is it?

A dry white wine made from a blend of grapes (Chardonnay, Parellada), with a portion fermented and matured in small French oak barrels

What does it taste like?

Light and fresh citrus aromas with a touch of oak, crisp and fresh on the palate

If you like this, then try with confidence . . .

Greater quality, greater intensity

Domaine Leflaive Puligny-Montrachet

Greater quality, less intensity

The very best from Mâcon, such as Mâcon Solutré Clos des Bertillones Denogent

Try something completely different

White wines from cru classé châteaux in Pessac-Léognan

Trapiche Malbec

Recommended	$	13.5%

What is it?

A dry red wine made from the Malbec grape grown in
Mendoza, Argentina, with subtle oak contact

What does it taste like?

Very deep in color, with brooding blackberry and prune
fruit and a touch of oak spice. Full-bodied and intense.

If you like this, then try with confidence . . .

Greater quality, greater intensity

Luigi Bosca Vistalba Malbec and Nicolas Catena Zapata
Malbec Argentino, then Flichman Parcelo 26 for the
ultimate monster Malbec

Greater quality, less intensity

Colomé Malbec or Yacochuya Estate from Salta, Bodegas Lagarde Agrelo and
Terrazas Afincado single-vineyard Malbecs

Try something completely different

Cahors from Clos Triguedina or Tannat Castel La Puebla Dayman from Stagnari
in Uruguay

Trimbach Pinot Blanc

Recommended	$$	12.5%

What is it?

A dry white wine made from a blend of grapes
(80% Auxerrois, 20% Pinot Blanc) grown in
Alsace, France

What does it taste like?

Very approachable, with a soft, round mid-palate
and flavors of melon and red apple, finishing
clean with juicy acidity

If you like this, then try with confidence . . .

Greater quality, greater intensity

Trimbach Pinot Gris Réserve with a few years additional bottle-age

Greater quality, less intensity

JosMeyer Pinot Gris Le Fromenteau

Try something completely different

A good Soave such as Pieropan or Inama, perhaps even Chasselas from Blaise
Duboux in Switzerland or, for the very adventurous, a super-soft Koshu from
Japan, such as Misawa Private Reserve from Grace

Trimbach Riesling

Highly Recommended	$$	13%

What is it?
A dry white wine made from the Riesling grape grown in Alsace, France

What does it taste like?
Dry, with pronounced flavors of lime curd, green apple and white peach that linger

If you like this, then try with confidence . . .
Greater quality, greater intensity
Trimbach Riesling Cuvée Frédéric Émile
Greater quality, less intensity
Trimbach Riesling Clos Ste Hune

Try something completely different
Dry Australian Semillon, particularly from the Hunter Valley, with several years bottle-age

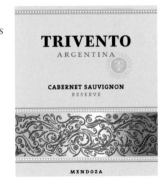

Trivento Reserve Cabernet Sauvignon

Recommended	$	14%

What is it?
A dry red wine made from the Cabernet Sauvignon grape grown in Mendoza, Argentina. Aged 6 months in used French oak barrels.

What does it taste like?
Smooth and fruity, with black raspberry jam flavors

If you like this, then try with confidence . . .
Greater quality, greater intensity
Catena Alta Cabernet Sauvignon
Greater quality, less intensity
Etchart Cafayate Cabernet Sauvignon

Try something completely different
Malbec, Argentina's signature red wine, from the best producers, such as Archával Ferrer, Catena, O Fournier and Tikal

Trivento Reserve Malbec

Recommended	$	14%

What is it?

A dry red wine made from the Malbec grape grown in Mendoza, Argentina. Aged 6 months in used French oak barrels.

What does it taste like?

Smooth and easy-drinking, with smoky raspberry fruit

If you like this, then try with confidence . . .

Greater quality, greater intensity

Luigi Bosca Vistalba Malbec and Nicolas Catena Zapata Malbec Argentino, then Flichman Parcelo 26 for the ultimate monster Malbec

Greater quality, less intensity

Colomé Malbec or Yacochuya Estate from Salta, Bodegas Lagarde Agrelo and Terrazas Afincado single-vineyard Malbecs

Try something completely different

Cahors from Clos Triguedina or Tannat Castel La Puebla Dayman from Stagnari in Uruguay

Trivento Reserve Syrah

Recommended	$	14%

What is it?

A dry red wine made from the Syrah grape grown in Mendoza, Argentina. Aged 6 months in used American oak barrels.

What does it taste like?

Sweet, smoky fruit, straightforward and juicy

If you like this, then try with confidence . . .

Greater quality, greater intensity

Hermitage from Chapoutier (especially l'Ermite) and Marc Sorrel (Gréal), or fuller-style Côte Rôtie such as those by Guigal (Château d'Ampuis and the single-vineyard bottlings)

Greater quality, less intensity

René Rostaing and Yves Montez produce Côte Rôtie of exceptional quality, in a more elegant style and emphasizing freshness and florality.

Try something completely different

California Petite Sirah, the very best of which include Rosenblum Rockpile, Turley Cellars Hayne Vineyard or Lava Cap Grand Hill

Trivento Reserve Torrontés

Recommended	$	13%

What is it?

A dry white wine made from the Torrontés grape grown in Mendoza, Argentina

What does it taste like?

Just off-dry, with a very intense floral nose of roses, jasmine, lychee and peaches with a clean finish

If you like this, then try with confidence . . .

Greater quality, greater intensity

Off-dry, fully fledged Muscat d'Alsace such as Rolly Gassmann

Greater quality, less intensity

Alsace Klevner de Heiligenstein starting with Zeyssolff L'Opaline

Try something completely different

Spicy-floral rather than fruity-floral, such as the lighter Gewürztraminer d'Alsace, such as JosMeyer Les Folastries

Turning Leaf Cabernet Sauvignon

Recommended	$	13%

What is it?

A dry red wine made from the Cabernet Sauvignon grape grown in California with subtle oak influence

What does it taste like?

Black fruit and sweet spice aromas with mild tannins and a clean finish

If you like this, then try with confidence . . .

Greater quality, greater intensity

Caymus Special Selection Cabernet Sauvignon or Dunn Vineyards Howell Mountain Cabernet Sauvignon

Greater quality, less intensity

Stag's Leap Cask 23 Estate Cabernet Sauvignon

Try something completely different

For a classic Bordeaux to match the intensity and voluptuousness of top California Cabernet Sauvignon, try a Merlot-dominated Pomerol such as châteaux L'Evangile, La Fleur-Pétrus, Latour à Pomerol, Petit-Village, Trotanoy and, if you can afford them, Pétrus and Le Pin

Turning Leaf Chardonnay

Recommended	$	13.5%

What is it?

A dry white wine made from the Chardonnay grape grown in California with subtle oak influence

What does it taste like?

Smooth and soft wine, with creamy vanilla and peach flavors

If you like this, then try with confidence . . .

Greater quality, greater intensity

Jacob's Creek Chardonnay Adelaide Hills

Greater quality, less intensity

The very best from the basic Mâcon-Villages appellation, such as Mâcon Solutré Clos des Bertillones Denogent

Try something completely different

The best Pinot Blanc from Alsace, starting with Domaine Weinbach or Collio Pinot Blanco from Schiopetto from Veneto in Italy

Turning Leaf Merlot

Recommended	$	13.5%

What is it?

A dry red wine made from the Merlot grape grown in California with subtle oak influence

What does it taste like?

Sweet plum fruit with a velvety tannin structure

If you like this, then try with confidence . . .

Greater quality, greater intensity

Great Merlot from California (Pahlmeyer, Paloma and Pride) or Washington (L'Ecole No. 41, Leonetti, Seven Hills and Woodward Canyon)

Greater quality, less intensity

Raphael Rosé of Merlot from Long Island

Try something completely different

Great Merlot-dominated blends from Pomerol, such as châteaux L'Evangile, La Fleur-Pétrus, Latour à Pomerol, Petit-Village, Trotanoy and, if you can afford them, Pétrus and Le Pin

Turning Leaf Pinot Grigio

Recommended	$	12.5%

What is it?
A dry white wine made from the Pinot Grigio
grape grown in California

What does it taste like?
Just off-dry, with baked apples and refreshing
acidity

If you like this, then try with confidence . . .
Greater quality, greater intensity
JosMeyer Pinot Gris 1854 Fondation or Trimbach
Pinot Gris Réserve with a few years bottle-age
Greater quality, less intensity
JosMeyer Pinot Blanc Les Lutins or Domaine Weinbach Pinot Blanc

Try something completely different
A good Soave such as Pieropan or Inama, perhaps even Chasselas from Blaise
Duboux in Switzerland or, for the very adventurous, a super-soft Koshu from
Japan, such as Misawa Private Reserve from Grace

TURNING LEAF.

PINOT GRIGIO
CALIFORNIA

Turning Leaf Pinot Noir

Recommended	$	13%

What is it?
A dry red wine made from the Pinot Noir grape
grown in California

What does it taste like?
Good intensity of fruit, with red cherry and
strawberry flavors and fresh acidity

If you like this, then try with confidence . . .
Greater quality, greater intensity
La Bauge au Dessus and other Pinot Noir from Au
Bon Climat in Santa Barbara, California, or Le
Grand Clos Pinot Noir from Le Clos Jordanne in
Niagara, Canada
Greater quality, less intensity
The more elegant Oregon Pinot Noir, starting with Adelsheim, Bethel Heights
and Rex Hill

Try something completely different
Fruit-driven Nebbiolo, such as Cascina Adelaide di Amabile Drocco Barolo
Fossati, Aldo Conterno Barolo Cicala, Parusso Barolo Le Coste-Mosconi
or G. D. Vajra Barolo Albe

TURNING LEAF.

PINOT NOIR
CALIFORNIA

Veuve Clicquot NV Brut Yellow Label

Recommended	$$$	12%

What is it?

A dry sparkling wine made from a blend of grapes (Pinot Noir, Chardonnay and Meunier) grown in Champagne, France. Traditional Method with lees aging for a minimum of 3 years.

What does it taste like?

Red apple, pastry and hints of nuts and creamy caramel, round and soft on the palate

If you like this, then try with confidence . . .

Greater quality, greater intensity
Veuve Clicquot Vintage
Greater quality, less intensity
Veuve Clicquot La Grande Dame

Try something completely different

The top sparkling wines from England (Camel Valley, Henners, Herbert Hall, Nyetimber, Ridgeview) and Tasmania (Bay of Fires, Clover Hill, Jansz, Stefano Lubiana, Pirie, Relbia)

Vidal-Fleury Châteauneuf-du-Pape

Highly Recommended	$$$	14.5%

What is it?

A dry red wine made from a blend of grapes (85% Grenache, 10% Syrah, 5% Mourvèdre) grown in Châteauneuf-du-Pape, Southern Rhône, France. Aged on the lees in large French oak barrels for 12 months.

What does it taste like?

Thick, meaty wine with potent baked red berry fruit, hints of heather and lavender, and a dark mineral streak on the finish

If you like this, then try with confidence . . .

Greater quality, greater intensity
Domaine Pierre Usseglio Châteauneuf-du-Pape, then Château Rayas
Greater quality, less intensity
Domaine du Vieux Télégraphe Châteauneuf-du-Pape, then Château de Beaucastel Châteauneuf-du-Pape Hommage à Jacques Perrin

Try something completely different

Pure Grenache from Australia (Yalumba Bush Vine Grenache, Kilikanoon The Duke Clare Valley Grenache) or France (Mas Foulaquier Le Petit Duc)

Vidal-Fleury Condrieu

Highly Recommended $$$ 13.5%

What is it?

A dry white wine made from the Viognier grape grown in Condrieu, Northern Rhône, France. Half of the wine was fermented in stainless steel tanks and the other half in large French oak barrels. 100% of the wine underwent malolactic fermentation and spent 12 months in new French oak barrels on the lees with lees stirring to impart creaminess and texture.

What does it taste like?

Extremely aromatic, with aromas of orange blossom, jasmine, and honeysuckle plus fresh apricots. Full-bodied, with a creamy texture and low acidity.

If you like this, then try with confidence . . .

Greater quality, greater intensity
Condrieu from Cuilleron (Le Ayguets, Les Chaillets) or Alain Paret (Lys de Volan)
Greater quality, less intensity
More restrained styles of Condrieu, starting with Les Vins de Vienne, then those of Georges Vernay and François Villard, plus Château Grillet

Try something completely different

Muscat d'Alsace from Rolly Gassmann

| **To Die For** | **$$$** | 13% |

What is it?

A dry red wine made from the Syrah grape grown in Côte Rôtie, Northern Rhône, France. Aged on the lees for 4 years in large French oak barrels.

What does it taste like?

Pronounced, complex aromas of black pepper, smoked meat and purity of fruit. Perfectly balanced, with great oak integration and an unctuous texture.

If you like this, then try with confidence . . .

Greater quality, greater intensity

Hermitage from Chapoutier (especially l'Ermite) and Marc Sorrel (Gréal), or fuller-style Côte Rôtie such as those by Guigal (Château d'Ampuis and the single-vineyard bottlings)

Greater quality, less intensity

René Rostaing and Yves Montez produce Côte Rôtie of exceptional quality, in a more elegant style and emphasizing freshness and florality.

Try something completely different

California Petite Sirah, the very best of which include Rosenblum Rockpile, Turley Cellars Hayne Vineyard or Lava Cap Grand Hill

Vidal-Fleury Côtes-du-Rhône Blanc

| **Highly Recommended** | **$$** | 13.5% |

What is it?

A dry white wine made from a blend of grapes (Viognier 75%, Grenache Blanc 15%, Others 10%) grown in Côtes-du-Rhône, France with no oak influence

What does it taste like?

Very perfumed, with white grape, peach and honeysuckle aromas. Quite rich and dense, with a clean, lasting finish.

If you like this, then try with confidence . . .

Greater quality, greater intensity

Coudoulet de Beaucastel Blanc, then Château de Beaucastel Blanc Vieilles Vignes

Greater quality, less intensity

Vieux Manoir du Frigoulas Côtes-du-Rhône Villages Blanc

Try something completely different

Rutherglen Estates Renaissance Viognier Roussanne Marsanne

Vidal-Fleury Côtes-du-Rhône

Highly Recommended	$$	13.5%

What is it?

A dry red wine made from a blend of grapes (65% Grenache, 20% Syrah, 10% Mourvèdre, 5% Carignan) grown in Côtes-du-Rhône, France. Aged on the lees (70% in stainless steel tanks and 30% in large French oak barrels).

What does it taste like?

Full and rich, packed with dark red fruits, plus pepper and wild herb complexity. Excellent typicity.

If you like this, then try with confidence . . .

Greater quality, greater intensity
Domaine Pierre Usseglio Châteauneuf-du-Pape, then Château Rayas
Greater quality, less intensity
E. Guigal Châteauneuf-du-Pape, then Domaine du Vieux Télégraphe Châteauneuf-du-Pape

Try something completely different

Pure Grenache from Australia (Yalumba Bush Vine Grenache, Kilikanoon The Duke Clare Valley Grenache) or France (Mas Foulaquier Le Petit Duc)

Vidal-Fleury Crozes-Hermitage

Recommended	$$	13.5%

What is it?

A dry red wine made from the Syrah grape grown in Crozes-Hermitage, Northern Rhône, France. Aged 6 months in large French oak barrels.

What does it taste like?

Polished and flashy style, with very ripe black fruits

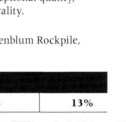

If you like this, then try with confidence . . .

Greater quality, greater intensity

Hermitage from Chapoutier (especially l'Ermite) and Marc Sorrel (Gréal), or fuller-style Côte Rôtie such as those by Guigal (Château d'Ampuis and the single-vineyard bottlings)

Greater quality, less intensity

René Rostaing and Yves Montez produce Côte Rôtie of exceptional quality, in a more elegant style and emphasizing freshness and florality.

Try something completely different

California Petite Sirah, the very best of which include Rosenblum Rockpile, Turley Cellars Hayne Vineyard or Lava Cap Grand Hill

Vidal-Fleury Saint-Joseph

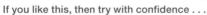

Highly Recommended	$$	13%

What is it?

A dry red wine made from the Syrah grape grown in St. Joseph, Northern Rhône, France. Aged 12 months in large French oak barrels.

What does it taste like?

Modern style, with rich, ripe blueberry and blackberry aromas, hints of violet and balanced, juicy acidity

If you like this, then try with confidence . . .

Greater quality, greater intensity

Hermitage from Chapoutier (especially l'Ermite) and Marc Sorrel (Gréal), or fuller-style Côte Rôtie such as those by Guigal (Château d'Ampuis and the single-vineyard bottlings)

Greater quality, less intensity

René Rostaing and Yves Montez produce Côte Rôtie of exceptional quality, in a more elegant style and emphasizing freshness and florality.

Try something completely different

California Petite Sirah, the very best of which include Rosenblum Rockpile, Turley Cellars Hayne Vineyard or Lava Cap Grand Hill

Villa Antinori Toscana

Highly Recommended	**$$**	**13.5%**

What is it?

A dry red wine made from a blend of grapes (55% Sangiovese, 25% Cabernet Sauvignon, 15% Merlot, 5% Syrah) grown in Tuscany, Italy. Aged in small French, Hungarian and American oak barrels for 12 months, followed by 8 months in bottle prior to release.

What does it taste like?

Aromas of dried red cherry, cocoa and raisin, on a medium-bodied frame with integrated oak structure and good length

If you like this, then try with confidence . . .

Greater quality, greater intensity

The best, richest Chianti Classico (Castello di Ama, Poggio al Sole Casasilia, Querciabella) and Brunello di Montalcino (Casanova di Neri, Case Basse, Mastrojanne, Siro Pacenti)

Greater quality, less intensity

Lighter and fruitier with Yalumba Y Series Sangiovese Rosé or Mitolo Jester McLaren Vale Sangiovese Rosé

Try something completely different

Montepulciano d'Abruzzo (Valentini is best)

Villa Maria Chardonnay East Coast Private Bin

Recommended	**$$**	**13.5%**

What is it?

A dry, lightly oaked white wine made from the Chardonnay grape grown in Hawkes Bay, New Zealand. A small proportion of French oak is used.

What does it taste like?

Smooth, rich, creamy yellow fruits, with cashew nuts and oak adding complexity on the finish

If you like this, then try with confidence . . .

Greater quality, greater intensity

Any white Burgundy from Domaine (not Olivier) Leflaive

Greater quality, less intensity

The very best from the basic Mâcon-Villages appellation, such as Mâcon Solutré Clos des Bertillones Denogent

Try something completely different

The best Pinot Blanc from Alsace, starting with Domaine Weinbach or Collio Pinot Blanco from Schiopetto from Veneto in Italy

Villa Maria Chardonnay Marlborough Cellar Selection

Recommended	$$$	13.5%

What is it?

A dry, oaked white wine made from the Chardonnay grape grown in Marlborough, New Zealand. Aged in a mix of old and new French oak for a minimum of 10 months.

What does it taste like?

Usually the richest and most complex of Villa Maria Chardonnays, but not always the best. Needs a cheese platter to shine.

If you like this, then try with confidence . . .

Greater quality, greater intensity

Any white Burgundy from Domaine (not Olivier) Leflaive

Greater quality, less intensity

The very best from the basic Mâcon-Villages appellation, such as Mâcon Solutré Clos des Bertillones Denogent

Try something completely different

The best Pinot Blanc from Alsace, starting with Domaine Weinbach or Collio Pinot Blanco from Schiopetto from Veneto in Italy

Villa Maria Chardonnay Marlborough Reserve

Highly Recommended	$$	13.5%

What is it?

A dry, oaked white wine made from the Chardonnay grape grown in Marlborough, New Zealand. Aged in a mix of old and new French oak for a minimum of 12 months.

What does it taste like?

Beautifully focused, fine citrus fruit, with elegant, lingering minerality and fine acids

If you like this, then try with confidence . . .

Greater quality, greater intensity

Any white Burgundy from Domaine (not Olivier) Leflaive

Greater quality, less intensity

The very best from the basic Mâcon-Villages appellation, such as Mâcon Solutré Clos des Bertillones Denogent

Try something completely different

The best Pinot Blanc from Alsace, starting with Domaine Weinbach or Collio Pinot Blanco from Schiopetto from Veneto in Italy

Villa Maria Dry Riesling Private Bin

Highly Recommended $$ | **12.5%**

What is it?
A dry white wine made from the Riesling grape grown in Marlborough, New Zealand

What does it taste like?
Extraordinarily good for entry-level Riesling. Off-dry, lime-dominated citrus fruits. Elegant, excellent minerality.

If you like this, then try with confidence . . .
Greater quality, greater intensity
Pressing Matters R0 from Tasmania
Greater quality, less intensity
Observatory Hill Vintner's Reserve or, for a leaner, more linear Riesling, Puddleduck from Tasmania

Try something completely different
Dry Australian Semillon, particularly from the Hunter Valley, with several years bottle-age

Villa Maria Merlot Reserve

To Die For $$ | **13.5%**

What is it?
A dry red wine made from the Merlot grape grown in Hawkes Bay, New Zealand. Aged in a mix of old and new French oak for a minimum of 18 months.

What does it taste like?
Voluptuous red wine of multilayered red and black soft fruits, velvety textured. Delicious!

If you like this, then try with confidence . . .
Greater quality, greater intensity
Blake Family Redd Gravels Merlot-dominated blend, Clearview Estate Merlot-Malbec, Delegat's Merlot Reserve, Kumeu River Merlot, Goldwater Esslin Merlot and Saint Clair Marlborough Premium Merlot
Greater quality, less intensity
Eradus Merlot Rosé from Gisborne

Try something completely different
Great Merlot-dominated blends from Pomerol, such as châteaux L'Evangile, La Fleur-Pétrus, Latour à Pomerol, Petit-Village, Trotanoy and, if you can afford them, Pétrus and Le Pin

Villa Maria Pinot Gris Cellar Selection

Recommended	$$$	13.3%

What is it?

A dry wine made from the Pinot Gris grape grown in the Awatere Valley of Marlborough, New Zealand

What does it taste like?

More banana-spice than the Private Bin, but with a similar grippy finish

If you like this, then try with confidence . . .

Greater quality, greater intensity

JosMeyer Pinot Gris 1854 Fondation or Trimbach Pinot Gris Réserve with a few years additional bottle-age

Greater quality, less intensity

JosMeyer Pinot Blanc Les Lutins or Domaine Weinbach Pinot Blanc

Try something completely different

A good Soave such as Pieropan or Inama, perhaps even Chasselas from Blaise Duboux in Switzerland or, for the very adventurous, a super-soft Koshu from Japan, such as Misawa Private Reserve from Grace

Villa Maria Pinot Gris East Coast Private Bin

Recommended	$$	13%

What is it?

A dry wine made from the Pinot Gris grape grown in and blended from three different regions (Gisborne, Marlborough and Hawkes Bay) of New Zealand

What does it taste like?

Floral-banana aromas that become slightly spicy with time in bottle, with firm red apple and banana fruit on palate, and good grip on the finish

If you like this, then try with confidence . . .

Greater quality, greater intensity

JosMeyer Pinot Gris 1854 Fondation or Trimbach Pinot Gris Réserve with a few years additional bottle-age

Greater quality, less intensity

JosMeyer Pinot Blanc Les Lutins or Domaine Weinbach Pinot Blanc

Try something completely different

A good Soave such as Pieropan or Inama, perhaps even Chasselas from Blaise Duboux in Switzerland or, for the very adventurous, a super-soft Koshu from Japan, such as Misawa Private Reserve from Grace

Villa Maria Pinot Noir Cellar Selection

Highly Recommended $$$ 14%

What is it?

A dry red wine made from the Pinot Noir grape grown in Marlborough, New Zealand. Aged in a mix of old and new French oak for a minimum of 12 months.

What does it taste like?

A rich, plump and seductively succulent, top-drawer Marlborough Pinot Noir. Silky tannins. Lovely finesse.

If you like this, then try with confidence . . .

Greater quality, greater intensity

Pinot Noir from Akarua, Ata Rangi, Craggy Range Te Muna, Felton Road and Twin Paddocks

Greater quality, less intensity

Kim Crawford Marlborough New Zealand Pansy Rosé

Try something completely different

Fruit-driven Nebbiolo, such as Cascina Adelaide di Amabile Drocco Barolo Fossati, Aldo Conterno Barolo Cicala, Parusso Barolo Le Coste-Mosconi or G. D. Vajra Barolo Albe

Villa Maria Pinot Noir Private Bin

Recommended $$ 13.5%

What is it?

A dry red wine made from the Pinot Noir grape grown in Marlborough, New Zealand. Aged in French oak for 10 months.

What does it taste like?

Typical Marlborough Pinot Noir, with more red cherries than black, but soft tannins make the fruit in this wine accessible.

If you like this, then try with confidence . . .

Greater quality, greater intensity

Pinot Noir from Akarua, Ata Rangi, Craggy Range Te Muna, Felton Road and Twin Paddocks

Greater quality, less intensity

Kim Crawford Marlborough New Zealand Pansy Rosé

Try something completely different

Fruit-driven Nebbiolo, such as Cascina Adelaide di Amabile Drocco Barolo Fossati, Aldo Conterno Barolo Cicala, Parusso Barolo Le Coste-Mosconi or G. D. Vajra Barolo Albe

Villa Maria Pinot Noir Reserve

Highly Recommended	$$	14%

What is it?

A dry red wine made from the Pinot Noir grape grown in
Marlborough, New Zealand. Aged in French oak (almost
30% new) for 14 months.

What does it taste like?

The fruit is really quite plump and elegant, with red and
black cherries, spiced plums and softly textured tannins

If you like this, then try with confidence . . .

Greater quality, greater intensity
Pinot Noir from Akarua, Ata Rangi, Craggy Range Te
Muna, Felton Road and Twin Paddocks
Greater quality, less intensity
Kim Crawford Marlborough New Zealand Pansy Rosé

Try something completely different

Fruit-driven Nebbiolo, such as Cascina Adelaide di Amabile Drocco Barolo
Fossati, Aldo Conterno Barolo Cicala, Parusso Barolo Le Coste-Mosconi
or G. D. Vajra Barolo Albe

Villa Maria Riesling Cellar Selection

Highly Recommended	$$$	12.5%

What is it?

A dry white wine made from the Riesling grape grown in
Marlborough, New Zealand

What does it taste like?

As complex as youthful Riesling can get, the lime
influence here is subdued, more general citrus with
hints of mandarin. Intense yet delicate. Very fine.

If you like this, then try with confidence . . .

Greater quality, greater intensity
Pressing Matters R0 from Tasmania
Greater quality, less intensity
Observatory Hill Vintner's Reserve or, for a leaner, more linear Riesling,
Puddleduck from Tasmania

Try something completely different

Dry Australian Semillon, particularly from the Hunter Valley, with several years
bottle-age

Villa Maria Riesling Reserve

Highly Recommended $$ 12%

What is it?
A dry white wine made from the Riesling grape grown in Marlborough, New Zealand

What does it taste like?
Almost dry, crisply rich, tangy, lime-dominated citrus fruits

If you like this, then try with confidence . . .
Greater quality, greater intensity
Pressing Matters R0 from Tasmania
Greater quality, less intensity
Observatory Hill Vintner's Reserve or, for a leaner, more linear Riesling, Puddleduck from Tasmania

Try something completely different
Dry Australian Semillon, particularly from the Hunter Valley, with several years bottle-age

Villa Maria Sauvignon Blanc Cellar Selection

Recommended $$$ 13.5%

What is it?
A dry white wine made from the Sauvignon Blanc grape grown in Marlborough, New Zealand

What does it taste like?
Combines intensity with softness, leaning closer to citrus than passion fruit

If you like this, then try with confidence . . .
Greater quality, greater intensity
Iconic Marlborough Sauvignon Blanc, such as Cloudy Bay, Craggy Range Avery Vineyard, Hunter's, Isabel Estate, Koura Whaleback, Nobilo Icon and Palliser Estate
Greater quality, less intensity
The finest, most elegant Pouilly-Fumé, such as Didier Dagueneau Silex and Pur Sang

Try something completely different
Lean, linear Riesling from Alsace (Trimbach Clos Ste Hune or JosMeyer Grand Cru Hengst) and Mosel (Maximin Grünhaus Abtsberg Alte Reben Trocken)

Villa Maria Sauvignon Blanc Private Bin

Highly Recommended	$$	13.5%

What is it?

A dry white wine made from the Sauvignon Blanc grape grown in Marlborough, New Zealand

What does it taste like?

Excellent typicity featuring vibrant acidity, medium body, with flavors of gooseberry, grapefruit and passion fruit, and a deliciously dry and tangy finish

If you like this, then try with confidence . . .

Greater quality, greater intensity

Iconic Marlborough Sauvignon Blanc, such as Cloudy Bay, Craggy Range Avery Vineyard, Hunter's, Isabel Estate, Koura Whaleback, Nobilo Icon and Palliser Estate

Greater quality, less intensity

The finest, most elegant Pouilly-Fumé, such as Didier Dagueneau Silex and Pur Sang

Try something completely different

Lean, linear Riesling from Alsace (Trimbach Clos Ste Hune or JosMeyer Grand Cru Hengst) and Mosel (Maximin Grünhaus Abtsberg Alte Reben Trocken)

Villa Maria Sauvignon Blanc Reserve Clifford Bay

Highly Recommended	$$	13%

What is it?

A dry white wine made from the Sauvignon Blanc grape grown in Clifford Bay in the Ataware Valley, Marlborough, New Zealand

What does it taste like?

Fresh, vibrant, and juicy, with more elderflower than gooseberry, and intense citrus flavors on the finish

If you like this, then try with confidence . . .

Greater quality, greater intensity

Iconic Marlborough Sauvignon Blanc, such as Cloudy Bay, Craggy Range Avery Vineyard, Hunter's, Isabel Estate, Koura Whaleback, Nobilo Icon and Palliser Estate

Greater quality, less intensity

The finest, most elegant Pouilly-Fumé, such as Didier Dagueneau Silex and Pur Sang

Try something completely different

Lean, linear Riesling from Alsace (Trimbach Clos Ste Hune or JosMeyer Grand Cru Hengst) and Mosel (Maximin Grünhaus Abtsberg Alte Reben Trocken)

Villa Maria Sauvignon Blanc Reserve Wairau Valley

Highly Recommended	$$	13%

What is it?

A dry white wine made from the Sauvignon Blanc grape grown in the Wairau Valley, Canterbury, New Zealand

What does it taste like?

Deliciously ripe gooseberry fruit, with the greater intensity of grapefruit dominating the wine

If you like this, then try with confidence . . .

Greater quality, greater intensity

Iconic Marlborough Sauvignon Blanc, such as Cloudy Bay, Craggy Range Avery Vineyard, Hunter's, Isabel Estate, Koura Whaleback, Nobilo Icon and Palliser Estate

Greater quality, less intensity

The finest, most elegant Pouilly-Fumé, such as Didier Dagueneau Silex and Pur Sang

Try something completely different

Lean, linear Riesling from Alsace (Trimbach Clos Ste Hune or JosMeyer Grand Cru Hengst) and Mosel (Maximin Grünhaus Abtsberg Alte Reben Trocken)

Wolf Blass Gold Label Cabernet Sauvignon

Highly Recommended	$$	14.5%

What is it?

A dry red wine made from the Cabernet Sauvignon grape grown in Coonawarra, South Australia. Aged in French oak (20% new) for 18 months.

What does it taste like?

Pronounced eucalyptus, black cherry and black currant flavors with big, fine-grained tannins. Nicely balanced.

If you like this, then try with confidence . . .

Greater quality, greater intensity

Wynns Coonawarra Estate John Riddoch Cabernet Sauvignon

Greater quality, less intensity

Wynns Coonawarra Estate The Siding Cabernet Sauvignon

Try something completely different

Washington Merlot from the best producers, such as L'Ecole No. 41, Leonetti, Seven Hills and Woodward Canyon

Wolf Blass Gold Label Riesling

Highly Recommended	$$	13%

What is it?

A dry white wine made from the Riesling grape grown in Eden Valley, South Australia

What does it taste like?

Steely, dry style with pure flavors of fresh green apples and a bit of lime zest. Really lovely.

If you like this, then try with confidence . . .

Greater quality, greater intensity

Pewsey Vale Riesling The Contours Museum Reserve, Grosset Polish Hill and Pressing Matters (R0 or R9)

Greater quality, less intensity

Observatory Hill Vintner's Reserve or, for a leaner, more linear Riesling, Puddleduck from Tasmania

Try something completely different

Dry Australian Semillon, particularly from the Hunter Valley, with several years bottle-age

Wolf Blass Platinum Label Shiraz

| Highly Recommended | $$$ | 14.5% |

What is it?

A dry red wine made from the Shiraz grape grown in Barossa, South Australia. Aged in new French oak for 22 months.

What does it taste like?

Dark and smoky, tarry almost, with thick blackberry and fig flavors and firm tannins

If you like this, then try with confidence . . .

Greater quality, greater intensity

Penfolds St Henri and various Bin numbers (28, 128, 150, 389), culminating in RWT and Grange or Henschke Hill of Grace

Greater quality, less intensity

Clonakilla Shiraz-Viognier

Try something completely different

Zinfandel (especially those by Ridge), Petite Syrah (Ridge Vineyards Dynamite Hill, Rosenblum Rockpile, Turley Cellars Hayne Vineyard or Lava Cap Grand Hill) or even an Australian Zinfandel (such as Cape Mentelle)

Wolf Blass Yellow Label Cabernet Sauvignon

Recommended	$$	13.5%

What is it?

A dry red wine made from the Cabernet Sauvignon grape grown in South Australia. A portion of the wine was matured in a mix of French and American oak.

What does it taste like?

Intense black cherry fruit, with prominent toast and vanilla oak flavors

If you like this, then try with confidence . . .

Greater quality, greater intensity
Wolf Blass Gold Label Cabernet Sauvignon
Greater quality, less intensity
Wolf Blass Grey Label Langhorne Creek Cabernet Sauvignon

Try something completely different

Washington Merlot from the best producers, such as L'Ecole No. 41, Leonetti, Seven Hills and Woodward Canyon

Wolf Blass Yellow Label Chardonnay

Recommended	$$	13.5%

What is it?

A dry white wine made from the Chardonnay grape grown in South Australia. A portion was matured in French oak for 6 months.

What does it taste like?

Red apple, vanilla and melon flavors, with a generous, mouth-filling, creamy texture

If you like this, then try with confidence . . .

Greater quality, greater intensity

Wolf Blass White Label Specially Aged Release Adelaide Hills Chardonnay

Greater quality, less intensity

Wolf Blass Gold Label Adelaide Hills Chardonnay

Try something completely different

Fabulous Australian Marsanne, Roussanne and Marsanne-Roussanne blends from Yeringberg

Wolf Blass Yellow Label Shiraz

Recommended	$$	13.5%

What is it?

A dry red wine made from the Shiraz grape grown in South Australia. A portion was matured in American oak for 8 months.

What does it taste like?

Big dollop of ripe blackberry and plum fruit, supported by spicy, toasty oak. Powerful, full-bodied red.

If you like this, then try with confidence . . .

Greater quality, greater intensity

Penfolds St Henri and various Bin numbers (28, 128, 150, 389), culminating in RWT and Grange or Henschke Hill of Grace

Greater quality, less intensity

Clonakilla Shiraz-Viognier

Try something completely different

Zinfandel (especially those by Ridge), Petite Syrah (Ridge Vineyards Dynamite Hill, Rosenblum Rockpile, Turley Cellars Hayne Vineyard or Lava Cap Grand Hill) or even an Australian Zinfandel (such as Cape Mentelle)

Woodbridge Cabernet Sauvignon

Recommended   **$**   **13.5%**

What is it?

A dry red wine made from a blend of grapes (76% Cabernet Sauvignon, 6% Merlot and 18% other varieties) grown in California and aged in a mix of French and American oak

What does it taste like?

Dark cherry fruit with some hints of tobacco, cedar and toast, smooth tannins

If you like this, then try with confidence . . .

Greater quality, greater intensity

Caymus Special Selection Cabernet Sauvignon or Dunn Vineyards Howell Mountain Cabernet Sauvignon

Greater quality, less intensity

Stag's Leap Cask 23 Estate Cabernet Sauvignon

Try something completely different

For a classic Bordeaux to match the intensity and voluptuousness of top California Cabernet Sauvignon, try a Merlot-dominated Pomerol such as châteaux L'Evangile, La Fleur-Pétrus, Latour à Pomerol, Petit-Village, Trotanoy and, if you can afford them, Pétrus and Le Pin

Woodbridge Chardonnay

Recommended   **$**   **13.5%**

What is it?

A dry white wine made from a blend of grapes (76% Chardonnay, 18% Colombard and 6% other varieties) grown in California. Only a small part undergoes malolactic fermentation, and the wine is aged for 6 months on its lees in oak.

What does it taste like?

Tropical pineapple and banana, with a touch of cream and toast. This is rich-textured and generous.

If you like this, then try with confidence . . .

Greater quality, greater intensity

Jacob's Creek Chardonnay Adelaide Hills

Greater quality, less intensity

The very best from the basic Mâcon-Villages appellation, such as Mâcon Solutré Clos des Bertillones Denogent

Try something completely different

The best Pinot Blanc from Alsace, starting with Domaine Weinbach or Collio Pinot Blanco from Schiopetto from Veneto in Italy

Woodbridge Sauvignon Blanc

Recommended	$	13%

What is it?
A dry white wine made from a blend of grapes (76% Sauvignon Blanc, 15% Colombard and 9% other varieties) grown in California, fermented in stainless steel and aged on its lees

What does it taste like?
Fresh grapefruit and grassy aromas, and very zesty and fresh on the palate

If you like this, then try with confidence . . .
Greater quality, greater intensity
Cru classé Graves from Pessac-Léognan, culminating in Domaine de Chevalier
Greater quality, less intensity
Château Bonnet Blanc Entre-Deux-Mers

Try something completely different
Riesling from Hugel or Trimbach in Alsace, France, and dry Rieslings from Von Bühl and Bassermann Jordan in the Pfalz, Germany

Wyndham Estate Bin 222 Chardonnay

Recommended	$	13%

What is it?
A dry white wine made from the Chardonnay grape grown in Southeastern Australia. A portion was matured in French oak for 6 months.

What does it taste like?
Consistently satisfying peach, mango and melon fruit with a touch of fig and a subtle balance of oak

If you like this, then try with confidence . . .
Greater quality, greater intensity
Hardy's Eileen Hardy Chardonnay
Greater quality, less intensity
Hardy's HRB Chardonnay

Try something completely different
Fabulous Australian Marsanne, Roussanne and Marsanne-Roussanne blends from Yeringberg

Wyndham Estate Bin 555 Shiraz

Recommended	$$	13.5%

What is it?
A dry red wine made from the Shiraz grape grown in Southeastern Australia. Aged in large, used American and French oak barrels for 12 months.

What does it taste like?
Meaty, with blackberry, black pepper notes, bright acidity and a smooth finish

If you like this, then try with confidence . . .
Greater quality, greater intensity
Penfolds St Henri and various Bin numbers (28, 128, 150, 389), culminating in RWT and Grange or Henschke Hill of Grace
Greater quality, less intensity
Clonakilla Shiraz-Viognier

Try something completely different
Zinfandel (especially those by Ridge), Petite Syrah (Ridge Vineyards Dynamite Hill, Rosenblum Rockpile, Turley Cellars Hayne Vineyard or Lava Cap Grand Hill) or even an Australian Zinfandel (such as Cape Mentelle)

Yalumba Bush Vine Grenache

Highly Recommended	$$	14%

What is it?
A dry red wine made from the Grenache grape grown in Barossa, Australia. Aged 8 months in used American, French and Hungarian oak barrels.

What does it taste like?
A Grenache with character. White pepper, fresh strawberry, raspberry jam, hints of bramble and mint. Full-bodied yet very well-balanced, not heavy.

If you like this, then try with confidence . . .
Greater quality, greater intensity
Kilikanoon The Duke Clare Valley Grenache
Greater quality, less intensity
Mas Foulaquier Le Petit Duc

Try something completely different
The finest French Grenache-based blends, such as Domaine Pierre Usseglio Châteauneuf-du-Pape, then Château Rayas

Yalumba Eden Valley Viognier

Highly Recommended	**$$**	**13.5%**

What is it?
A dry white wine made from the Viognier grape grown in Eden Valley, South Australia. Fermented and aged in used French oak for 10 months.

What does it taste like?
Nutty, honeyed, rich and pure with good acidity

If you like this, then try with confidence . . .
Greater quality, greater intensity
Yalumba Viognier The Virgilius
Greater quality, less intensity
Clonakilla Canberra District Viognier or Petaluma Adelaide Hills Viognier

Try something completely different
Muscat d'Alsace from Rolly Gassmann

Yalumba The Signature

To Die For	**$$$**	**14.5%**

What is it?
A dry red wine made from a blend of grapes (typically around 60% Cabernet Sauvignon, 40% Shiraz) grown in Barossa, South Australia. Aged 22 months in a mix of new and used French, American and Hungarian oak barrels.

What does it taste like?
Gorgeous, classic wine with intense aromas of licorice, eucalyptus, black cherry, chocolate, blueberry, meat, and vanilla and tobacco. A complete, full and supple wine.

If you like this, then try with confidence . . .
Greater quality, greater intensity
Wolf Blass Black Label Cabernet Sauvignon Shiraz Malbec
Greater quality, less intensity
Brangayne of Orange Tristan Cabernet Sauvignon Shiraz Merlot

Try something completely different
Pure Cabernet Sauvignon from Washington (Andrew Will, Woodward Canyon), Australia (Houghton's Jack Mann, Balnaves The Tally) and Spain (Marqués de Griñon)

Yellow Tail Chardonnay

Recommended	$	12.5%

What is it?

A dry white wine made from the Chardonnay grape grown in Southeastern Australia

What does it taste like?

Pineapple and mango dominate the ripe tropical fruit in this round-textured and generous wine

If you like this, then try with confidence . . .

Greater quality, greater intensity
Hardy's Eileen Hardy Chardonnay
Greater quality, less intensity
Hardy's HRB Chardonnay

Try something completely different

Fabulous Australian Marsanne, Roussanne and Marsanne-Roussanne blends from Yeringberg

Yellow Tail Shiraz

Recommended	$	13.5%

What is it?

A dry red wine made from the Shiraz grape grown in Southeastern Australia

What does it taste like?

Ripe blackberries and blueberries, with a hint of eucalyptus. Intense flavors and rich texture.

If you like this, then try with confidence . . .

Greater quality, greater intensity

Penfolds St Henri and various Bin numbers (28, 128, 150, 389), culminating in RWT and Grange or Henschke Hill of Grace

Greater quality, less intensity

Clonakilla Shiraz-Viognier

Try something completely different

Zinfandel (especially those by Ridge), Petite Syrah (Ridge Vineyards Dynamite Hill, Rosenblum Rockpile, Turley Cellars Hayne Vineyard or Lava Cap Grand Hill) or even an Australian Zinfandel (such as Cape Mentelle)

Ysios Rioja Reserva

Highly Recommended	**$$**	**13.5%**

What is it?

A dry red wine made from the Tempranillo grape grown in the Alavesa district of Rioja, Spain. Aged in French, American and Hungarian oak barrels for a minimum of 14 months, with at least a further 22 months in the bottle.

What does it taste like?

Attractively perfumed, with seductively soft red and black cherries on the palate and spiced, chocolaty fruit on the finish. Excellent freshness and acidity.

If you like this, then try with confidence . . .

Greater quality, greater intensity

Rioja from Finca Allende, Artadi, Lealtanza, Manzanos, Marqués de Griñon, Nekeas, Palacios Remondo, La Rioja Alta, San Vicente and Bodegas Ysios, then the very best wines of Barón de Ley, Luis Canas, Contino, Marqués de Murrieta, Marqués de Riscal and Bodegas Muga for ultimate quality

Greater quality, less intensity

Reserva and Gran Reserva from La Rioja Alta Viña Ardanza, Marqués de Cáceres and Viña Tondonia Rioja or any rosado from a top Rioja producer

Try something completely different

Numanthia Termes then Numanthia Termanthia from Toro

Zardetto Prosecco Treviso

Recommended	**$**	**11.5%**

What is it?

An off-dry sparkling white wine made from the Glera grape grown in Prosecco, in the Veneto region of northeastern Italy. Charmat method with no lees aging to retain fresh fruit character.

What does it taste like?

Gushing with freshness, the citrus element to the fruit here sets Zardetto apart from most other Prosecco

If you like this, then try with confidence . . .

Greater quality, greater intensity

Champagne Mumm Demi-Sec

Greater quality, less intensity

Champagne De Venoge Vin du Paradis

Try something completely different

Veuve Clicquot Vintage Rich

Zonin Amarone della Valpolicella

Highly Recommended   **$$**   **14%**

What is it?

A dry red wine made from a blend of grapes (Corvina and Rondinella) grown in Valpolicella, in the Veneto region of Italy. Made from dried grapes. Aged in large Slavonian oak barrels for 2 years.

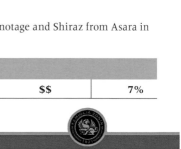

What does it taste like?

Spicy fig nose leads to a full-bodied, intense palate with firm tannins and a long finish

If you like this, then try with confidence . . .

Greater quality, greater intensity
Quintarelli Amarone della Valpolicella
Greater quality, less intensity
Corte Sant'Alda Amarone della Valpolicella

Try something completely different

Avalon, a quirky Amarone-inspired blend of Pinotage and Shiraz from Asara in Stellenbosch, South Africa

Zonin Moscato Puglia

Highly Recommended   **$$**   **7%**

What is it?

A sweet white semi-sparkling wine made from Moscato grapes grown in Puglia, Italy

What does it taste like?

Fresh, floral, sweet and grapey. Easy to drink.

If you like this, then try with confidence . . .

Greater quality, greater intensity
Richer, fully sparkling Asti from the very finest producers, such as Romano Dogliotti Asti La Selvatica or Cerutti Asti Cesare
Greater quality, less intensity
Marchesi di Grésy Moscato d'Asti

Try something completely different

The light-as-a-dime fortified Muscat de Beaumes-de-Venise from top producers such as Domaine des Bernardins or Durban

Zonin Prosecco

Recommended	$	11%

What is it?

An off-dry sparkling white wine made from the Glera grape grown in Prosecco, in the Veneto region of northeastern Italy. Charmat method with no lees aging to retain fresh fruit character.

What does it taste like?

Fairly neutral, but pleasant with apple skin and ripe melon flavors with just a touch of sweetness

If you like this, then try with confidence . . .

Greater quality, greater intensity
Champagne Mumm Demi-Sec
Greater quality, less intensity
Champagne De Venoge Vin du Paradis

Try something completely different
Veuve Clicquot Vintage Rich

Zonin Valpolicella Ripasso Superiore

Highly Recommended	$$	13%

What is it?

A dry red wine made from a blend of grapes (Corvina and Rondinella) grown in Valpolicella, in the Veneto region of Italy. Fermented using the ripasso method. Aged in large Slavonian oak barrels for 1 year.

What does it taste like?

Fresh and dried red cherry, raisin and sweet spice aromas and flavors. Medium-bodied, with good mid-palate richness and uplifting acidity on the finish.

If you like this, then try with confidence . . .

Greater quality, greater intensity
Zonin Amarone della Valpolicella
Greater quality, less intensity
Corte Sant'Alda Valpolicella Classico

Try something completely different
Margan Family Special Reserve Ripasso, a splendid Australian take on this classic wine

PART 3

THE 20 MOST USEFUL WINE TIPS

T he following is a digest of the most useful tips I know. Some of the longer ones might be off-putting for those who really do not want to start learning about wine, but even if that is you, the odds are that you will wonder what to do in some of these situations, so simply ignore the section until, if ever, you need it.

1 How to search for a specific wine

Use wine-searcher.com, which at the time of writing listed 5.4 million wines from more than 36,000 wine retailers around the world. The free version does not yield as comprehensive a list of retailers for each search as the Pro version, but it is the most comprehensive free wine locating service in existence.

2 How to store wine

Most people have no need to store wine, and buy wines to drink, not to store. However, if you want to keep a few bottles for convenience, common sense will tell you to place them somewhere relatively cool, dark and free from fluctuations in temperature. The kitchen is the very worst place to store wine.

3 How to drink wine at the correct temperature

Traditionally, white wines have been served chilled and red wines at room temperature. At higher temperatures, the odorous compounds in wine are more volatile and the tactile impression of tannin is softened, so the practice of serving full-bodied red wines at room temperature releases more aromatics into the bouquet, softens the tannins, and allows the fruit to show through. The colder a red wine is served, the more tannic and less fruity it will taste. One major effect of chilling wine is that more carbonic gas is retained, which enhances the crispness and freshness of a white wine, and with no tannins to act as a barrier this tends to liven the impression of fruit on the palate. It is thus beneficial to chill a youthful white wine and absolutely vital to serve a sparkling wine well chilled, as this keeps it bubbling longer. However, the term *room-temperature* dates back to well before central heating became commonplace, when houses in Northern Europe were relatively cold and drafty. Consequently red wines are often now served much too warm, and with the widespread use of the fridge, white

wines are frequently served too cold. If you have the ideal cellar at a constant 50–55°F (10–12.5°C), this would be the perfect temperature for a rosé wine, and rather than rely on anything as pompous as a wine thermometer to serve different styles of wine at precise temperatures, I prefer to think of serving whites with the "chill on" and reds with the "chill off," edging colder for sparkling wines and warmer for fuller-bodied reds.

4 How to chill wine

Over-chilling a wine kills its flavor and aroma, but there are few things worse than a tepid white wine or more dangerous than trying to open a warm bottle of sparkling wine. If you use a bucket of ice, the ice is useless unless it has the all-enveloping medium of water through which to transmit its chilling effect. You need plenty of ice, but you need more water than ice. A few minutes before opening the wine, carefully invert the bottle in the bucket, particularly if it's a sparkling wine, as the one place not in contact with the freezing water is the top of the neck where the free gas is waiting to explode. It is fine to chill wine in a fridge for up to a few days, but not long term because initially the wax covering on some corks might adhere to the inside of the bottle neck and eventually the refrigeration process will suck the moisture from the cork, causing it to shrink and let in air to promote oxidation. If you have been unable to plan ahead, then ten to fifteen minutes in a freezer has never done a wine any harm. At the height of summer, this might have to be increased to as long as twenty to thirty minutes. If anyone tells you that this practice can "burn" a wine, you can ignore them, as such claims are unfounded; the cold creeps evenly into the bottle by exactly the same principle as with rapid-chill sheaths (which take even less time and should be considered the number one wine chilling tip). If there is one occasion when you should over-chill a wine, it is when pouring for a large number of people, particularly if everyone is packed into one room. The more people there are, the longer it will take to pour the wine, allowing the wine to warm up; the smaller the room the hotter the atmosphere, so it always pays to start out too cold

5 How to bring a wine up to room temperature

Using direct heat on a bottle of wine is unwise. Whether you stand a bottle in front of radiant heat (which also happens to be dangerous) or put it under a hot tap, some of the wine gets too hot, leaving the rest too cold. The best way of "taking the chill off" is thirty to ninety seconds in a microwave on low to medium power. The duration and power setting will depend on the storage temperature of the wine, personal preference (which itself can change according to the climate and time of year) and, of course, the power of the microwave in question. A microwave is ideal because the process is so gentle, involving no heat as such, merely the vibration of water molecules, which warm up the wine as they rub together.

6 How to cope with sediment in wine

With increasing age, many wines—especially but not exclusively reds—throw a natural sediment of tannins, tartrates and coloring pigments that collect in the base or along the side of the bottle. Most sediment is loose and fine, but you may encounter a thin film of dark-colored sediment adhering to the inside of the bottle. The technical description of this bloom is an insoluble complex polymer of pigmented tannins and protein. It is not known why it affects some wines and not others, but it does appear to be most commonly found in high-pH red wines from exceptional vintages or hotter climes. Both red and white wines, particularly white, can also shed a crystalline deposit due to a precipitation of tartrates. These precipitations can also appear on the end of the cork that is in contact with the wine. Although harmless, their appearance is distracting and drinking wine that contains sediment is not pleasant, thus decanting will be necessary to remove it.

7 How to decant a wine

Several hours prior to decanting, move the bottle into an upright position, as this allows the sediment lying along the side of the bottle to fall to the bottom. Cut away the top ¼ inch (.5 cm) or so of the foil capsule. This could well reveal a penicillin growth or, if the wine is an old vintage, a fine black deposit, neither of which will have had contact with the wine, but to avoid any unintentional contamination when removing the cork it is wise to wipe the lip of the bottle neck and the top of the cork with a clean, damp cloth. Insert a corkscrew and gently withdraw the cork. Place a clean finger covered in tissue inside the top of the bottle and carefully remove any pieces of sediment, cork or any tartrate crystals adhering to the inside of the neck, then wipe the lip of the bottle neck with a clean, dry cloth. Lift the bottle slowly in one hand and the decanter in the other and bring them together over a light source, such as a candle or flashlight, to reveal any sediment as the wine is poured. Aim to pour the wine in a slow, steady flow so that the bottle does not jerk and wine does not "gulp for air." Such mishaps will disturb the sediment, spreading it through a greater volume of liquid. Stop decanting once you notice the sediment approaching the neck of the bottle. If you are very skilled, you can be left with very little wine, but you should always err on the side of caution and there are some instances, such as those with a bloom on the bottle, in which you will be forced to stop with a lot of wine remaining in the bottle. To render such wine drinkable, pour the cloudy dregs through a fine-grade coffee filter paper. Some snobs claim to be able to taste the filter paper, but in every blind test I have set up for such people, no one has ever been able to tell the difference between filtered and decanted. So why not filter everything? Because it's a pain and the more heavily sedimented the wine, the longer it takes to drip through fine-grade coffee filter paper. Once the wine is decanted, the next question is whether to serve it in a decanter or to rinse out the bottle, allow it to stand upside down to drip dry, then refill the original bottle. There can be a time and a place for using a decanter, but the original bottle is as good as any other vessel from which to pour a wine, and its label allows people to see what they are drinking.

8 How to allow a wine to breathe

Is this breathing business just pretentious nonsense? No, not at all. Wine "feeds" on the small amount of air trapped inside the bottle between the wine and the cork, and on the oxygen naturally absorbed by the wine itself. It is during this slow oxidation that various elements and compounds are formed or changed in a complex chemical process known as maturation. By the time a wine is ready to drink, the only oxygen present will be microscopic amounts that enter the wine through its closure, whether that is a cork, a synthetic or a screwcap. At this time, all the biochemical paths are loaded and cocked. They just need some oxygen to kick start the process, and opening a bottle achieves that. The fact that restaurants invariably decant older vintages has given rise to a belief that older vintages must be allowed to breathe. Some older, finer wines do benefit from breathing, but generally the older the wine, the sooner you should start drinking it after opening, as it is more likely that it will start losing fruit. If it doesn't, if it starts to build in the glass, then you can relax and let it breathe, but breathing usually has the most dramatic effect on young wines, particularly young, full-bodied, tannic reds. The top tip for making the most of youthful reds is to make sure they are roughly the right temperature (*see* items 3 and 5) and then pour the wine into a jug from a height of six to nine inches, then back into the bottle using a funnel, and leave it for thirty minutes.

9 How to open a bottle of wine without a corkscrew

Slowly but surely push the cork into the bottle using the knuckle of your index finger. This might not be easy, but it is not as hard as it sounds as the bottle neck widens a bit. Then, take a length of string and tie a bunch of knots at the end of it. Lower the knots into the neck of the bottle and, using anything thin enough to enter the neck (a table knife, knitting needle, etc.), push the knots under the floating cork. Once the knots are lodged there, wrap the other end of the string around your hand. Pull up on the string, guiding the top end of the cork back into the neck and making sure that the knots remain lodged under the cork. As soon as the cork is aligned with the neck, it is relatively easy to pull it out with the string.

10 How to open a Champagne bottle

This applies to any sparkling wine, of course. First remove the foil from the top inch or so to reveal the wire cage. Find the circular end of the wire, which will be twisted and folded upwards. Simply pull it outwards, untwist the wire, and unravel the cage. A good tip is not to remove the cage, not only because that is when most bottles fire their corks prematurely, but also because it acts as a good grip, which is always useful but will be essential when the bottle is slippery, particularly if the cork is stuck tight. As you do this, hold the bottle upright at an angle away from the body, with the cork pointing at no person or anything breakable. As you untwist the end of the wire and loosen the cage with one hand, make sure that you keep the other hand firmly on the cork and the top of the cage. This ensures that it will not surprise you by shooting out as you unravel the cage. If you used your best hand to loosen the wire, transfer your grip on the cork to the other hand, and completely enclose the cork and cage. Holding the base of the bottle with your other hand, twist both ends in opposite directions. This is the point where others advise that you twist the bottle, not the cork because the more pressure you place on the cork, the greater the likelihood that the head of the cork will break. Nonsense. Basic physics determine that the pressure on the cork is the same whichever end you twist and it is easier to exert and control pressure on the cork, with the cage providing grip, than it is to grasp the slippery base end of a bottle. Whichever end you twist, you just have to be careful. As soon as you feel pressure forcing the cork out, try to hold it in, but continue the twisting operation until, almost reluctantly, you release the cork from the bottle. The mark of a professional is that the cork comes out with a sigh, not a bang.

11 How to pour Champagne

Pour a little into each glass first. If you try to fill each glass one at a time, it will take forever for the foam to subside, but if you pour a little into each glass, by the time you get to the last glass, the foam on the first glass will have subsided, making it easy to top up. Never fill to the brim. If using a flûte, two-thirds is ideal. If using a more conventional wine glass, one-third will suffice. The convention is to pour any sparkling wine directly into a standing glass, not to tilt the glass as if you are pouring a lager. Recent research and common sense tell us that the "lager method" will preserve the carbonic gas content of a Champagne, but the mousse of a youthful nonvintage can be a little aggressive and consequently benefits from a little taming by pouring into a standing glass rather than preserving the harshest element of the mousse.

12 How to react to wines sealed with a screwcap

For many wine critics and, indeed, most wine consumers in the UK, Australia and New Zealand, the screwcap is the preferred—much preferred—closure for premium quality wines, although this is not so in the USA and France, where it is still considered synonymous with cheap, poor-quality wine. This was also the attitude in the UK until the most recent turn of the century, when the British became so fed up with cork taint (*see* item 13 below) that consumers were ready to embrace all forms of alternative closure. Initially, synthetic corks were the most widely used, but although some excellent products by two American companies, Nomacorc and Neocorc, were available and are still excelling to this day, much cheaper and inferior synthetic closures quickly dominated and consequently were not well received. When almost all New Zealand wines exported to the UK arrived with screwcaps virtually overnight, this type of closure became instantly acceptable. This was due in no small part to the fact that sales of New Zealand wines were soaring despite having the highest average price of wines from any country on the UK market. But it was not before time. The pharmaceutical industry long ago concluded that a lump of tree bark was neither the most efficient, nor the most hygienic closure for a bottle of medicine, so why has it taken the wine industry so long? As for those who claim that screwcaps take the romance out of opening a bottle of wine, they obviously do not open enough wine bottles! My foot-dragging generation of wine consumers in the UK has a lot to answer for, but as soon as the vast majority of Australian and New Zealand wines switched to screwcap, the new, younger and better-informed generation of wine drinkers were easily persuaded to accept the change. Principally because it eradicates TCA, which is responsible for cork taint in wines, but also because it guarantees consistent maturation.

13 How to identify a corked wine

A corked wine smells unattractively dusty, and tastes similar to an earthy potato or carrot—not the potato or carrot part, just the earthiness in a potato or carrot (although that is caused by geosmin, which is something different). The cause of cork taint was first identified in 1981 by a Swiss research scientist, and by the 1990s its incidence had been quantified at such an alarmingly high percentage (8%) that a significant proportion of winemakers started looking for alternative closures. It was originally believed to be a mold infection of the cork, but such infections have always been extremely rare, and it was later found to be due to extremely low levels of various chloroanisoles, with 2,4,6-trichloroanisole (commonly referred to as TCA) the main culprit. Initially thought to be exclusively the unwanted by-product of sterilizing corks with chlorine, TCA has since been identified at source in cork oak trees, in oak barrels, wooden pallets, and wooden roof structures. If you are not sure what a corked wine smells like and anyone ever says they have a corked wine that is so bad that it leaps out of the glass (the cork taint in a lightly corked wine can be almost subliminal), you should ask to have a sniff because once smelled, never forgotten, and you will immediately start recognizing it at much lower concentrations. Until you can recognize the cork taint, and accept that you do not like it (some people are oblivious to it), don't worry: the amount of TCA in wine is in parts per trillion and will do you no harm.

14 How to order wine in a restaurant

At one time, the more expensive the restaurant, the more stuffy and snooty the sommelier (a.k.a. wine waiter), but it is quite different today. Gone are the days when they would steer you toward the most expensive wines on the list. The new generation of sommeliers continue to respect the traditional classics that have always dominated wine lists, but also rely heavily on much less expensive wines from all over the world. Much like the ethos of this guide, there is now a genuine desire to find out what sort of wines customers like, then guide them to something compatible and reasonably priced.

No revolution reaches every nook and cranny, so it is always possible to come across the occasional snooty wine waiter.

When shown the wine you have ordered, you should always examine the label to make sure it is precisely the wine and vintage you have ordered, and when offered the opportunity to taste, agree and draw the sommelier's attention to anything wrong. This is usually confined to faults such as a corked or oxidized wine, but might also simply be a matter of the temperature at which the wine is served. Is it too warm or too cold? Despite the advice given in item 3 above, the customer is always right. If you choose to ignore the advice and drink wines at a different temperature, that is your right and the sommelier should take immediate steps to raise or lower the temperature of the wine to meet your wishes, and to do this with the minimum of fuss. However, there are customers who claim not to know the difference between a fault and a wine they do not like, or who are reticent about suggesting there could be a fault, let alone daring to send back any wine. If that is you, I have the perfect solution, especially in those rare situations where you encounter an overbearing and intimidating wine waiter. When he pours out a small amount of wine for you to okay, keep up the conversation with your fellow diner or diners. Do not even look at the wine waiter. Just take your time to finish whatever you were saying to the other guests, then lift the glass and tilt it as if you are examining the color. It doesn't matter if you don't know what you are supposed to be looking for! Then put the glass under your nose for barely half a second. Do not taste it and again without looking at the wine waiter, just say "That's fine." You can even do a little circle with your index finger, to indicate that he should pour the wine. While he is pouring, continue your private conversation, as if the whole wine exercise is no big deal. When he has finished, give him a short look, a nod and a polite "Thank you" and once more return to your conversation. From now on, even the snootiest wine waiter will not be condescending because he will be absolutely convinced that you know more about wine than he does. As you would never dare send a wine back anyway, you have lost nothing by accepting it.

15 How to react to wine served in a basket

There is no reason for restaurants to use these pretentious hang-ups from the 1960s unless a bottle has sediment, and it is to prevent that sediment from moving. However, if a wine does have sediment, it should be decanted, not laid in a cradle, because no matter how careful the sommelier is, the constant topping up of glasses will cloud up a larger than necessary portion of the wine. If presented with a wine in a basket my advice is to ask for it to be properly decanted, if there is sediment, or stood upright, if there isn't.

16 How to approach food and wine pairing

Drink what you like, I say. For 90 percent of the time, drinking a wine you like with the food you like works well enough for most people. It is true that some combinations are made in heaven, but it requires a lot of effort to discover which of those suit both your personal food and wine preferences, and your personal thresholds for recognizing the active aromas and tastes, and you have to ask yourself, is it worth it? Is it worth going to all that trouble for one food and wine combination in ten? Especially when the alternative is perfectly acceptable? If the answer is no, read no further. If, however, you are still interested in honing your food and wine choices, read on. There are no rules that cannot be broken, but there are some useful food and wine combinations that have evolved over time. A good tip is to start with conventional food and wine combinations (e.g., Chablis or Muscadet with oysters), because to exist they must have worked for many people over the ages, so you are more likely to enjoy them than not. However, if you personally dislike a certain wine or food, it doesn't matter how many other people have enjoyed the combination. If any combination is okay, but not quite right for you, simply tweak the wine closer to your personal taste. Don't make a big stylistic change, just try a wine that is a little fuller, lighter, sweeter, more acidic or whatever it is you feel is not quite right, and edge your way towards something more personally acceptable. We all have different levels at which we detect tastes and aromas, therefore the perception of perfect balance of, say, acidity and sweetness is literally different from one person to another. On the whole these differences have little real effect on how we appreciate most food and wine combinations, which is why most conventional combinations work for most people. It is also why we can all agree that a strawberry tastes like a strawberry, not a raspberry. However, there are some detection levels that can have a radical effect on how we perceive tastes and aromas. Our ability to detect sugar, for example, can vary by a factor of ten, which gives a totally different twist to the notion of a "sweet tooth" because for some individuals ten spoonfuls of sugar in a cup of coffee tastes no sweeter than one spoonful for those at the other end of the sugar detection spectrum. That demonstrates why you should not be worried if you do not like any particular food and wine combination. There could be any number of physiological reasons. Or it could be purely aesthetic, that you simply have a personal dislike of a certain flavor, and there is nothing wrong with that. Perhaps the best way of avoiding these physiological and aesthetic issues is simply to keep to the guideline that the more delicately flavored the food, the more delicate the wine should be, whereas fuller-flavored foods can take fuller-flavored wines. When applying this, a good tip is not to consider the main ingredient, such as chicken or pasta, but to focus on the strongest flavors involved, which might be what the meat was basted in or the sauce with which it is served. If serving more than one wine at a meal, common sense tells us to ascend in quality and flavor, serving white before red, dry before sweet (which is why you should have the cheese before dessert), light-bodied before full-bodied, and young before old. Contrary to popular belief, white wines are generally better than reds with cheese, although some reds do go with certain cheeses, particularly hard cheeses. With dessert, there are only two tips worth remembering: always chose a wine that is sweeter than the dessert, and ignore almost everything the French recommend on the subject (because they serve Brut Champagne with dessert!).

17 How to choose wine glasses

One of the biggest wine tips of all is to buy decent glasses. Should you wonder whether the vessel you drink anything from really matters, try drinking hot chocolate from a Champagne flûte and Champagne from a chipped mug. If you still cannot appreciate the point, you are beyond help. For everyone else, read on. A decent wine glass does not have to be very expensive, but it is worth paying a small premium for a certain quality and size of glass, with sides that taper in slightly at the top, to gather the aromas, and a rim that should be as thin and fine as your budget will allow. The rim is the most important point. The finer it is, the more it increases the impression of finesse The thicker the rim, the more rustic a wine appears to be. Avoid straight-sided glasses, colored glass and cut-glass. Not all clear glasses are good, either, the so-called Paris goblet with bulbous rims being the worst. White wines, dessert wines and fortified wines are often served in glasses that are ridiculously small. They should all be served in the same good-sized glass in which the red wine is served.

18 How to wash wine glasses

You might not think there can be much of a tip for washing wine glasses, but if you ever bumped into a wine snob, there is a good chance that he or she would tell you to use only clean water, not detergent, and never use a dishwasher, but this is nonsense. You need to use warm water and detergent to clean any wine glass after use, particularly if it has any greasy marks from use at mealtime. Just make sure that the glasses are sufficiently rinsed in warm to hot water, and give them a good polish with a clean, odorless glass cloth (do not use a perfumed fabric conditioner when washing the glass cloths). Contrary to what the alarmists think, a dishwasher is fine for wine glasses, providing they are dishwasher proof, and as long as you do not use a perfumed finishing agent. A soon as the glasses come out of the dishwasher, use a glass cloth to dry and polish the glasses. Even glasses that come out of a dishwasher that dries through residual heat will require wiping the rims to prevent drip marks.

19 How to preserve the freshness of an open bottle of wine

Once a bottle of wine has been opened, you have to fight against oxidation and a loss of aromatics in order to maintain maximum freshness. Using proprietary blends of inert gas, such as nitrogen, CO_2 and argon, will work, but it's a hassle and costs money. I would never use a device that pumps air out of a bottle. They purport to protect the wine from oxidation, but I fear they actually create an environment in which the most volatile aromatics are literally sucked out of the wine.

Once a bottle has been opened and some of its contents poured, the wine left inside the bottle will absorb a significant volume of oxygen through exposure to the air, and oxidation will commence. For a few hours at the table, this can be beneficial (*see* item 8 above), but if allowed to continue at the same rate or faster for a matter of a day or more, it will soon begin to dull the aroma of the wine and will eventually form more distinctive and off-putting oxidative aromas. This process cannot be stopped, but it can be slowed by cutting off the supply of more oxygen and lowering the temperature. The easiest way to achieve this is to pour the wine into an empty plastic water bottle, squeeze the bottle until the wine is about to overflow, then reseal the bottle. It is easily possible to do this and not end up with even the tiniest bubble of air in the semi-crushed, entirely full plastic water bottle, which you then store in a fridge (even red wines should be stored in the fridge). You can use whites and rosés straight from the fridge, but should take the reds out a couple of hours in advance to acclimatize. If you want to keep leftover wine for cooking, just freeze it in cubes and store them in a freezer bag.

20 How to take notes at a wine tasting

There is no better way of finding out which wine you prefer than by tasting several together and picking out your favorite. Should there be an opportunity, you should take it. This might not be a geeky event, but could simply be a few wines opened and available to taste in a wine shop. Sometimes there will be a tasting sheet and sometimes there won't. Some people get worried when they are handed a tasting sheet and wonder what on earth they should write. If that's you, don't worry, you don't have to write anything. Here's a tip. Taste the first wine and give it a ✓ if you like it or an ✗ if you don't. Taste the second wine and do the same if you like it or dislike it equally. However, if you like it even more, give it two ✓s; if you dislike it more, give it two ✗s. If you like it even more than that, give it three ✓s; and if you dislike it even more than that, give it three ✗s. Repeat *ad nauseam*, giving as many ✓s and ✗s to individual wines as you like. If you encounter a wine that comes between two ratings, simply use a half-✓ or half-✗ (a ✓ or an ✗ over a horizontal line with the digit 2 underneath). If you discover that you happened to start off with one of the wines you like or dislike most, you might have to go back and convert the single ✓ or ✗ to multiple ✓s or ✗s. Should you go back and forth between the wines, do not worry if you change your mind and feel like adjusting some of your ratings. Quite often even an experienced taster distrusts his or her judgment for the first one or two wines tasted and will automatically return to recalibrate, if necessary. Furthermore, wines can taste better or worse when tasted immediately after different wines, so after completing the tasting, it can be instructive to taste some wines in a random order or even completely retaste every wine in reverse order. Finally, if you want to buy, say, just one wine and you have awarded your top rating to, say, two or three wines, have a taste-off. If you are still not sure, try just sniffing each one to see which you prefer "on the nose" (it is surprising how important the aroma becomes the more you drink a particular wine). If you are still not sure, taste each one again to see how long the core of flavor of the wine remains distinctly registered in the mouth (known as the length of a wine). Don't bother to time it, as you should easily notice if one wine has much greater (or much less) length. Choose the longest. Or if you still cannot make up your mind, buy them all and take the problem home with you!

All images courtesy of the wineries, except for the following: p. 292: © Kitch Bain/Shutterstock; p. 295: © Ina Peters/iStockphoto; p. 297: © schab/Shutterstock; p. 299: © allec/Dreamstime; p. 300: © Nomadsoul1/Dreamstime; p. 301: © Serge Bertasius/iStockphoto; p. 305: © Nikola Bilic/Dreamstime; p. 307: © Vasil Vasilev/Dreamstime; p. 308: © Chiyacat/Dreamstime

About Tom Stevenson

Tom Stevenson has been writing about wine for more than thirty years. Described by his colleagues as one of today's most prolific wine authors, Stevenson is regarded as the world's leading authority on Champagne. In *Christie's World Encyclopedia of Champagne & Sparkling Wine* he published a document dated December 17, 1662, written by Dr. Christopher Merret, proving that it was the English, not the French, who invented sparkling Champagne. He has written

twenty-three critically acclaimed books, the most important of which have been published internationally by more than fifty publishers and translated into over twenty-five languages. He is the winner of thirty-three literary awards, including Wine Writer of the Year three times and the Wine Literary Award (America's only lifetime achievement award for wine writers). Most recently, he was inducted into the Hall of Fame of the Wine Media Guild of New York. Stevenson has a regular column in *The World of Fine Wine* and has judged at wine competitions in the US, UK, France, Germany, Greece, Italy and Australia. He is best known as the author of *The Sotheby's Wine Encyclopedia*, which has been published continuously since 1988 and is used as a standard reference for Master of Wine and Master Sommelier examinations worldwide. It has sold more than 700,000 copies in fourteen major languages.